"Churches close daily due to poor pastoral leadership. This book offers pastors an answer to that problem—a biblical answer ... Chapter by chapter, Jones and Wilder ask, 'What about you?' It is a hint of the value and practicality of this work."

—**Gary J. Bredfeldt**, professor of leadership, Liberty University

"Ready to rethink pastoral leadership through a Scriptural lens? Jones and Wilder, with decades of pastoral leadership experience, have crafted a unique text on leadership for pastors."

—**Kenneth S. Coley**, senior professor of Christian education, director of Ed.D. studies, Southeastern Baptist Theological Seminary

"There are many leadership books available to the church, but few speak with a prophetic voice that addresses timely leadership issues ... The book you hold in your hands is such a voice. As churches continue to rise and often fall around the personality and charisma of one domineering leader, *The God Who Goes before You* is a needed voice to bring balance."

—**Brian Croft**, senior pastor, Auburndale Baptist Church, Louisville, KY

"In this outstanding book, Timothy Paul Jones and Michael Wilder have zeroed in on the central elements for Christian leadership: union with Christ, communion with Christ's people, and mission in the world."

—**Andrew M. Davis**, senior pastor, First Baptist Church of Durham, Durham, NC

"Do we really need another book on leadership? The answer is a heartfelt 'yes' when that book is a distinctively Christian, practically-designed, gospel-focused biblical theology of leadership. Timothy Paul Jones and Michael Wilder have provided so much more than another 'how-to' guide for pastors and CEOs. This highly recommended volume presents a thoughtful, integrative, and theologically shaped approach to leadership that calls for investing in people and in the shared calling of a faithful community for the glory of God."

—**David S. Dockery**, president, Trinity International University

"Michael Wilder and Timothy Paul Jones ... have provided deeply biblical and practical guidance on how to steward a congregation under Christ's leadership."

—**Kevin Ezell**, president, North American Mission Board

"From helpful explanations of leadership offices in the Old Testament, to the simple yet profound challenge that leadership for the believer is first followership, this book is filled with wisdom."

—**Eric Geiger**, senior pastor, Mariners Church, Irvine, CA

"Rich in content, impressive in scope, and practical in aim, Jones and Wilder have served local churches and the academy by contributing this work to the field of leadership."

—**Dave Harvey**, executive director, Sojourn Network, and teaching pastor, Summit Church, Naples, FL

"Written by two scholar-practitioners who love and serve the local church, this theology of leadership is accessible, fresh, and faithful—a gift to the church."

—**Andrew Hebert**, lead pastor, Paramount Baptist Church, Amarillo, TX

"Michael Wilder and Timothy Jones have profoundly shaped my view of biblical and pastoral leadership … Their unique blend of scholarship and pastoral experience makes them the capable guides we need to lead us to the biblical heart of true pastoral leadership."

—**Beau Hughes**, pastor, The Village Church Denton, Denton, TX

"Rather than laying a Christian veneer over secular principles, this book will challenge you to consider seriously what it means to draw your leadership practices from God's Word."

—**Jeff Iorg**, president, Gateway Seminary

"Reading this book is like feeling a cool, fresh breeze on a hot, humid summer day. Finally, someone has considered the whole counsel of God when considering leadership, Jesus, and the church."

—**Benjamin L. Merkle**, professor of New Testament and Greek, Southeastern Baptist Theological Seminary

"Every leader is still a follower. In *The God Who Goes before You*, Jones and Wilder connect the practice of leadership to the story of Scripture, pointing leaders toward a more biblical and faithful model than the self-focused leadership methods so prevalent today. This book will equip Christians to lead by teaching them to follow the way of the shepherd."

—**Russell Moore**, president, The Ethics and Religious Liberty Commission of the Southern Baptist Convention

"Readers will evaluate leadership motifs in light of the fact that all believers have full access to God's revelation. They will walk away asking, 'How can I best serve and care for the people in my community?' The authors submit (and rightly so) that it will take 'courage, creativity and conviction.'"

—**David D. Nemitz**, director, Center for the Advancement of Faculty Excellence, and associate professor of religion and instructional design, Liberty University

"Not every book about leadership written for a Christian audience is biblical, insightful, thorough, inspiring, and challenging. This one is! The ideal Christian leader is someone who has been shaped by the character of God and who follows the Lord so well that others are inspired to follow Christ."

—**Miguel Núñez**, pastor, Iglesia Bautista Internacional, Santo Domingo, Dominican Republic

"*The God Who Goes before You* is a gift to the church ... Wilder and Jones have given us a rich theology and gems of pastoral wisdom for stewarding leadership in the service of God's people."

—**Kevin Peck**, lead pastor, The Austin Stone Community Church, Austin, TX

"Jones and Wilder have given the church a valuable work on leadership that is ... defined and motivated by the work of Christ in the history of redemption. With great social intelligence, they offer a much-needed correction to current models of church leadership adapted from Wall Street."

—**Eric C. Redmond**, assistant professor of Bible, Moody Bible Institute

"If you're tired of Christian leadership books based merely on business practices and creational wisdom with a few Bible verses sprinkled throughout, then this book is for you! In *The God Who Goes before You*, Timothy Paul Jones and Michael Wilder argue from the entire storyline of Scripture that Christian leaders are, first and foremost, Christ-followers."

—**Juan R. Sanchez**, senior pastor, High Pointe Baptist Church, Austin, TX

"What a delight to read a book on pastoral leadership rooted in careful biblical exegesis and shaped by biblical theology."

—**Thomas R. Schreiner**, professor of New Testament interpretation, The Southern Baptist Theological Seminary

"The Christ-following leadership principles of this book provide a distinct biblical framework for leaders who guide churches, Christian universities, or faith-based organizations."

—**Timothy L. Smith**, president, University of Mobile

"There is so much that is commendable about this book—not least the esteeming of community, the exhortation to lead as under-shepherds of the one true and faithful Shepherd, the teaching about church discipline, and a much-needed corrective to typecasting leaders today as 'kingly,' 'prophetic,' or 'priestly.' But the heart-warming, action-inspiring, best thing about it is that, from beginning to end, *The God Who Goes before You* is beautifully punctuated by the truth of our union with Christ as that which informs and sustains all that we are and do."

—**Steve Timmis**, CEO, Acts 29

"*The God Who Goes before You* is the leadership book that I've longed to read. Jones and Wilder write theologically rich content rooted in years of pastoral experience. This book both critiques and considers the best leadership principles from Christian and secular leaders."

—**Jamaal Williams**, lead pastor, Sojourn Community Church Midtown, Louisville, KY

MICHAEL S. WILDER AND
TIMOTHY PAUL JONES

The

GOD

Who Goes

BEFORE YOU

PASTORAL LEADERSHIP AS CHRIST-CENTERED FOLLOWERSHIP

B&H
ACADEMIC
NASHVILLE, TENNESSEE

To the congregations we are privileged to serve:
First Southern Baptist Church, Floyds Knobs
and
Sojourn Community Church, Midtown

Week by week, we are blessed beyond measure to lead you, to serve you,
and to proclaim the Word of God among you.

CONTENTS

FOREWORD

R. Albert Mohler Jr.

C hristians are rightly and necessarily concerned about leadership, but many Christians seem to aim no higher than secular standards and visions of leadership.[1] We can learn a great deal from the secular world and its studies of leadership and its practices—but the last thing the church needs is warmed-over business theories decorated with Christian language.

Christian leaders are called to convictional leadership, and that means leadership defined by beliefs that are transformed into corporate action. The central role of belief is what *must* define any truly Christian understanding of leadership. What this means is that leadership is always a theological enterprise, in the sense that our most important beliefs and convictions are about God. If our beliefs about God are not true, everything we know and everything we are will be warped and contorted by that false knowledge—and this fact points to a huge problem.

The culture around us has its own concept of God, and it has little to do with the God of the Bible. Out in the fog of modern culture, God has been transformed into a concept, a therapist, a benign and indulgent patriarch, a user-friendly deity. As theologian David F. Wells states so powerfully, "We have turned to a God that we can use rather than a God we must obey; we have turned to a God who will fulfill our needs rather than to a God before whom we must surrender our rights to ourselves. He is a God for us, for our satisfaction, and we have come to assume that it must be so in the church as well. And so we transform the God of mercy into a God who is at our mercy. We imagine that he is benign, that he will acquiesce as we toy with his reality and co-opt him in the promotion of our ventures and careers."[2]

In the aftermath of this crisis in the knowledge of God, many essential truths are eclipsed or lost entirely, and one of those truths is the principle of stewardship.

Out in the secular world, the horizon of leadership is often no more distant than the next quarterly report or board meeting. For the Christian leader, the horizon and frame of reference for leadership is infinitely greater. We know that our leadership is set within the context of eternity. What we do matters now, of course, but what we do matters for eternity, precisely because we serve an eternal God and we lead human beings for whom he has an eternal purpose.

But the most important reality that frames our understanding of leadership is nothing less than the sovereignty of God. Human beings may claim to be sovereign, but no earthly leader is anything close to being truly sovereign. In Daniel chapter 4, we learn of Nebuchadnezzar, king of Babylon, one of the most powerful monarchs in human history. God judges Nebuchadnezzar for his arrogance and pride, and he takes Nebuchadnezzar's kingly sovereignty away from him. Later, after his humbling lesson, God restored Nebuchadnezzar to his greatness. Nebuchadnezzar spoke of the lesson he had learned about who really was sovereign, and he testified of God's true sovereignty, stating that "his dominion is an everlasting dominion, and his kingdom endures from generation to generation" (Dan 4:34). What Nebuchadnezzar recognized is that he was never truly sovereign. Sovereignty isn't sovereignty if a higher sovereign can take it away from you.

Like Nebuchadnezzar, today's Christian leaders know that God is sovereign, and we are not. And yet what does it really mean to affirm God's sovereignty as Christian leaders? It means that God rules over all space and time and history. It means that God created the world for his glory and directs the cosmos to his purpose. It means that no one can truly thwart his plans or frustrate his determination. It means that we are secure in the knowledge that God's sovereign purpose to redeem a people through the atonement accomplished by his Son will be fully realized. It also means that human leaders, no matter their title, rank, or job description, are not really in charge. The bottom line is this—we are merely stewards, not lords, of all that is put into our trust. The sovereignty of God puts us in our place, and that place is in God's service.

The biblical concept of a steward is amazingly simple and easy to understand. The steward is one who manages and leads what is not his own, and he leads knowing that he will give an account to the Lord as the owner and ruler of all.

Stewards are entrusted with responsibility. Indeed, stewards in the Bible are shown to have both great authority and great responsibility. Kings had stewards who administered their kingdoms—just think of Joseph as Pharaoh's steward in Egypt. Wealthy citizens hired stewards to serve as what amounted to chief executive officers of their enterprises—just think of the parable Jesus told about the wicked steward in Luke 16:1–8.

Paul describes ministers as "stewards of the mysteries of God" (1 Cor 4:1) and Peter spoke of all Christians as "good stewards of God's varied grace" (1 Pet 4:10). Clearly, this is a concept that is central to both Christian discipleship and Christian leadership. Christian leaders are invested with a stewardship of influence, authority, and trust we are called to fulfill. In one sense, this underlines just how much God entrusts to his human creatures, fallible and frail as we are. We are called to exercise dominion over creation, but not as ones who own what we are called to lead. Our assignment is to serve on behalf of another.

Think of the leadership failures and crises that regularly populate the headlines. Many, if not most, of those failures originated in the leader's arrogance or overreaching. Stewards cannot afford to be arrogant, and they must quickly learn the danger of overreaching. At the same time, stewards are charged to act, and not to stand by as passive observers. Leaders are not simply to lead; we are to lead knowing that we are leading on another's behalf. Leaders—no matter their title or magnitude—are servants, plain and simple.

The God Who Goes before You understands that leadership cannot be reduced to business-oriented best practices or pragmatic commitments. In this book, Timothy Paul Jones and Michael Wilder lay out a compelling and thoroughly theological vision for leadership that highlights the character of God and the centrality of the gospel in everything leaders do. This is an important book full of biblical insight and pastoral wisdom. As the church marches forward, these lessons on leadership must be heeded for the sake of the church and for our faithfulness in the kingdom.

ACKNOWLEDGMENTS

The two of us gladly serve as professors and administrators at The Southern Baptist Theological Seminary, and we are deeply grateful for the seminary's support as we have completed this project. We are particularly grateful for our provost, Dr. Randy Stinson, a man who models in an academic setting what it means to shepherd a faculty. Dr. Stinson has contributed deeply to our development as leaders and has graciously provided us with manifold opportunities to thrive in academic leadership.

Although we are both professors and seminary administrators, *The God Who Goes before You* is no mere academic exercise. Between the two of us, we are approaching sixty years of combined pastoral experience. This text was written as we each led churches in two very different contexts. Michael is a pastor at First Southern Baptist Church in Floyds Knobs, Indiana, a small-town congregation in the midst of an amazing growth and revitalization process. This revitalization has centered on gospel-focused worship, shared leadership, Scripture-driven prayer, intentional discipleship, missional fervency, and financial stability. The church is now growing an average of 12 percent per year. Timothy serves as one of the preaching pastors at the Midtown congregation of Sojourn Community Church, a congregation of nearly 1,500 people that gathers in an economically challenged urban neighborhood in Louisville. The Midtown congregation of Sojourn is in the midst of an intentional long-term movement toward ethnic diversity and racial reconciliation. Every page of this book has been shaped by our shared desire to be faithful to Scripture as we shepherd these two congregations.

Michael: This book has roots in a particular morning of prayer and Scripture reading when I was twenty-one years old. I was seeking greater clarity as to what the Lord would have me pursue in terms of ministry focus in the years to come. For the first time, 2 Tim 2:2 and Phil 2:15 came together as a guiding directive in ministry. As I began in the coming weeks to pray through those verses, I concluded that as long as the Lord gave me breath, my life would be focused on raising up a godly generation of leaders amidst a crooked and perverse society. This driving ambition to raise up a generation of leaders who are capable of replicating themselves has been my greatest desire throughout nearly thirty years of ministry. As I have thought about this way of investing my life, I have realized ministry can be complicated and difficult at times, but I have also recognized how much it comes down simply to shepherding the flock that God has assigned to you.

I am grateful for encouragement from those who call me pastor; I am blessed to serve the people of First Southern Baptist Church in Floyds Knobs, Indiana. I am also thankful for the opportunity to have co-labored with my friend and colleague Timothy Paul Jones in this project. His intelligence and depth is evident, just as his love for Christ and the church is inspiring. He is a true shepherd—a brother raised up among brothers and sisters to serve the body.

Finally, I am constantly delighted by my family's words of encouragement. My wife, Ginger, and our three daughters have spurred me on to complete this project. As I have thought about shepherding and leading in the church while working on this project, I have been regularly reminded that the home is the proving ground for one's ability to shepherd the church. I am confident that we have grown as a family during this season and am hopeful that I am a better shepherd today as a result of this study.

Timothy: Three of the chapters that I wrote for this book were not the chapters I had planned to write. My plan at the beginning of this project was to offer a slight corrective of the prophet, priest, and king leadership typology that I had heard from young church planters with whom I worked in the Sojourn Network and Acts 29. As I researched and wrote the first drafts of these chapters, I became convinced on the basis of my study of Scripture that the entire typology was functioning in a fundamentally flawed way. In the end, I rewrote chapters three, four, and five to reflect a revised—and, I pray, far more biblical—understanding of how old covenant positions of leadership should be applied among the new covenant people of God. Many thanks to my Love Thy Neighborhood intern Mary Helen Thompson, my assistant Michael Graham, my colleagues Gregg Allison and Peter Gentry, my coworker Garrick Bailey, and my fellow pastor Justin Karl for reading and critiquing early portions of this manuscript. The words that I contributed to this project were written at Quills Coffee on Baxter Avenue and at Starbucks on Frankfort Avenue in Louisville, as well as on a deck overlooking the saltwater marshes surrounding Hilton Head Island in South Carolina.

I am blessed to serve alongside my fellow pastors and other leaders at the Midtown congregation of Sojourn Community Church. Rarely a Sunday goes by that I do not find myself with a lump in my throat as I watch our congregation move toward a deep diversity that is increasingly reflective of John's vision of a "multitude . . . from every nation, tribe, people, and language" (Rev 7:9). When it comes to leadership, I am grateful for what I have seen and learned working alongside Michael Wilder for the past decade. What God is doing through his leadership in revitalizing a church has been truly marvelous to observe.

My wife Rayann and our four daughters have remained a steadfast encouragement to me throughout every step of this project. I rejoice in the work that God has given me to do, both at Southern Seminary and in Sojourn Community Church. And yet I am always eager to return to the place that my wife has made our home. There, each day, a family formed by a crazy complex of unexpected adoptions awaits me. None of these children match when it comes to the color of their skin or the places from which they came, but God has brought us together by his grace, and I stand in awe of the blessings that God has spun into my life through them all.

ABBREVIATIONS

ABC	Anchor Bible Commentary
BBR	*Bulletin of Biblical Research*
BDAG	Bauer's *Greek–English Lexicon of the New Testament and Other Early Christian Literature*
BECNT	Baker Exegetical Commentary on the New Testament
BSac	*Bibliotheca Sacra*
CBQ	*Catholic Biblical Quarterly*
EGGNT	Exegetical Guide to the Greek New Testament
EvQ	*Evangelical Quarterly*
HBT	*Horizons in Biblical Theology*
HTS	*Harvard Theological Studies*
IOS	*Israel Oriental Society*
JEA	*Journal of Egyptian Archaeology*
JETS	*Journal of the Evangelical Theological Society*
JSOT	*Journal for the Study of the Old Testament*
LXX	Septuagint
NAC	New American Commentary
NICNT	New International Commentary on the New Testament
NovT	*Novum Testamentum*
PL	*Patrologia Latina*
PNTC	Pillar New Testament Commentary
SBLSP	Society of Biblical Literature Seminar Papers
SJT	*Scottish Journal of Theology*
TDNT	*Theological Dictionary of the New Testament*
TNTC	Tyndale New Testament Commentaries
TrinJ	*Trinity Journal*
TynBul	*Tyndale Bulletin*
VT	*Vetus Testamentum*

JBL   *Journal of Biblical Literature*
WBC   Word Biblical Commentary
WTJ   *Westminster Theological Journal*

PART ONE

Foundations for Leadership through Followership

CHAPTER ONE

What If Jesus Didn't Lead like Jesus? Redefining Christian Leadership

"Jesus called them over and said to them, 'You know that those who are regarded as rulers of the Gentiles lord it over them, and those in high positions act as tyrants over them. But it is not so among you.'"

Mark 10:42–43

▶ Chapter One Key Point

The power that a leader exercises is not the leader's but Christ's; the truth that the leader is called to proclaim is not the leader's vision but God's revelation; and the position to which the leader is called is not sovereignty over the community but stewardship within the community, submitted to the leadership of Christ. ◀

Jesus has been showing up in some unexpected locations lately.

Well, not Jesus himself, but images and objects that—at least in the eyes of some beholders—happen to look like Jesus.

Two separate families have spotted the face of Jesus in splotches of mold on their shower walls. "It gives me inspiration just to do better," one individual said after his bathroom epiphany. Some saw these images as divine signs, while others looked into the face of Jesus and saw dollar signs. One man sawed out his image of Jesus and sold the moldy sheetrock to a casino for nearly two thousand dollars.

In another supposed sighting of Jesus, a bank teller fell asleep while frying some bacon. When he awoke, he was shocked to find his apartment filled with smoke, but his biggest surprise came when he scraped the scorched pork into the sink. There, imprinted in grease in the blackened pan, was an image that looked to him like the face of Jesus. "It's going to take pride of place on a wall," the teller replied when asked about his pan. "I might get a glass cabinet to put it in. . . . Someone's looking over me."[1]

Jesus, CEO?

There is another unusual spot where Jesus has been showing up as well— one that, for many people, may seem almost as incongruous as his alleged appearances in bacon grease and bathroom mold. For a couple of decades now, Jesus has been showing up on bookstore shelves and in online searches not only in the usual categories like "Christian living" and "theology" but also under less expected headings such as "leadership" and "management."

The book titles in this genre range from *Jesus, CEO* and *The Management Methods of Jesus* to *Lead like Jesus* and *Jesus on Leadership*. Nearly all of these texts follow a similar strategy in their quest to extract leadership tips from Scripture. Examples from the life of Jesus are selected from the biblical text; then these bits of sacred writ are distilled into universal principles guaranteed to boost leadership skills today.

The author of *The Management Methods of Jesus* claims, for example, to unveil the "principles of management practiced" by Jesus, "the greatest manager the world has ever known." Principles practiced by Jesus, according to this text, encompass everything from maintaining "good logistical support" to displaying generosity whenever followers deserve to be rewarded.[2] A similar text entitled *Lead like Jesus* shot to the top berth on the *New York Times* bestseller list with the guarantee that following the leadership style of Jesus will result in "right and effective" decisions.[3] According to this book, a heart that imitates the leadership style of Jesus will be inclined toward right preparation of successors, a right perspective on who should lead, and the recognition of feedback from followers as a gift. Another such text, *Jesus, CEO*, suggests that imitating Jesus's methods of leadership can enable business leaders to harness "spiritual energy" so they will become more "empowered."[4]

These leadership texts are undoubtedly well intended. After all, doesn't every Christian leader long to lead in a way that honors Jesus? And shouldn't we feel compelled to pay attention to the perspective of Scripture on every topic, including leadership? Of course! And yet it is our contention that most of these quests to extract timeless and universally transferable leadership principles from Scripture are as misguided as searching for Jesus in scorched frying pans and moldy shower walls.

People believe they've glimpsed Jesus in bacon grease and bathroom mold because they see splotches that fit their preconceived notions of what Jesus might look like, based on everything from classic paintings to cartoon sketches. Similarly, if we open the Scriptures seeking moralistic principles to sustain our practices of leadership, what we tend to notice are patterns that fit our preconceived assumptions about leadership. The result is that patterns observed in biblical texts are excised from their canonical contexts and elevated to the level of divinely inspired prescriptions. When that happens, the biblical text functions not as the revelation of the kingdom of God in Christ but as a collection of humanly achievable principles that fit preconceived notions of leadership.

What If Jesus Didn't Lead like Jesus?

The problem is not that the resulting leadership principles do not work. In fact, many of these principles do represent effective techniques for aiming an organization toward a leader's objectives. Some of them may even be usable in Christian organizations. The problem is that these principles are presented as if they derive from the biblical metanarrative—and, in particular, from the life and teachings of Jesus—when, in fact, they are the result of human observations of patterns in the created order. The Scriptures are used in ways that are selective, decontextualized, and—in many instances—not even distinctly Christian. According to *Lead like Jesus,* for example, imitating the leadership style of Jesus requires leaders to treat feedback from their followers as a gift. Yet the authors conveniently sidestep those moments when Jesus seems not to have followed this principle at all—such as the time when Peter provided Jesus with feedback on his claim that the Messiah must be crucified. "This will never happen to you!" was Peter's feedback (Matt 16:22–23). Jesus replied, "Get behind me, Satan! You are a hindrance,"

apparently unaware that leading like Jesus means always receiving followers' feedback as a gift. If *Lead like Jesus* is right about how to lead like Jesus,
sometimes Jesus didn't lead very much like Jesus.

The author of *The Management Methods of Jesus* conveniently limits
his examples to patterns that are humanly attainable and not uniquely or
necessarily grounded in the supernatural works and character of Jesus.
In the process, Jesus is presented as the supreme exemplar of a manager
who maintains strong logistical support. But the book's declaration that
leaders today should imitate the logistical skills of Jesus never grapples
with those moments when Jesus supernaturally created his own logistical support systems. Faced with a shortage of wine at a wedding, Jesus
transformed six jars of water into the finest vintage the guests had ever
tasted (John 2:1–10). Later, faced with a lack of lunch supplies, Jesus
caused ordinary baskets to spawn sufficient sardines and dinner rolls to
feed thousands of people (Matt 14:13–21; 15:32–39). And yet none of
the books about Jesus's style of leadership suggests that leaders should imitate Jesus by miraculously metamorphosing a picnic lunch or a few water
bottles into a free-for-all food and drink buffet—and that is not what we
are suggesting either.

Our point is that leading like Jesus can't be reduced to the imitation of
humanly attainable principles that are as true of Buddha as they are of the
Son of God.[5] If these universalized leadership principles do indeed work, it
is not because of anything that God has accomplished through the incarnation, crucifixion, and resurrection of the second person of the Trinity.[6] It is,
instead, because they represent patterns that have been woven into creation
itself. If a leadership principle could have originated as easily from a fortune
cookie as from the Bible, that principle is probably not going to prepare you
to lead like Jesus.[7]

To find biblical texts that call for "leadership" in any way approximat-
ing what that term implies in Western cultures, one is forced "to begin with
such concepts of leadership and then try to tie Bible verses to them in a non-
contextual or barely contextual way."[8] Some of the resulting observations
about leadership may turn out to be accurate. And yet it is equally possible
that these principles represent human observations of sin-distorted patterns
in a cosmos that is groaning for a glory yet to come (Rom 8:20–22).[9] In
many cases, seeking universal leadership principles in Scripture results in

radical distortions of the meaning of the biblical text.[10] Such principles may manage to smear a veneer of religiosity over the surface of our existing patterns of leadership, but they cannot conform our leadership to the character of Jesus or fill our leadership with the power of his Spirit.

Christian Leadership and the Story Line of Scripture

Does this mean, then, that Jesus has nothing to teach us about how to lead? Are biblical writings "profitable for teaching, for rebuking, for correcting, for training in righteousness" (2 Tim 3:16) but irrelevant for administration? If so, where should a pastor glean wisdom to lead his flock? For that matter, how does a Christian CEO learn to manage her employees in ways that reflect her commitment to Christ? How can administrators in Christian nonprofit organizations make certain that their leadership practices express God's design?

We are convinced that Jesus has much to teach us about how to lead. Yet these lessons will be missed if we merely attempt to distill a few practices described in the Gospels into universal leadership principles. *What's misplaced in such a process is the centeredness of Jesus's leadership in the cross and resurrection, as well as the positioning of his story within the broader story line of God's work with Israel and the world.* The leadership practices of Jesus only make sense when treated in the context of the whole canon of Scripture. As Scot McKnight reminds us in *The King Jesus Gospel,*

> The Story of Jesus makes sense only as it follows and completes the Story of Israel. . . . The apostles' gospel was the Story of Jesus resolving the Story of Israel. The texts the apostles quoted from the Old Testament weren't props; they were light posts to help Israel find its way from Abraham to Jesus.[11]

God's work with humanity is a single glorious river that rolls from Eden to the new Jerusalem, and we are privileged to be caught in its currents.[12] The story of Jesus is the apex within this vast metanarrative that stretches from the beginning of time to the end. It is the story of a kingdom lost in Eden, misplaced again in Israel's exile, then inaugurated and guaranteed anew through a cross and an empty tomb.

The canonical Scriptures are the written revelation of this single divine plan to flood every crest and crevasse in the cosmos with the glories of God's reign. Since the canon is a coherent whole that tells a single story, every biblical text should be interpreted on its own terms as it stands in the context of the entire canon.[13] The Bible "is not an inspired book of moralisms or a book of virtues; it is, from cover to cover, a book about the glory of God in Jesus Christ through the redemption of his people who will dwell in the kingdom of Christ forever."[14]

That is the central reason why the texts that tell the story of Jesus must never be treated as decontextualized fragments that can be distilled into timeless principles to improve our personal leadership skills. The story of Jesus is part of a comprehensive metanarrative that God has provided to teach us, to warn us, and to transform us (Rom 15:4; 1 Cor 10:11). Separating the story of Jesus from the larger story line of Scripture is like beginning a baseball game with the seventh-inning stretch, launching your reading of a trilogy by studying the final chapter in the final volume, or expecting an airplane to land at your destination without first taking off from your point of departure.

When it comes to leadership, there *is* much to be learned from empirical research and from the intuitive reflections of marketplace leaders—but, without the whole canon of Scripture as our supreme and sufficient authority, flawed views of divine purposes and human capacities will skew our view of leadership. That's why a Christ-centered, kingdom-focused, canonically shaped vision of leadership must precede any principles of leadership that derive from human wisdom. Unless our foundational vision for leadership is grounded in the metanarrative of Scripture that culminates in the kingdom inaugurated through Jesus Christ, we will not be able to separate the wisdom of the world from the wisdom of Christ.

Our goal in this book is to provide a foundation for the study of leadership that looks at the subject with both feet firmly planted in the whole of Scripture, not in a few isolated and extracted examples of leadership. Our focus will be on church leadership, and particularly on the character and practices of pastoral leaders. Many of the truths we highlight will be, however, equally applicable to the lives of Christian leaders in the marketplace. This vision for Christian leadership has emerged from examining the story line of Scripture comprehensively, interpreting biblical texts in light of their historical, epochal, and canonical contexts.[15]

1. *Interpreting the Scriptures in their historical contexts means exploring each text in light of its grammar, genre, and original setting.* This is a crucial first step whenever we study the Scriptures. Our interpretation should never, however, stop at this horizon, because neither Jesus nor the inspired authors of Scripture ever stopped there (Luke 24:27, 44; for examples, see Matt 2:15, 18; John 19:24, 28–30). The earliest Christians moved beyond how the text would have been understood by the first hearers to ask what the text means in light of Jesus Christ and the whole canon of Scripture.

2. *Interpreting the Scriptures in their epochal context means recognizing that God did not reveal everything to his people at once.* Particularly in the Old Testament, the Scriptures are pregnant with implications that were not recognized until later, and authors frequently seem to have been unaware of the full implications of their own Spirit-inspired declarations. These later implications never, however, correct or contradict earlier texts. Inspired intentions that were hidden like tiny seeds in earlier biblical texts blossom in light of later events into meanings that the original human authors never imagined.[16]

3. *Interpreting the Scriptures in their canonical context calls us to seek God's intention for each text by reading the text as part of a single, unified, Spirit-inspired canon centered in the revelation of God's kingdom in Jesus Christ.*[17] "We all hold confidently," Augustine of Hippo declared in the fifth century, "to the firm belief that these historical events and the narrative of them always have some foreshadowing of things to come, and are always to be interpreted with reference to Christ and his church."[18]

Dynamics of Christian Leadership

As the two of us have taught, studied, and practiced leadership over the past several years, this approach has yielded a series of observations that will be woven throughout every part of this book:[19]

1. *Leadership calls for the pursuit of God's justice in the context of a covenant community.* This is the *moral* orientation of leadership, and it is grounded in our common creation in God's image and in our union with Christ.
2. *Leadership calls for right use of divinely delegated authority.* This is the *power* component of leadership, and this component shapes our relationships with the people we lead.
3. *Leadership calls for declaration of a truth and vision that is greater than ourselves.* This is the foundation of *truth*, and it provides direction for our mission in the world.[20]

In the following chapters, you will see these observations developed into three distinct dynamics of Christian leadership:

1. *The position to which the leader is called is not sovereignty above the community but stewardship within the community.* The proper position of the Christian leader is a position of presence and guidance among the people, not one of separation from or lordship over the people. This observation emerges from the moral dynamic of leadership.
2. *The power that the leader exercises is not the leader's but Christ's, and this power must be expressed according to God's design for a diverse community of Spirit-equipped servants.* Any power that the leader exercises is given by God. The purpose of this divinely delegated power is not to provide a leader with a platform for personal fulfillment or professional advancement. It is to guide the people of God toward the mission of God for the glory of God. This observation is grounded in the power dynamic of leadership.
3. *The truth that the leader is called to proclaim is not the leader's vision but God's revelation.* The leader's goal is not for the people to submit to a pursuit of the leader's dreams; it is to guard and to guide the people in such a way that they seek and submit to the authority of God. This observation is tied to the truth dynamic of leadership.

The single proposition that ties these threads together is the recognition that the leader's pursuit of God always takes precedence over the leader's positional authority. Before we are leaders, we must be followers—followers of a God who goes before us. "When we look at the Bible, we shouldn't be looking for a list of leadership principles. What we should be looking for is the God who leads. The Bible focuses far more on *who God is* than on *what we need to be.*"[21]

In the old covenant, the people of God pursued God by following God-called mediators—prophets and judges, priests and kings—and by living faithfully according to God's covenant. In the new covenant, the lives of all believers have been joined with the life of the crucified and risen Christ. The leader's calling within this Christ-formed community is not to live as an old-covenant mediator but to take the lead in orienting people's attention and affections toward Jesus Christ the mediator and overseer who goes before us (John 10:4; 1 Tim 2:5; Heb 2:11; 1 Pet 2:25).

Leadership as Moral Practice	Leadership calls for the pursuit of God's justice.	The position to which the leader is called is not sovereignty above or separation from the community but stewardship within the community in union with Christ.
Leadership as Right Appropriation of Power	Leadership calls for the right use of divinely delegated authority.	The power that the leader exercises is not the leader's but Christ's, and this power must be expressed according to God's design for a diverse community of Spirit-equipped servants.
Leadership as Proclamation of Truth	Leadership calls for the declaration of a truth and vision that is greater than ourselves.	The truth that the leader is called to proclaim is not the leader's vision but God's revelation.

Our goal in *The God Who Goes before You* is not to present timeless principles that would work as well in a synagogue or a mosque as in the life of a follower of Jesus. Our purpose is to highlight patterns that are uniquely rooted in God's revelation of himself in the whole of his written Word and, supremely, in Jesus Christ. Moralistic principles distilled from incidents in the lives of religious sages may work to accomplish human objectives in an organization. Yet they will do little to lead us toward patterns of leadership that are shaped by the Triune God and grounded in our union with Christ. One of our teaching colleagues is known for placing this challenge before fledgling preachers: "Did Jesus have to be raised from the dead for your sermon to work? If not, start over."[22] We've asked ourselves a similar question throughout every stage of developing this book: "Did Jesus have to be raised from the dead for this truth about leadership to work? If not, start over."

Marketplace Definitions of Leaders and Leadership

"Leadership is a process whereby an individual influences a group of individuals to achieve a common goal."[23]

—Peter Northouse

"The only definition of a leader is someone who has followers."[24]

—Peter Drucker

"Leadership is the capacity to translate vision into reality."[25]

—Warren Bennis

"Leadership is influence—nothing more, nothing less."[26]

—John Maxwell

"Leadership is a process of social influence, which maximizes the efforts of others, towards the achievement of a goal."[27]

—Kevin Kruse

What common themes do you notice in this list of definitions? Which of these definitions is most helpful for Christian leadership? Which one is least helpful?

The Struggle to Define "Leadership"

But how should "leadership" be defined?

Bernard Bass, a well-known leadership scholar, has suggested that "the search for the one and only proper and true definition of leadership seems to be fruitless"—and he's probably right.[28] Scholarly definitions of leadership have tended toward ambiguity, while practitioners' perspectives have typically relied on intuition rather than research.[29] This reliance on intuition has resulted in many memorable but reductionistic definitions of leadership. Consider, for example, John Maxwell's understanding of leadership as "influence—nothing more, nothing less," or Peter Drucker's claim that "the only thing you can say about a leader is that a leader is somebody who has followers."[30] Leadership certainly includes followers and influence, but the definition of a leader can hardly be reduced to either one.

Our intent is to present a definition that is holistic rather than reductionistic, and Christ-centered rather than universal, with both scholarly foundations and clear practical application. This definition is not meant to stand as "the one and only proper and true definition of leadership." Our goal is far more modest. What we plan to present is a distinctly Christian definition of the role of a pastoral leader based on specific leadership dynamics that have emerged through a study of the Scriptures.

Before providing this operative description of a leader, however, it will be helpful to sketch out the precise position of our definition in relation to earlier understandings of leaders and leadership. Most definitions of leaders and leadership over the past century or so have fallen into one of three categories: leader centered, leader directed, or leader/follower focused.[31]

1. *Leader centered.* Leader-centered definitions of leadership see everything in the organization rising or falling based on the leader's character and competence. Early twentieth-century research in the field of leadership was strongly leader centered. In this era, studies of leadership focused on the leader's capacity to shape opinions through written and oral communication as well as through persuasive behavior ("persuasion without coercion").[32] The "great man" theory of leadership, as well as early situational leadership theories, exemplifies this approach that defines leadership in terms of the acts and character of the leader.

2. *Leader directed.* Leader-directed definitions are concerned with the ways that a leader casts vision, sets goals, enforces compliance, and evaluates performance. Leader-directed descriptions of leadership tend to focus on the achievement of measurable results.

3. *Leader/follower focused.* Leader/follower definitions of leadership have been concerned with the interactions between leaders and followers. In this perspective, leadership is seen as a process. Important aspects of this process include how influence is exerted, how power and roles are differentiated, and how people connect emotionally with one another, as well as dynamics of distance between leaders and followers. In the leader/follower approach, the leader serves as a model to be imitated.[33]

Here's another way to look at the contours of leadership research over the past several decades: In the early twentieth century, leadership was primarily defined in terms of "control and the centralization of power."[34] Writers in the 1930s reacted against this perspective and highlighted the importance of successful mutual interactions between leaders and followers. By the 1960s, the attention had shifted to the influence of the leader's behavior on the accomplishment of democratically determined goals. The 1980s saw a surge of published works on leadership. Definitions of leadership became more multifaceted, but the theme of leadership as excellent management still dominated much of the literature. Leadership was, in some sense, singing the tune of industrialism at this point.[35]

More recently, leadership literature has increasingly distinguished between leadership and management. This is not to suggest, of course, that effective leadership does not require management skills. The vast majority of leaders must operate both as managers and leaders.[36] These functions have been, however, increasingly recognized as distinct. The most recent trends have focused on leadership as a social process,[37] and it is likely that future leadership research will continue to seek a better understanding of the social interactions between leaders and groups.[38]

Throughout the history of leadership studies, the dominant theories of leadership have been rooted in perspectives that have overlooked persons of color. Some of the greatest leaders of the twentieth century have been African Americans. And yet it has only been in the past few decades that significant research has explored the distinct contours of African American leadership—and even less research has been pursued in relation to Hispanic and Asian leaders.[39] To gain a more nuanced and multifaceted understanding of leadership, future scholars and practitioners of leadership must listen more carefully to a far broader range of cultures and ethnicities.[40]

Common Themes in Definitions of Leadership

Peter Northouse has identified four common themes in definitions of leadership:

1. Leadership is a process.
2. Leadership involves influence.
3. Leadership occurs in a group context.
4. Leadership involves goal attainment.[41]

From the perspective of a Christian leader, what is missing from this list? What do you find most useful? What is least useful?

Christian Definitions of Leaders and Leadership

"Leadership is all about putting the right beliefs into action, and knowing, on the basis of convictions, what those right beliefs and actions are."[42]

—R. Albert Mohler Jr.

"Leadership is influence, the ability of one person to influence others to follow his or her lead. . . . The personality of the spiritual leader influences others because it is irradiated, penetrated, and empowered by the Holy Spirit."[43]

—J. Oswald Sanders

"Christian leadership [is] inspiring, challenging, or empowering people or groups to join God's mission of redemption and healing."[44]

—Arthur Boers

"A leader is one who influences a specific group of people to move in a God-given direction."[45]

—J. Robert Clinton

"Christian leaders are servants with credibility and capabilities who are able to influence people in a particular context to pursue their God-given direction."[46]

—Aubrey Malphurs

"Spiritual leadership is knowing where God wants people to be and taking the initiative to get them there by God's means in reliance on God's power."[47]

—John Piper

Which of these definitions is most helpful to you as a Christian leader? Why? Which one is least helpful?

An Operative Definition of the Role and Practices of a Christian Leader

It's at this point that our definition provides a unique perspective. Ours is a definition that not only prioritizes an objective foundation for leadership in Scripture but also takes both leaders and followers into account and explicitly seeks to develop communities that are ethnically, generationally, and socioeconomically diverse.[48] Instead of defining leadership as an abstract concept, our definition is more concrete, focusing on the leader's role and practices within the community. With all these factors in mind, here's how we have chosen to define the Christian leader's function and calling:

> *The Christ-following leader—living as a bearer of God's image in union with Christ and his people—develops a diverse community of fellow laborers who are equipped and empowered to pursue shared goals that fulfill the creation mandate and the Great Commission in submission to the Word of God.*[49]

This definition calls Christian leaders—and church leaders in particular—to interact with the people they lead on the foundational basis of their common creation in God's image. This foundation does not remove the need for leadership, but it does relativize leadership by recognizing our shared identity as bearers of God's image as well as the supremacy of Christ over leaders and followers alike. This understanding of leadership is "leader centered"—but the central leader is Jesus Christ, not any mere human being. It includes aspects that are "leader directed"—but the goals toward which the leader directs his people are conformed to God's revelation, not to the leader's personal vision. It takes "leader/follower" interactions into account—but it grounds these interactions in the objective realities of creation in God's image and re-creation in union with Christ.

So how should this definition reshape our practices of leadership?

The final paragraphs of this chapter will unpack a few foundational implications of this definition for the life and work of the Christian leader. We'll begin by looking at the person of the leader, then we will move to the functions of a leader. Lastly, we will tie the definition to a triad of leadership dynamics that will form a framework for the remainder of the book.

Creation Mandate

The creation mandate is God's command to humanity to "be fruitful, multiply, fill the earth, and subdue it" (Gen 1:28). "Be fruitful, multiply, fill the earth" suggests cultivation of the social world, calling humanity to build families, churches, schools, cities, governments, laws. "Subdue the earth" includes stewardship of the natural world, calling us to plant crops, build bridges, design computers, paint canvases, convert ink and paper into books, compose music, construct cabinetry—all in ways that value and sustain the earth's resources. This biblical command is sometimes also called the *cultural mandate*, because it lays the foundation for the formation of culture.[50]

Great Commission

The Great Commission is Christ's command to his followers to "Go . . . and make disciples of all nations, baptizing them in the name of the Father and of the Son and of the Holy Spirit, teaching them to observe everything I have commanded you" (Matt 28:19–20).

The Identity of the Leader: A Bearer of God's Image Living in Union with Christ

A Christian leader is one who has been redeemed by the blood of Jesus, united with him through the work of the Holy Spirit, and called to guide fellow bearers of God's image. Put another way, the life of the Christian leader is marked by *union* with Christ, *communion* with others, and a *mission* to exercise dominion over some specific aspect of God's creation. The result of this gift of union, communion, and mission should be holy ambition to multiply the manifest fame of God's name and to see people formed into the image of Christ. A Christ-following leader embraces these privileges with humility, seeing these gifts as undeserved opportunities to participate in the growth of God's kingdom.

When leaders are set free from the need to be glorified, the door is opened for deep love and sincere respect for the people they lead. A high ethic of care drives such leaders to guide followers in right paths not simply for the accomplishment of organizational goals but for the flourishing and formation of each individual. Driven by this ethic of care, leaders can personify a combination of godly ambition and humble dominion in their leadership (Acts 20:28; 1 Cor 11:1; Heb 13:7; 1 Pet 5:3).[51]

Union with Christ

The leader's union with Christ will be a foundational theme throughout this exploration of leadership. Union with Christ is identification with God's Son that leads to participation in God's life and to incorporation into the communion of God's people (Rom 5:17; 6:11; Col 3:3). "Those who are in Christ act out Christ's obedient sonship, attesting to his death and resurrection in every scene they play."[52] What this means for a believer's daily life is that, from the moment we first place our faith in Christ,[53] the Holy Spirit joins us with Jesus in such a way that we enjoy the same relationship with the Father that Jesus does.[54]

The Function of the Leader: One Who Empowers Fellow Laborers

Leaders are also called to create environments that are conducive to high levels of personal motivation, resulting in increased effectiveness and joy among followers. One overlooked aspect in the formation of such an environment is a passion for excellence and beauty.[55] God is surrounded by "strength and beauty," and his primeval creation was a place of manifold beauty (Gen 1:4, 10, 12, 18, 20–31; Ps 96:6). In his creation of the world, it is as if our Creator has gone off

on one wild, specific tangent after another, or millions simultane-
ously, with an exuberance that would seem to be unwarranted, and
with an abandoned energy sprung from an unfathomable font. . . .
The point of the dragonfly's terrible lip, the giant water bug, bird-
song, or the beautiful dazzle and flash of sunlighted minnows is . . .
that it all flows so freely wild, like the creek, that it all surges in such
a free, fringed tangle . . . : the [Creator] loves pizzazz.[56]

The fall distorted the beauty of God's creation, but our pizzazz-loving
Creator's passion for creational splendor never ceased. He made this continuing concern for beauty clear in his instructions for Israel's worship
(Exod 28:2, 40). Even when veiled in flesh, Jesus provided his disciples with
a momentary glimpse of his radiant beauty (Matt 17:2). In the closing chapters of the biblical canon, the Holy Spirit inspired John to depict the consummation of God's plan for the ages as a golden city with splendor "like a
precious jewel" (Rev 21:11; 22:1).

A leader's passion for excellence and beauty may include the formation
of aesthetically pleasing environments—but beautiful leadership isn't merely
about physical aesthetics. Beauty in leadership means choosing to value not
only quantifiable objectives but also intangible outcomes—outcomes that
contribute to human flourishing in ways that can't be counted or measured.
If indeed humanity's chief purpose is "to glorify God and to enjoy him forever,"[57] our approach to leadership should provoke Creator-glorifying joy in
the lives of the people we lead. At the very least, people should sense that we
value intangible aspects of human thriving and that we are striving to create contexts where they can flourish. This recognition moves leaders from
merely wondering, "How can we complete this task?" to asking, "What is
the most beautiful way that we can pursue this goal together?"[58]

Leadership Definition, Dynamics, and Diagnostics

	Leadership Definition	Leadership Dynamic	Leadership Diagnostics
Union with Christ	*The Christ-following leader—living as a bearer of God's image in union with Christ and his people—*	The position to which the leader is called is not sovereignty above or separation from the community but stewardship within the community in union with Christ.	Are there areas of your leadership where you are not clearly recognizing that any power you may possess is a stewardship delegated by God?
Communion with Christ's People	*develops a diverse community of fellow laborers who are equipped and empowered to pursue shared goals*	The power that the leader exercises is not the leader's but Christ's, and this power must be expressed according to God's design for a diverse community of Spirit-equipped servants.	Do you imagine possibilities for ethnic, cultural, and socioeconomic diversity in your community that do not yet exist? How are you empowering others to shape the organization's vision and to hold one another—and you—accountable to pursue this vision?
Mission in the World	*that fulfill the creation mandate and the Great Commission in submission to the Word of God.*	The truth that the leader is called to proclaim is not the leader's vision but God's revelation.	In what areas are you most tempted not to proclaim God's truth with boldness and integrity? What risks are you taking for the sake of seeking to fulfill the creation mandate and the Great Commission?

Followership, Delegated Power, and the Necessity of Community

When we bring together our definition of leadership with the three dynamics that we mentioned earlier (see "Leadership Definition, Dynamics, and Diagnostics" in this chapter), we see that (1) *A Christian leader is, first and foremost, a follower*. Research into followership has been largely overlooked in contemporary leadership literature, but followership is central to every aspect of what we have written in *The God Who Goes before You*.[59] "The Christ-following leader"—according to our definition—lives "as a bearer of God's image in union with Christ and his people." Because Christian leadership is at its very core "followership," Christ-following leaders must never pretend that they possess sovereignty above or separation from the people they serve. We are fellow bearers of God's image with the people we lead, and Christ himself has united us with them.

For the Christian leader, followership means that everyone, even the leader, is always being led.[60] When the Israelites were making their way through the wilderness, God repeatedly revealed himself as the God who goes before his people; old covenant leaders led the people by following the God who went before them (Exod 13:21; 23:23; 32:34; Num 14:14; Deut 1:30–33; 31:8; Josh 3:6, 11). This revelation of God's ways in the wilderness pointed forward to the call of Jesus to follow him and to his promise to forge the way before us all the way to the end (Matt 4:19; 8:22; 9:9; 10:38; 16:23–24; 19:21; 20:29; 26:32; 28:7; Heb 12:2).

We are not called to lead like Jesus in the sense of attempting to imitate his precise practices of management or administration; instead, we are called to lead as followers of Jesus. In fact, in one sense, the people we lead should not be following us at all. We are followers of God, and the people we lead should follow God *through* us—that is to say, they should look at us and glimpse not our own personal whims and visions but God's will, God's way, and God's passion for the fame of his own name. "Leaders . . . lead as they are led by Christ; they teach as they are taught of Christ; they build in the manner by which they have been instructed by Christ; and they labor for the glory, not of themselves, but for the glory of the one to whom belongs all glory and honor and praise."[61] We are stewards of Christ's mission who have answered his call, and Christ himself goes before us as the only proper focus of our contemplation and direction.

The claim that a leader is a follower first and never ceases to be a follower is radically counterintuitive. "Did you ever stop," one character muses in the classic comedy film *Road to Utopia,* "to think of one of those dog sled teams? The lead dog is the only one that ever gets a change of scenery."[62] The unspoken assumption is that the most desirable place to be is always ahead of everyone else, separate and at the front of the pack. Otherwise, all that you see will be the backside of whoever is in front of you. But, as Moses discovered in the cleft of Mount Sinai, the "back" of the God who goes before us is a glorious sight to behold and to follow (Exod 33:23).

> Before leaders can presume the right to teach people God's Word or to create visions of growth and destiny for them, they must embody personally the ideals of the covenant relationship to which the people have bound themselves. This may call for a modification of [John] Maxwell's favorite leadership proverb, "He who thinks he leads, but has no followers, is only taking a walk." Actually, leaders in the church *must* be taking a walk, walking according to God's Word so that they may learn to fear the Lord and obey his will. In this way they can model for the people the direct link between knowing the Word and fearing and obeying the Lord.[63]

Christian leaders are not soloists or free agents who forge paths for our organizations according to our own independent hopes and whims. We are accountable to the people around us in the church, and we are called to follow in the footsteps of the God who goes before us.

(2) Second, *leadership is inseparable from community.* "Where there is community," Dietrich Bonhoeffer observed, "there is leadership."[64] That's why we have chosen to define leadership not in individual terms but in terms of seeking to develop a diverse group of fellow laborers who are equipped and empowered for the pursuit of shared goals. Viewed from a Christian perspective, every community everywhere is—at the very least—a collection of persons created in God's image, clustered together because of the creation mandate and common grace. In the neighborhood where you live, both believers and unbelievers are drawn together by a God-given yearning for community. Your city's baseball team attracts thousands of people to a stadium and incites complete strangers to high-five one another after a home run because God formed us all with a love for organizing leisure through games.[65] Even if the content taught in your local community

college rejects the very idea of God, that college pulls people together into classrooms because of a longing for knowledge that God has etched into the soul of every human being. Every gathering of humanity hints at the reality of a God who exists in perfect community and who created human beings for community.

If a particular gathering of human beings also happens to be a local church, this community constitutes a visible expression of the bride of Christ—a group of Christ-following sojourners gathered around the Scriptures rightly taught and the sacraments rightly administered to honor the Triune God and to proclaim the good news of Christ's kingdom.[66] It is in the context of our local churches that Christian leaders are equipped to glorify God; this happens as we mourn and rejoice together, as we are admonished and taught, encouraged and rebuked. Christian leaders in the marketplace pursue this goal *from* the context of their local churches, strengthened and sharpened for mission by means of the fellowship they find among those who gather there. Leaders in the church lead not only *from* but also *in* these local communities of faith. Such leadership—whether in the church or in the marketplace—can be seen as followership exercised with biblical wisdom in the context of a community for which God has given us responsibility.

Seeking to develop a diverse group of fellow laborers—as we have chosen to define leadership in the context of community—includes pointing people toward a future in which their local church grows in depth, diversity, and passion for the spread of the gospel. Every congregation of believers should be actively pursuing diversity that is at least as variegated as its community, and this diversity should take the shape not only of a multiplicity of ethnicities but also of generational and socioeconomic diversity. Such diversity is, as Derwin Gray has pointed out, "a sign to the world that [God's] kingdom has broken through the darkness, establishing peace between enemies."[67] Diversity declares to the world that God is doing something among his people that can only happen through his power. As churches become more diverse—and particularly when diversity extends to the highest levels of leadership—those in the majority culture begin to glimpse systemic patterns of privilege and inequality around them. When that happens, God's people begin to recognize the biblical truth that the right use of privilege and power is not hoarding or self-protection but purposeful deployment of power to seek justice for the oppressed (Ps 82:2–4).

But, of course, leadership is far more than mere followership in community. God has also called leaders to exercise real authority with courage, creativity, and conviction—but this authority is never our own property to be used as we please. (3) *Authority is divinely delegated to us for a purpose greater than ourselves.* Power and authority belong to God, not to us (Ps 62:11). The purpose of any authority we may possess is to propel persons toward the creation mandate and the Great Commission in a manner that joyfully submits to the supreme authority of God's revelation. One day, all leaders—even if they are not followers of Jesus—will be called to give an account to the Sovereign King as to whether their authority functioned in harmony with God's revelation (Heb 13:17; 1 Pet 4:5). The standard by which leaders will be judged will be nothing less than Jesus Christ himself. Authentic and legitimate authority among God's people "can be attained only by the servant of Jesus who seeks no power of his own, who himself is a brother among brothers, submitted to the authority of the Word."[68]

Leadership That Magnifies God's Glory

"The kind of leadership that magnifies God's glory is a humble leadership; it's a leadership that does not seek to impress and to be admired; that does not set out to dazzle people with its own wisdom or to gain advantage and position, but devotes itself to the good of others and is willing to be looked down on and criticized and despised. Leadership that is faithful to the word of the cross is not about the pursuit and accumulation of glory."[69]

—David Starling

How can fixing our attention on the God who goes before us help us as Christian leaders to avoid patterns of leadership that seek to accumulate glory for ourselves or our churches?

Further Reading

Boers, Arthur. *Servants and Fools*. Nashville: Abingdon, 2015.
Gray, Derwin. *The High-Definition Leader*. Nashville: Nelson, 2015.
Loritts, Bryan. *Right Color, Wrong Culture*. Chicago: Moody, 2014.
Tidball, Derek. *Skillful Shepherds*. Grand Rapids: Zondervan, 1986.

What about You?

Reflect on this definition of leadership for a few moments:

The Christ-following leader—
living as a bearer of God's image in union with Christ and his people—
    develops a diverse community of fellow laborers who are
    equipped and empowered to pursue shared goals that fulfill
        the creation mandate and
        the Great Commission
            in submission to the Word of God.

Think about several approaches to leadership you have observed in the past. Then consider your own present practices of leadership in whatever context God has placed you, whether in the church, the home, or the marketplace. Which practices fit most clearly within this definition of leadership? What are some approaches you have observed or practiced that clearly fall outside this definition of leadership? If you are a leader in the broader marketplace, you may not be able to lead people to fulfill the Great Commission—but you can still lead people to pursue the creation mandate in ways that are congruent with God's truth.

CHAPTER TWO

The King Says:
Foundations for Leadership in the
Creation, Fall, and Exodus

"Then God said, 'Let us make man in our image, according to our likeness. They will rule.'"

Genesis 1:26

"The LORD went ahead of them in a pillar of cloud to lead them on their way during the day and in a pillar of fire to give them light at night, so that they could travel day or night."

Exodus 13:21

"The LORD your God who goes before you will fight for you, just as you saw him do for you in Egypt. And you saw in the wilderness how the LORD your God carried you as a man carries his son all along the way you traveled until you reached this place."

Deuteronomy 1:30–31

▶ Chapter Two Key Point

Leadership as followership was part of God's design from the beginning. Faithful leadership relies on the faithfulness, presence, and power of God. ◀

S imon Says" is one of the most familiar games children play—and it's one
that's been around a long time.[1] The current form of the game seems to
have started no fewer than eight hundred years ago. Yet even after centuries
of play, the rules of the game haven't changed much.

You do remember how to play "Simon Says," don't you?

Someone at the front of the room delivers commands that can range
from "touch your toes" to "put your finger on your neighbor's nose." You
follow the instructions—but only if they're preceded by the clause "Simon
says." The key to being a "Simon Says" champion is to listen carefully for
Simon's name. If you follow instructions that Simon didn't say, you'll find
yourself on the sidelines.

This game is a good reminder of one particular truth about leadership:
All of us are called to follow someone's instructions. Effective leadership
is not forging a solo path ahead of others; it's learning to follow the right
instructions from the right leader at the right time. None of us is a sovereign
ruler who answers only to self. It's true in "Simon Says," and it's true in our
lives as leaders.

> Human beings may claim to be sovereign, but no earthly leader is
> anything close to being truly sovereign. . . . Human leaders, no mat-
> ter their title, rank, or job description, are not really in charge. . . .
> We are merely stewards, not lords, of all that is put in our trust.
> The sovereignty of God puts us in our place, and that place is in
> God's service.[2]

Bob Dylan was right—no matter who you are, "you're gonna have to
serve somebody."[3]

If you happened to play "Simon Says" with a group of Hebrew-speaking
children, the game would likely be known not as "Simon Says" but as
"*Hamelekh 'Amar*"—"The King Says." Even though this name for the game
isn't meant to be a reference to God, it stands as a further reminder of our
unique calling as Christian leaders. Christian leadership is, first and foremost, following the lead of the Sovereign King of all creation.

Some leaders seem to think leadership means hauling a flag ahead of
their followers, independently plotting courses and strategies for the organization. Such leaders fail to recognize that every leader is first a follower
and that leadership was never meant to be a solo endeavor. The positions to

which we are called never privilege us with sovereignty above or separation from the people. Instead, they provide us with opportunities for stewardship among these people that we are privileged to lead. Followership and accountability in community are essential foundations for effective leadership. Dysfunctions in Christian leadership were typically dysfunctions in followership long before they became dysfunctions in leadership.

No matter how high Christian leaders may rise in an organization, we never cease to be servants. Any power we possess is delegated to us by someone, and all power ultimately derives from God. In this chapter, we will trace the initial contours of what it means to lead as a follower, drawing primarily from God's primeval design in Genesis and from God's rescue of his people in Exodus. What we will see is that effective stewardship of leadership is grounded in deliberate dependence on God's faithfulness, presence, and power.

Vicegerent

from Latin, *vicus* (place, office) + *gerere* (to hold, to carry)

Ruler appointed and empowered to govern as a representative of a sovereign or supreme ruler. In the beginning, Adam was created in covenant with God as a son and vicegerent over the world. From Adam until Christ, every God-appointed vicegerent failed to be faithful to his covenant with God. Christ alone was perfectly faithful to God's covenants.[4]

God's Design for Leadership

God's plan from the beginning was for human beings to live as both rulers and followers. Leadership was not something that God added after sin entered the world in an attempt to fix his blemished creation. Like marriage and community, leadership is a good gift that God wove into the fabric of creation from the very beginning.[5]

Immediately before he formed the first man and woman, God declared his intention to make them in his own "image," according to his "likeness," so that they would "rule" (Gen 1:26).[6] In ancient Near Eastern contexts, creation in the image and likeness of a deity implied *sonship* and *rulership*.

The divine image defines human life (ontologically—not just func-
tionally) in terms of a covenant relationship with the creator God
on the one hand, and with the creation on the other. The former
may be captured by the term *sonship*. . . . The latter relationship,
. . . between humans and the creation, may be reflected in the terms
kingship and *servanthood*.[7]

The first two human beings were designed to live as heirs of God's love
and as rulers of God's world. To be identified as God's likeness was to be
sons of God; to be crafted in God's image was to be royal vicegerents, ruling the King's domain in a manner that fulfilled the King's will.[8] The first
human being is, therefore,

set in the midst of creation as God's statue. He is evidence that
God is the Lord of creation; but as God's steward he also exerts his
rule, fulfilling his task not in arbitrary despotism but as a responsible agent. His rule and his duty to rule are not autonomous; they
are copies.[9]

In God's eyes, all of humankind is royalty. Every child of Adam and Eve
from every ethnicity and culture is, therefore, equally and infinitely valuable.[10] As a result, the people we lead must be defined in our minds first and
foremost "by their creation in the image of God. . . . They are not problems
to be fixed, but mysteries to be honored and revered."[11]

This shared status of sonship and rulership did not, however, preclude
the possibility of hierarchies, ranks, or distinct responsibilities among the
first human beings. Even before sin pierced the cosmos, God designed a
structure of headship for the flourishing of the social order in his world. The
opening chapters of Genesis mark the first man as a leader by crafting the
woman from the man and by highlighting the man's naming of the woman
(Gen 1:27; 2:18–23).[12] The man in the primeval garden "has a leadership
role while the woman has a 'followship' position. . . . Some think that submission was unknown until the fall, . . . but leadership-followship is a creation ordinance."[13] From the creation of primeval humanity until their fall
into iniquity, the man and the woman shared dominion as equal partners
with complementary roles (Gen 1:26).

Primeval humanity's vicegerency entailed not only kingly stewardship
but also priestly service.[14] The Holy Spirit inspired Moses to depict Adam's

cultivation of the garden in terms that would be applied later to the work of priests (Gen 2:15; Num 3:7–8; 8:26; 18:5–6). This pattern made it clear that the manual labor of tending and expanding the garden was neither menial nor meaningless. Adam was a priest in a garden sanctuary. He was called to nurture the garden as a living context for worship and to learn God's ways so that he could exercise God's rule as God himself would. Before their fall into sin, humanity constituted a royal priesthood, unfallen heirs of the Sovereign King, untainted by sin and free from death's sting. Kingship and priesthood were present in God's creation from the beginning, and the man and the woman ruled in holy complementarity. Their work was a royal labor that pointed to God's goodness and reflected God's glory.

This exalted status never, however, opened the door for any mere mortal to ascend to a status of total autocracy.[15] Human dominion was comprehensive and complementary but never independent or absolute. When God commanded the man and the woman to "rule the fish of the sea, the birds of the sky, and every creature that crawls on the earth," he spoke of this rulership in the plural (Gen 1:26, 28–29). In the more detailed recounting of humanity's creation in the second chapter of Genesis, God placed explicit boundaries around humanity's sovereignty by setting aside a single tree in the center of the garden and declaring this tree to be God's own exclusive possession (Gen 2:16–17; 3:3).[16] From the beginning, the privilege of leadership came with a mandate to submit to the Creator's words.[17] "Even in the garden of Eden he who would be lord of all [was to] be servant of all."[18]

Before designating the man and the woman as vicegerents, the Creator revealed himself to be the God who goes before his people. He did this by preparing the garden as a temple for his glory and by establishing his rightful role as sovereign Lord. Humanity's dominion was to be exercised in community, and this dominion was explicitly constrained by the will of a greater sovereign, the King over all. The leadership to which we are called is never sovereignty above or separation from the rest of humanity but stewardship within the community for the glory of God.

Work as God's Assignment for the Service of Others

"The material creation was made by God to be developed, cultivated, and cared for in an endless number of ways through human labor. But even the simplest of these ways is important. Without them all, human life cannot flourish. . . . We are continuing God's work of forming, filling, and subduing. Whenever we bring order out of chaos, whenever we draw out creative potential, whenever we elaborate and 'unfold' creation beyond where it was when we found it, we are following God's pattern of creative cultural development. . . . Our daily work can be a calling only if it is re-conceived as God's assignment to serve others. And that is exactly how the Bible teaches us to view work. . . . If God's purpose for your job is that you serve the human community, then the way to serve God best is to do the job as well as it can be done."[19]

—Tim Keller

How can you "re-conceive" of labor as God's assignment to serve others? Are there forms of honest labor that you fail to see as assignments from God? Do you look down on some forms of labor? Do you respond to waiters and waitresses with honor and respect even when they are slow, or do you objectify them as servants whose purpose is to meet your needs? Do you greet and get to know janitors, security guards, and delivery truck drivers that you encounter, or do you overlook and ignore them? Each of them is created in God's image, and their labor matters to God. The character of a leader is revealed by how the leader treats men and women who do the work that the world sees as menial. Because their labor matters to God, they and their labor should matter to you as well.

Leadership in the Shadow of the Fall

But humanity refused to be satisfied with anything less than total sovereignty. The resulting rebellion birthed not only personal iniquity but also the spread of sin in social structures, resulting in systemic injustice and oppression. "When Adam chose willful rebellion against the law of God," Eric Mason writes,

> he was choosing to forfeit his birthright by rejecting his calling to represent, be responsible, and enjoy his relationship with God, his wife, and the rest of creation. This single act placed in motion the initial and progressive fall of creation and its order, one whose effects still ravage every facet of the world today.[20]

Beginning beneath that tree in the center of the garden and continuing to this very day, leader after leader has perverted godly dominion into ungodly despotism.[21] Dictators hoard wealth for themselves while poverty and disease destroy their subjects; law enforcement systems perpetuate injustice by judging individuals differently based on their socioeconomic status or the amount of melanin in their skin; pastors pervert their positions for the sake of personal pleasure or profit. Even among leaders who sincerely long to follow God, depravity runs so deep that we are capable of deceiving ourselves into thinking we are pursuing God's way when we are exploiting others and running headlong down our own deadly paths.

All of these perversions of leadership represent attempts to usurp the sovereignty and power that belong to God alone. Adam and Eve, patriarchs and judges, priests and prophets and kings—all of them and all of us have swallowed the same seductive lie: "You will be like God" (Gen 3:5). This lie taints every aspect of our lives and leadership. Thus our lineage from Adam and Eve is—in the words of C. S. Lewis—"both honor enough to erect the head of the poorest beggar, and shame enough to bow the shoulders of the greatest emperor on earth."[22]

Every expression of leadership that fails to follow God first and foremost is either a distortion or a dim reflection of God's primeval design for leadership. A dictatorial leader, for example, may successfully aim people toward achieving his goals, but only by elevating himself to a level of sovereignty that is the rightful property of God alone. A gracious but unbelieving leader may, on the other hand, substitute transcendent ideals such as servanthood or fairness or justice for the Word of the living God. This sort of leadership can contribute to human flourishing even though the unbelieving leader may be unaware of God's goodness. How? The leader's ideals represent sin-dimmed reflections of the goodness that is God's alone, even if the leader is ignorant of the true origin of this goodness. Every good endeavor that humanity undertakes and every great story that we repeat represents—to borrow a phrase from J. R. R. Tolkien—"a splintered fragment of the true light, the eternal truth that is with God," even if that endeavor is undertaken by an unbeliever.[23]

Christian leaders must not, however, allow themselves to be satisfied with dim fragments of God's good design. We have glimpsed the true light, and we know that the very cosmos is orderly only because it is held together by the power of Christ (Col 1:16–17; 1 John 2:7–11). He is the light that illumines our practices of leadership.

But how, in a sin-darkened world, can Christian leaders remain centered in God's way?

The foundation for following God first is not found in any practice that we can achieve. In fact, it is not found in us at all! Our capacity to live as God-following leaders is rooted wholly in the character and promises of God. When moments of uncertainty arise—and they will!—we as Christian leaders are not called to dig deeper within ourselves to summon certitude and strength. Instead, we are called to cling to the covenant faithfulness, the unfailing presence, and the sovereign power of the God who goes before us. With that in mind, let's look closely at how God revealed his faithfulness, presence, and power in the life and leadership of Abraham and Moses.[24]

What about You?

Study Genesis 12–15.

Imagine yourself as Abraham. God has promised you a son and called you to follow him to an unknown place (Gen 12:1–3; 15:4)—but God has also revealed that your descendants will spend four centuries in a foreign land, enslaved and oppressed (15:13). How will you respond? In faith or in fear?

Abraham does both.

Abraham is a man with no premises on which to build a home, only promises that God will build a nation through him and his wife. Abraham follows the God who goes before him, but he also asks questions: "Lord GOD, what can you give me, since I am childless?" "Lord GOD, how can I know that I will possess it?" "Can a child be born to a hundred-year-old man?" (15:2, 8; 17:17). God reassures Abraham that his words will come true—but many decades will pass before most of these promises are fulfilled, and some promises will still remain unfulfilled when Abraham draws his last breath.

Today, God has assured us once and for all in Jesus Christ that every promise will be fulfilled. "Every one of God's promises is 'Yes' in him" (2 Cor 1:20). Because of God's decisive work in and through Jesus Christ, we can lead with patient confidence that God will do among his people everything that he has promised.

Following the God Who Is Faithful

The opening verses of Exodus invite readers into a story that stretches backward through Abraham to the very beginning of time. Moses wrote that "the Israelites were fruitful, increased rapidly, multiplied, and became extremely numerous" (Exod 1:7). When Moses wrote these words, he was reminding his readers that God never forgot the purposes he had when he created Adam or the promises he made when he called Abraham (compare Gen 1:28; 9:7; 17:6; 28:3; 35:11; 47:27; 48:4).[25] Neither Israel's slavery nor Israel's suffering had come as a surprise to God. When God made his covenant with Abraham, he had informed the man from Mesopotamia that his offspring would "be . . . enslaved and oppressed. However"—God promised—"I will judge the nation they serve, and afterward they will go out with many possessions" (Gen 15:13–14).

And so, at precisely the right time, God designated Moses as his servant and called the nation of Israel to become the priestly son and king that Adam had failed to be (Exod 4:22; 19:5–6).[26] He gave Moses the wisdom he needed to judge his people and turned Moses into a prophet like no other (Exod 18:13–26; Deut 34:10–12). The truth that sustains godly leadership is not a vision for the future that we develop in our own power; it is wisdom that comes through the gracious revelation and the sovereign power of God.

God's Plan Has Never Depended on Your Competence

When Moses protested his divine calling at the burning bush, "God could have tried to prove that Moses was the right man for the job. . . . No one in the whole world was better prepared to lead Israel out of Egypt than Moses, who was Egyptian enough to confront the Egyptians and Hebrew enough to love the Hebrews. All of that was true, but it was not the answer God gave. If he had shown Moses that he was fully qualified for his calling, that would have led Moses to trust in his gifts rather than in his God. The real question was not who Moses was but who God was, for 'God said, "I will be with you"' (Exod 3:12). The exodus did not depend on the competence of Moses but on the presence of God."[27]

—Philip Graham Ryken

Are there areas of your life and leadership in which you act as if God's plan depends on your competence? Meditate on God's message to Moses. Ask God to reveal and to remove the pride that presumes his plan depends on you.

Following the God Who Is with Us

When the time came for his people to be rescued, God raised up an unlikely leader—Moses, a felon who had spent four decades as a shepherd after fleeing the consequences of a capital crime in Egypt. God called Moses to fulfill this impossible task by igniting a scrap of desert vegetation. While the burning bush spilled over with the manifest glory of God the holy arsonist, Moses spilled out defensiveness and doubt. "Who am I? . . . What should I tell them? . . . What if they won't believe?" Moses asked. Then he informed the King of all creation—as if God didn't already know!—"my mouth and my tongue are sluggish" (Exod 3:11, 13; 4:1, 10). Before the bush stopped burning, Moses could be heard begging, "Please, Lord, send someone else" (4:13).

No matter what God declared to him, Moses could not imagine that he might be the leader God had selected to rescue his people. Moses objected to God's call a total of five times—but God never pointed Moses's attention to his own human capacities. God never said, "Be more self-confident, Moses; you've got this under control!" Instead, God responded to Moses's excuses by declaring a series of truths about his own nature and actions. God refused to allow "fear from the past . . . to thwart the redemptive promise of the future."[28] Here's a summary of the truths that God declared in Exodus as he prepared Moses to lead Israel:

- "I am the God of your father, the God of Abraham, the God of Isaac, the God of Jacob" (3:6).
- "I have observed the misery of my people" (3:7).
- "I have come down to rescue them . . . and to bring them . . . to a good and spacious land" (3:8).
- "I will certainly be with you" (3:12).
- "I AM WHO I AM" (3:14).[29]
- "But when I stretch out my hand and strike Egypt . . ." (3:20).
- "And I will give these people such favor with the Egyptians that when you go, you will not go empty-handed." (3:21).

- "This will take place . . . so they will believe that the Lᴏʀᴅ, the God of their fathers, the God of Abraham, the God of Isaac, and the God of Jacob, has appeared to you" (4:5).
- "I will help you speak and I will teach you what to say" (4:12).
- "I will help both you and him [Aaron] to speak and will teach you both what to do" (4:15).

"Neither previous faith nor any other personal endowment had the slightest part to play in preparing [this] man who was called to stand before Yahweh for his vocation."[30] Everything Moses needed to accomplish the task to which he was called, God provided through his own perfect presence. He still does. Because God is present with us in Christ, we as Christian leaders possess every resource we need to accomplish every task to which God calls us (Phil 4:10–20).

The centeredness of this calling in the power of God is clear throughout every line of this exchange between God and Moses. Near the center of his dialogue with Moses, God described himself as "I AM WHO I AM" and promised he would "be with" Moses (Exod 3:12, 14). This promise of God's continuing presence was probably meant to remind Moses of God's previous promises to remain with Abraham, Isaac, and Jacob (Gen 17:4; 26:3; 28:15). Later, the Lord God would repeat and expand this same promise to Moses: "My presence will go with you" (Exod 33:14). When God spoke these words, Moses clung so tightly to the promise that he responded, "If your presence does not go, . . . don't make us go up from here" (33:15).

> To lead the people effectively, Moses needed to know the very mind of God. He didn't want God simply to send down orders; he wanted to know the thinking behind God's plans—his ways with his people. To that end, Moses wanted to remain in constant communication with God. This was essential to his spiritual leadership.[31]

Moses understood that true leadership on his part was first and foremost followership. If God did not lead with his own presence, Moses saw that it was better not to proceed at all. In response to Moses's request, God not only sent a representative ahead of his people (Exod 23:20–21; 33:2) but also remained present among his people (33:15–17). Over and over, the God of Israel revealed himself to this leader of his people as the God who goes before us.

Today, God has revealed his presence once and for all in Jesus Christ, and he has promised to be with us "always, to the end of the age" through our union with Christ and through the presence of his Spirit (Matt 28:20). Because God is present in us and among us, we are never left alone, to lead in our own power; we lead the people of God by the power of the Spirit of God. If we are not dependent on God's presence within us through his Holy Spirit in every part of our leadership—not only in the ends but also in the means, methods, and motivations—our leadership is a failure, regardless of the external results.

The Call to Service and the Presence of God

"The call to God's service always comes with the promise of God's presence. . . . When Joshua inherited the mantle of spiritual leadership, God promised him, 'As I was with Moses, so I will be with you; I will never leave you or forsake you' (Josh 1:5). God made the same promise to Gideon, who was too timid to lead the troops into battle. God said, 'I will be with you' (Judg 6:16). God also promised to be with Jeremiah, who was only a youngster when he became a prophet: 'Do not be afraid . . . for I am with you' (Jer 1:8)."[32]

—Philip Graham Ryken

God has promised his presence to every believer in Jesus Christ, and he has personally provided this presence through the Holy Spirit, who unites us with Christ (Matt 28:20; John 14:15–21; Heb 13:5–6). In what particular areas in your life and leadership do you need a reminder of God's presence? Pray for a renewed awareness of God's continuing presence with you. Surround yourself with godly men and women in whom the presence of God's Spirit is apparent and authentic.

Following the God of Power

God's past faithfulness to his covenants reminds leaders that God still keeps his promises. God's unfailing presence empowers us to wait patiently for gifts and guidance that God alone can provide. But what if this ever-present and ever-faithful God happened to be powerless? If God were an impotent deity, every fragment of comfort and confidence in him would immediately vanish. Thankfully, the phrase "impotent God" has no place in the vocabulary of those who trust the words of Scripture. The God we follow is a God of power.

- God demonstrated his creation power by speaking all things into existence and by sustaining all things through his Word (Heb 1:3; 11:3; Col 1:17).
- When Adam and Eve rebelled against him, God revealed his redemption power by pointing their attention toward a rescuer who would deliver a death-blow to the serpent's skull (Gen 3:15). God fulfilled this promise in small ways through each godly prophet, priest, judge, and king in his people's history. Then he fulfilled this promise once and for all in the life, death, and resurrection of Jesus Christ. This is the power by which we as Christian leaders live and lead today.
- One day, God will display his consummation power when he makes all things right and new at the end of time. Every expression of God-honoring justice from the fall of humanity to the end of time points forward to this final judgment.[33]

God made his power particularly clear in the exodus when he waged war on Pharaoh's idolatry for the sake of his covenant people. The plagues inflicted on Egypt displayed God's saving power and acted as avenues for God's judgment on Pharaoh's stubborn refusal to release Israel.[34] God meant this judgment to force Pharaoh to recognize that the God of Israel alone was the Lord and that he alone was worthy of absolute obedience. The real battle was not between Israel and Egypt; the real struggle was for the fame of the one true God against the false gods of Egypt.[35]

So what does God's power have to do with our leadership?

Paradoxically, God's power refines our leadership by reminding us that God's plans do not depend on our leadership. God does not call us to lead because he is powerless without us. As Christian leaders, we are privileged to participate in a glorious plan that God is able to accomplish without us but that he nevertheless chooses to share with us. Simply put, God does not need you—and that's good news! This fact frees leaders from the tyranny of living as "functional atheists," acting as if God's plans depend on our performance.[36] If God's plan depended on you or me or any other fallen human being, his purposes would fail. "All authority . . . in heaven and on earth" has been given to Jesus, and he has promised to build his church in his power and in his way (Matt 16:18; 28:18). Any power that the leader deploys to fulfill God's plan in God's way is not the leader's power but Christ's (Phil 2:13).

Precisely because God's purposes will proceed with or without our leadership, we can wait with patience and prayer on the power of the God who goes before us. Patience is a crucial discipline for pastoral leaders—but it is a difficult discipline to practice when our culture and sometimes even our churches clamor for constant busyness. "Both our flesh and our culture scream against spending an hour on our knees beside a desk piled with papers," John Piper writes. "And sometimes I fear that our seminaries conform to this deadly pragmatism that stresses management and maneuvering as ways to get things done with a token mention of prayer and reliance on the Holy Spirit."[37] Through prayerful patience, we recognize that our leadership is meaningless apart from the power of God, and we can reject the urge to forge ahead in our own feeble strength.

What about You?

Study 1 Sam 13:6–15.

One of the first failures of Israel's first king was his impatient decision to offer a sacrifice on his own that he had been forbidden to make until the prophet arrived. Think about a specific pivotal moment of decision that you've faced as a leader. When you made the decision, were you confident in God's plan? Did you pray and wait for clear guidance from God? Or did you make a decision under pressure, relying on your own strength?

Sometimes it's difficult to proclaim to ourselves the good news of God's unfailing presence and perfect plan. Instead of waiting until clear confidence emerges in the context of a godly community, we're prone to launch out in our own power. When faced with these challenges, the leader who follows God is able first to wait and pray. Such a leader knows that God is at work and that his plan is never too early or too late. What this awareness produces is not self-absorbed passivity but God-saturated patience. When you can't see the future clearly, patiently seek God through his Word, through prayer, and through the counsel of godly believers. "Be gentle to everyone, able to teach, and patient" (2 Tim 2:24). Be willing to wait for the guidance of the God who goes before you. Waiting in prayer represents the Christian leader's disciplined refusal to act before God acts.[38]

The God Who Goes before Us

When Israel left Egypt after the last of the ten plagues, God provided an opportunity for the Israelites to recognize him as the God who quite literally went before them:

> They set out from Succoth and camped at Etham on the edge of the wilderness. The LORD went ahead of them in a pillar of cloud to lead them on their way during the day and in a pillar of fire to give them light at night, so that they could travel day or night. The pillar of cloud by day and the pillar of fire by night never left its place in front of the people. (Exod 13:20–22)

From the moment they left Egypt until they reached the land of promise, God's manifest presence went before his people. The people followed God's way by plodding after a pillar of cloud or fire. Later, God would command the people to follow the ark of the covenant—the symbol of his presence among them—in a similar manner "so that you can see the way to go, for you haven't traveled this way before" (Josh 3:4). Time after time, God revealed himself as the God who goes before his people.

The route that God plotted for his people was almost certainly not the path that they would have selected based on their own wisdom. If the Israelites had headed straight for Canaan, they would probably have arrived there in less than a month.[39] And yet instead of leading them on a direct route from Egypt to the Promised Land, God "led the people around toward the Red Sea along the road of the wilderness" (Exod 13:18). He did this, at least in part, to avoid a clash between the Israelites and the Philistines (13:17)—but this route fulfilled a greater purpose as well. The roundabout path to the Promised Land provided the perfect setting for God to rescue his people "with an outstretched arm and greats acts of judgment," just as he had promised (Exod 6:6). By routing his people around the Red Sea, God placed them in a situation where they would be trapped between an uncrossable sea and an unbeatable army. There, the Lord revealed his great power by obliterating Pharaoh's army.

So why did God guide his people out of Egypt through such a round-about route?

God led his people on the pathway that would bring him the greatest glory by providing the greatest glimpse of his power.

Even though it may have seemed absurd at the time, the pillar of fire and cloud took the Israelites on a far more glorious route than they could ever have planned in their own power or wisdom. Still today, God leads his people in the paths that will bring him the greatest glory. He does not typically guide us with pillars of cloud or fire; he leads us instead through the power of his Holy Spirit. "God gives us all the divine guidance we need, and in a much better form. He has given us the fire of his Spirit, and now we have his glorious presence with us all day and all night. It is as if the column of cloud and the pillar of fire have come right inside of us!"[40] God is always seeking his glory, and we his followers are most blessed whenever he is most glorified. Sometimes this blessing comes in the form of deepened faith or growth in our understanding of our Savior. Other times this blessing may place us—like Israel—on a path where God alone can rescue us.

Sometimes following God's way may even place us on a path that doesn't produce fruit in our own lifetime. When the Israelites left Egypt, "Moses took the bones of Joseph with him, because Joseph had made the Israelites swear a solemn oath, saying, 'God will certainly come to your aid; then you must take my bones with you from this place'" (Exod 13:19). Centuries earlier, Joseph had trusted God's promise to Abraham (Gen 15:13–14) and made plans that would call for a response from a generation not yet born.[41] According to legendary filmmaker George Lucas, "You can't do it unless you imagine it"—and there is an extent to which these words are true.[42] And yet as leaders who serve a God whose plans extend far beyond anything we can know or imagine in this life, we may be called at times to undertake tasks that contribute to a vision that we cannot yet imagine and that may not even find its fulfillment in our lifetimes.

It's easy as leaders to take a perspective that's too limited in terms of time. We may think in terms of days, months, even years—but we rarely think in terms of decades or generations. As a result, we demand immediate relief from our problems and immediate gratification for our successes. God, however, is "from eternity to eternity" (Ps 90:2). We and our children and our children's children will flit ever so briefly across the face of this earth before being swept away into eternity—but God has all the time in this world and the next, and he is enacting a plan that will far outlast the rise and fall of all the kingdoms of the earth. When we lead with the long run in mind, we can take a multigenerational perspective on God's plans for the people we serve. Particularly when making changes in your church, be patient and structure the changes incrementally.

The God who goes before us never forgets those on whom he has set his love. Nothing takes him by surprise, and he always raises up the right leaders at the right time. "When the time came to completion," God himself came to earth as the only perfect king and priest, servant and son (Gal 4:4). Through union with Christ, Christians have been joined with him and filled with his power in a manner greater than Moses ever imagined. Because God is faithful not only to do what is right but also to empower those he calls, we can trust that he will provide us with all we need in order to do whatever he calls us to do.

The Pillar That Went before the Israelites

"We make our way to the light of the dwelling place on high with the grace of Christ lighting our way and guiding us. That light and column of fire that both protected [the Israelites] throughout the whole of their journey from the darkness of the nights and led them by a sure path to the promised homes of the fatherland also prefigured the light of this grace."[43]

—Bede

In the exodus, a sign of God's presence went before his people in a pillar of cloud or fire. What are some specific ways that God's presence has gone before you as a leader in the past? What does this suggest about the ways that God may work in your life and leadership in the future?

Leadership Definition, Dynamics, and Diagnostics

	Leadership Definition	*Leadership Dynamic*	*Leadership Diagnostics*
Union with Christ	*The Christ-following leader—living as a bearer of God's image in union with Christ and his people—*	The position to which the leader is called is not sovereignty above or separation from the community but stewardship within the community in union with Christ.	If you have been united with Christ, God never ceases to be present with you. How should this truth shape your leadership? How should leadership as a servant and heir of God change the ways that you use authority?
Communion with Christ's People	*develops a diverse community of fellow laborers who are equipped and empowered to pursue shared goals*	The power that the leader exercises is not the leader's but Christ's, and this power must be expressed according to God's design for a diverse community of Spirit-equipped servants.	God's power extends far beyond the possibilities that you may pursue in your lifetime. Do you dream not only about what your congregation might become under your leadership but also about what God might do in your community far beyond your lifetime? How can you instill in your congregation a vision to develop foundations for possibilities that may not even happen in their lifetimes? How can your congregation move toward tangible recognition and realization of God's vision for ethnic and socioeconomic diversity in your congregation?

Mission in the World	*that fulfill the creation mandate and the Great Commission in submission to the Word of God.*	The truth that the leader is called to proclaim is not the leader's vision but God's revelation.	God is faithful to empower those that he calls to do what he has called them to do. Are there areas of ministry where you have lacked boldness in fulfilling God's plan in God's way due to fear or to an awareness of your powerlessness? How might you rely more strongly on God's faithfulness and take risks for the sake of proclaiming God's good news and seeking justice for the oppressed?

Followers First and Foremost

Effective leadership, much like a rousing round of "Simon Says," requires us to follow the right instructions from the right leader at the right time. God created human beings to reflect his glory by representing his authority and by governing his world in his way. And yet from the moment our first parents tasted that fateful piece of forbidden fruit, we have all wanted to set our own rules.

"I just wanna be God," shock rocker Alice Cooper once sang.[44] Deep inside, so do we all. That's why we as leaders are constantly tempted to pervert our positions by setting ourselves up as sovereigns or by defining success according to our own standards and schedules. Neither our power nor our positions are, however, our property to be used as we please. Any power we possess is God's power first, and our leadership is a sacred stewardship that must be shaped by the faithfulness, presence, and power of God.

When we play "Simon Says," Simon sometimes gives commands that make no sense—yet if we fail to follow these commands, we'll find ourselves on the sidelines. *Don't* hear us saying that a single failed step in your practices of leadership disqualifies you from leadership! *Do* hear us saying that Christian leaders never possess the freedom to make independent decisions about how to lead. Christian leaders are first and foremost followers of Christ the King. Godly leadership—whether in the church or in the marketplace—is followership exercised with biblical wisdom for the good and the guidance of a community for which God has given us responsibility. In some cases, our King's directions may seem counterintuitive or even crazy, but we are still called to follow his lead. In other times and places, his directions may not arrive according to our timetables.

But here's the wonderful news that we sometimes forget: In many cases, the more we are committed to following the leadership of the King, the more committed our teams will become to follow both his leadership and ours. The more we rely on the faithfulness, presence, and power of God, the more his glorious beauty will be revealed to the people around us. And the more that people around us learn to delight in the glories of God, the more likely they will be to join us as we follow him.

In the Old Testament, some of the most significant expressions of leadership came through the offices of judge, priest, prophet, and king.[45] Kingship and priesthood were part of God's plan from the beginning, when he created Adam and Eve. Judges were established as part of God's covenant in the exodus to protect and to promote justice among the people (Deut 16:18–20). God provided prophets in response to his people's request at Mount Sinai (Deut 18:15-17). Woven throughout these offices was the pivotal analogy of the shepherd.[46] Through each of these offices, God paved a path before us, revealing the way of leadership through his works and through his Word. In the next section of *The God Who Goes before You*, we will provide a Christ-centered examination of each of these roles and show how each one is relevant for the lives of leaders today.

What about You?

In light of the biblical truths about God's nature, promises, and actions that are demonstrated in Genesis and Exodus, what would change about your leadership if you followed God first and waited on him?

Think deeply about this question.

Now let's consider a few specific aspects of your life as a leader:

- In what specific areas of your life are you tempted to see your pathway as better than God's pathway?
- In what specific areas of your life do you lack confidence that God will be faithful to do what he has promised?
- How might you be focusing your attention on immediate results instead of taking a generational perspective?
- In what specific areas in your leadership do you lack patience?
- Where in your home or community are you falling short when it comes to following God first?

Follow God first, because his pathway is far more glorious individually and corporately than your plans could ever be. Saturate your life with his Word, because his words are your surest guide. Take the long view, because the results that matter most may not be the ones you see in your lifetime.

Worshiping the God Who Goes before Us

Guide me, O Thou great Jehovah,
Pilgrim through this barren land;
I am weak, but Thou art mighty,
Hold me with Thy pow'rful hand.

Bread of heaven, Bread of heaven,
Feed me till I want no more;
Feed me till I want no more.

Open now the crystal fountain,
Whence the healing stream doth flow;
Let the fire and cloudy pillar
Lead me all my journey through.

Strong Deliv'rer, strong Deliv'rer,
Be Thou still my Strength and Shield;
Be Thou still my Strength and Shield.

When I tread the verge of Jordan,
Bid my anxious fears subside;
Death of death and hell's Destruction,
Land me safe on Canaan's side.

Songs of praises, songs of praises,
I will ever give to Thee;
I will ever give to Thee.
—William Williams, 1745

Responding to the God Who Goes before Us

Lead us, great God and strong Deliverer, and make us faithful followers
    whose faithfulness reveals your greater faithfulness,
    whose leadership is submitted to your all-surpassing power, and
    whose fellowship with the people you have redeemed echoes
        the eternal fellowship of Father, Son, and Holy Spirit,
        one God forever and ever,
        world without end. Amen.

Further Reading

Keller, Timothy, with Katherine Leary Alsdorf. *Every Good Endeavor.* New York: Penguin, 2012.

Kilner, John. *Dignity and Destiny.* Grand Rapids: Eerdmans, 2015.

Loritts, Crawford. *Leadership as an Identity.* 2nd edition. Chicago: Moody, 2009.

Ryken, Philip Graham. *Exodus: Saved for God's Glory.* Wheaton: Crossway, 2005.

PART TWO

Old Covenant Precedents for Leadership through Followership

Timothy Paul Jones

"Touch not mine anointed.' That's what this book says!" the chapel speaker stormed, flapping his King James Bible above his head. "There are people in this church right now who are trying to touch God's anointed—but I won't let them stretch their hands against me!"

I was fourteen years old, and common sense was in short supply for me at the time. Still, something about the chapel sermon that day in this tiny Christian school didn't seem right. The chapel preacher for the day was the school principal, who also happened to be the church's associate pastor. The trouble had started when this principal and associate pastor was caught secretly watching high school girls as they changed clothes before gym class. It soon became apparent that this may not have been all that he was doing with girls in the church and the school.

This day's chapel message was the principal's retort to those who had called for him to resign. His message began with David's refusal to overthrow King Saul. "Who can stretch forth his hand against the Lord's anointed?" David had said (1 Sam 26:9 KJV). The principal identified himself as a man anointed by the Lord to be a pastor; then he pointed out how David remained king even after committing adultery and murder. Before it was over, the principal had made his way to Ps 105:15 and declared that, because God had anointed him as a pastor, God would punish anyone who tried to remove him from his leadership position.

At the time, I wasn't able to articulate all the problems with the principal's hermeneutical acrobatics. Yet it occurred to me even as a folly-prone fourteen-year-old that the associate pastor of a church was not precisely analogous to the anointed monarch of Israel. Nevertheless, instead of confronting his sin and reporting his crimes, the congregation was convinced by his rhetoric and did nothing at all. In the end, he was hired by another church and school about forty miles away where similar patterns of abuse were, I later discovered, repeated.[1]

Perhaps it was this past experience with a leader who claimed an anointed role that triggered my queasiness when I began to hear well-meaning seminary students use terms like "kingly leaders" or "priestly types" to refer to themselves. "I'm not really preparing to do pastoral care," one of them commented to me over lunch when I asked him about his counseling skills. "I'm more a king than a priest, you know. So someone else will need to do the caregiving when I become a pastor." Another pastor in training put it this way: "I'm more of a prophetic teacher, so I'm looking for a kingly type to supplement my style by taking care of the church's strategy and vision." Church planters in particular seemed eager to pigeonhole themselves and their fellow leaders into anointed categories of prophet, priest, or king.

When I pressed these individuals further, it became clear that they were operating with a leadership model that seemed, at first glance, to be well-grounded in the Scriptures. From the perspective of these students, to lead like Jesus was to imitate one or more of the Old Testament offices that Jesus fulfilled. As they saw it, the threefold office of prophet, priest, and king provided a typology for church leadership. According to their application of this triad, every church leader possessed prophetic, priestly, or kingly gifts in differing degrees.

This perspective on leadership raised some of the same questions that had crossed my mind as a fourteen-year-old in that chapel service. How should leadership offices in ancient Israel shape the New Testament church—or should they? Does Old Testament kingship or priesthood connect at all with practices of pastoral leadership today? If so, how? Which aspects of leadership bridge the gap between the old and new covenants? And how should we make the connections between them?

Munus Triplex

Latin, "threefold office"

Munus triplex refers to three Old Testament roles—prophet, priest, and king—that were fulfilled in the one person of Jesus.[2] In the Old Testament, appointment to one of these offices could involve anointing—an act that signified the empowerment of an individual for a divinely designated duty (Exod 28:41; Lev 4:3–16; 6:22; 1 Sam 12:3–5; 16:6, 13; 1 Kgs 19:16).[3] Over time, the triad of prophet, priest, and king shaped Jewish expectations for a "Messiah" or "Anointed One."[4] At least as early as the fourth century AD, Christians already viewed the work of Jesus through the lens of this triad. The church historian Eusebius of Caesarea identified Jesus as "the only High Priest of all, the only King of every creature, and the Father's only High Prophet of prophets."[5] In modern times, the triad has been most prevalent in the theology of John Calvin and his theological heirs,[6] but the threefold office is also foundational in contemporary Roman Catholic ecclesiology.[7]

Prophet, Priest, King, and Judge— a Typology for Christian Leadership?

One version of this leadership typology encourages church leaders to pursue and to practice all three offices of prophet, priest, and king at once.[8] Another variation—represented by several of my students who were eagerly classifying one another as prophets, priests, or kings—connects each anointed role with a certain type of church leader. Those with strong teaching gifts are considered prophets; counselors and caregivers are classified as priests; those who can lead organizations effectively are identified as kings.[9] One further variation of this perspective specifically ties prophecy to the work of the church's teaching elders, while priesthood is linked to deacons, and kingly functions are correlated with ruling elders.[10] According to Vern Poythress,

> All the gifts mentioned in Romans 12, 1 Corinthians 12, and Ephesians 4 can be roughly classified as prophetic, kingly, or priestly. . . . Where speaking gifts are strong, people become recognized teachers. . . . Where ruling gifts are strong, people become recognized elders or shepherds. . . . Where serving gifts are strong,

people become recognized as servers and givers of mercy. Some have suggested that we may correlate this service particularly with the ministry of deacons.[11]

Seen in this way, different church officers possess prophetic, priestly, or kingly capacities in differing degrees, and the most appropriate role for each one depends on which of these capacities happens to be strongest. Research in the *Journal of Applied Christian Leadership* has added yet another role to the mix. Prophets, priests, and kings are presented as opposable types of moral leadership that can be integrated "with help from a fourth type, the judge" who fosters dialogue in the organization.[12]

But what biblical warrant is there for clustering church leaders into categories of priest or prophet, judge or king?

Here's what we will suggest throughout this exploration of leadership in the Old Testament: Although the *munus triplex* itself is a venerable and biblical structure, the appropriation of prophet, priest, and king as a typology for church leadership is not.[13] In fact, this usage of the *munus triplex* falls far short when it comes to biblical support. Particularly absent in Scripture is any clear identification of these offices with specific traits that different church leaders possess in differing degrees.[14]

This is not to suggest that Old Testament offices such as prophet, priest, king, and judge have nothing to do with Christian leadership! We are, in fact, quite convinced that these Old Testament roles are relevant for Christian leadership and church polity today—but not as leadership types that leaders possess in varying degrees.[15] The *munus triplex* shapes leadership best when the three offices are seen first and foremost as functions that have been fulfilled in Christ and conveyed to the whole people of God through union with Christ. Understanding these roles in light of their fulfillment in Christ reminds us that the positions to which leaders are called never situate us as sovereigns above the communities we serve but as stewards among a people that God in Christ has purchased.

Deuteronomy, the Centerpoint of Old Testament Theology

This exploration of these roles will extend throughout the entire Old Testament, but the focus will be—by design—on the book of Deuteronomy.

Both in terms of the story and the theology of the Old Testament, the book of Deuteronomy stands squarely at the center of God's work with the physical descendants of Abraham.[16] It was in Deuteronomy that Moses defined the offices of judge, king, and prophet and articulated the place of the priesthood in relation to these roles. The words of Moses in Deuteronomy provided the people of Israel with the standards by which judges would be appointed, kings would be judged, and prophets would be recognized as true or false (Deut 16:18–18:22).

With that in mind, let's take a step back in time to the plains of Moab in the closing centuries of the ancient Near Eastern Bronze Age. Let's listen as an aged shepherd speaks his final words to a nation that is preparing to enter a long-promised land. His words will form the foundation for our understanding of leadership that follows the God who goes before us.

The Quest for Justice: Judges and Kings in Israel

"Appoint judges and officials for your tribes in all your towns the Lord *your God is giving you. They are to judge the people with righteous judgment. Do not deny justice or show partiality to anyone. Do not accept a bribe, for it blinds the eyes of the wise and twists the words of the righteous. Pursue justice and justice alone, so that you will live and possess the land the* Lord *your God is giving you."*

Deuteronomy 16:18–20

"When Samuel grew old, he appointed his sons as judges over Israel. . . . However, his sons did not walk in his ways—they turned toward dishonest profit, took bribes, and perverted justice. So all the elders of Israel gathered together and went to Samuel at Ramah. They said to him, 'Look, you are old, and your sons do not walk in your ways. Therefore, appoint a king to judge us the same as all the other nations have.'"

1 Samuel 8:1–5

▶ Chapter Three Key Point

United with Christ the righteous Judge and King, believers today participate in God's kingdom and pursue God's passion for justice through faithful practices of church discipline. Church leaders follow the God who has gone before them by leading congregations to participate in the righteous judgments of God. ◀

The children of Israel stand poised on the precipice of the land of promise.

A generation earlier, their parents reached this point but failed to take the land. Now a new generation blankets the plains east of the Jordan River like grains of sand on the shore. Their eyes are centered on the figure who stands like a sentinel on a stony bulge in the earth.

This is Moses, the only leader of Israel who has conversed with God "face to face, just as a man speaks with his friend" (Exod 33:11). No leader like him has ever arisen before, and no leader like him will emerge again until the generation comes when a divine descendant of Abraham arrives to shatter the power of sin (Deut 18:15; 34:10–12). Moses is more than a century old, yet his eyes remain as sharp as a young archer's and the vigor of his youth has never faded (Deut 34:7). Here in the stony plains of Moab, he speaks his final words to Israel. The words that he speaks will not merely leave a legacy; they will shape a nation.

In his final address before the Israelites turn westward into the Promised Land, Moses first reviews the history that he has shared with these people (Deuteronomy 1–4). He urges the new generation of Israelites to love their God and to engrave God's truth in the lives of their children (4–11). Then he provides stipulations for living in covenant with the living God (12–26), before presenting the people with a last will and testament (27–33).

Like many ancient speeches, the structure chosen for this speech conveyed as much meaning as the content.[1] The form that God inspired Moses to use for his address mirrored ancient treaties that ratified the relationship between a suzerain and his vassals.[2] When the people of Israel agreed to the terms that Moses declared in Deuteronomy, they were doing far more than acknowledging their leader's last words. They were recognizing the Lord God as their sovereign suzerain and participating anew in the covenant of love that God had made with their ancestors.[3] In time, this gathering on the plains of Moab came to signify a time and a place "where the past and future of Israel coalesce in a single moment, . . . where the decision to follow Yahweh must be reaffirmed in every generation."[4]

The Ten Commandments and the Structure of Deuteronomy

Ten Commandments in Deuteronomy	Examples of Coordinating Detailed Stipulations in Deuteronomy
"Do not have other gods" (Deut 5:7). "Do not make an idol" (Deut 5:8–10). "Do not misuse the name of the Lord" (Deut 5:11).	"Destroy completely all the places where the nations that you are driving out worship their gods. . . . Cut down the carved images of their gods. . . . You are to eat . . . in the presence of the LORD your God at the place where he chooses to have his name dwell" (Deut 12–14).
"You are to labor six days and do all your work, but the seventh day is a Sabbath. . . . Remember that you were a slave in the land of Egypt, and the LORD your God brought you out of there with a strong hand and an outstretched arm" (Deut 5:12–15).	"At the end of every seven years you must cancel debts. . . . Celebrate the Passover. . . . Celebrate the Festival of Weeks. . . . Celebrate the Festival of Booths. . . . Remember that you were a slave in the land of Egypt and the LORD your God redeemed you" (Deut 15–16).
"Honor your father and your mother . . . so that you may live long and so that you may prosper in the land" (Deut 5:16).	"Appoint judges and officials. . . . Pursue justice and justice alone, so that you will live long and possess the land. . . . You are to appoint over you the king the LORD your God chooses. . . . The Levitical priests, the whole tribe of Levi, will have no portion or inheritance with Israel. . . . The LORD your God will raise up for you a prophet" (Deut 16–18).
"Do not murder" (Deut 5:17).	"Here is the law concerning a case of someone who kills a person" (Deut 19–22).
"Do not commit adultery" (Deut 5:18).	"If a man is discovered having sexual relations with another man's wife, both the man who had sex with the woman and the woman must die" (Deut 22–23).

"Do not steal" (Deut 5:19). "Do not give dishonest testimony" (Deut 5:20). "Do not covet your neighbor's wife or desire your neighbor's house . . . or anything that belongs to your neighbor" (Deut 5:21).	"Do not charge your brother interest. . . . If you make a vow to the LORD your God, do not be slow to keep it. . . . You must not put a sickle to your neighbor's grain. . . . When you make a loan of any kind to your neighbor, do not enter his house to collect what he offers as security" (Deut 23–26).

Some portions of this table adapted from James Hamilton, *God's Glory in Salvation through Judgment* (Wheaton: Crossway, 2010), 128.

Godly Leadership in the Home, Godly Leadership in the Nation

One particular section in ancient suzerain-vassal treaties was designated for detailed stipulations. That section is found in chapters 12 through 26 in the book of Deuteronomy. Moses carefully crafted this section of detailed stipulations so that the statutes in this section loosely followed the flow of the Ten Commandments. Throughout the section designated for detailed stipulations, each of the Ten Commandments was amplified through an expanded expression of God's concern for justice and faithfulness in that particular area of life (see "The Ten Commandments and the Structure of Deuteronomy").

The commandment that forbids carved images (5:8–10), for example, is expanded into an expectation that idols will be torn down (12:1–4). Similarly, the commandment to keep the Sabbath (5:12–15) is developed into a detailed description of Israel's sabbatical years and festivals (15:1–16:17). Most significant for the study of leadership, God's command to honor father and mother (5:16) is amplified into a detailed description of the primary leadership offices in Israel (16:18–18:22).

This link between honor for parents and the leadership of Israel shouldn't surprise us. Family was, after all, a fundamental building block in Israel's social order. It was through the flesh of a mother that God had promised to send the chosen seed who would crush the serpent's skull (Gen 3:15). Both before and after Moses described Israel's offices of leadership, he called fathers to engrave God's truth in their children's lives (Deut 4:9; 6:7, 20–21; 11:19; 31:13; 32:46). In later biblical texts, the metaphor of father described human prophets, priests, and kings, suggesting a clear tie between leadership in the household and leadership of the nation (Judg 18:19; 1 Sam 24:11; 2 Kgs 6:21).

For these tribes standing on the precipice of the land of promise, godly leadership was inseparable from family discipleship. The fruit of godly leadership in the nation depended on the root of godly leadership in the home. It makes sense, then, that Moses amplified the commandment to honor father and mother by providing detailed stipulations for four key leadership roles in Israel: judges, priests, kings, and prophets.

The words of Moses recorded in Deuteronomy did not create the offices of judge, prophet, priest or king. All of these offices were either practiced or predicted long before Moses stood before the people of Israel on the plains of Moab.[5] What Moses did in Deuteronomy was to situate these offices in the context of God's covenant with Israel. By constituting these roles in the context of the covenant, Moses called the Israelites to practice covenant faithfulness in every part of their lives—in their judgments, their worship, and their testimonies.

With this foundation in mind, let's take a careful look first at the meaning of the offices of judge and king for Israel and—through Christ—for us.

Judges and Officers: Their High Calling and Shortfallings

During the plagues in Egypt and the early days of Israel's escape, Moses seems to have served as the sole judge of Israel. It was Moses's father-in-law who—seeing his son-in-law burdened beneath more decisions than one man could possibly bear—urged him to appoint "able men" to "judge the people" (Exod 18:21–22; see also Deut 1:15–18).[6] Four decades later, on the plains of Moab, Moses provided the people with clear guidelines to appoint "judges and officers" so that righteous judgments might continue after he was gone (Deut 16:18 NASB).[7] The precise meaning of the word "officers" is debated. The officers may have been leaders who had the capacity to maintain written records.[8] It is also possible that "officers" referred to a class of leaders to which judges belonged and that the phrase should be read "judges from among those who are officers."[9] Whatever the precise meaning of "officers," judges and officers shared a single purpose: the pursuit of justice (Deut 16:20; compare Mic 6:8).[10]

Judicial verdicts consistent with divine justice were a necessary condition for long life in the land (Deut 16:18, 20). If righteous verdicts faltered, the powerful would oppress the vulnerable, and vengeance would prevail over love (Lev 19:15–16). And so Moses provided the people with a triad of specific prohibitions that would promote the pursuit of righteousness (Deut 16:19; cf. 1:17):[11]

1. "Do not deny justice."
2. "Do not . . . show partiality."
3. "Do not accept a bribe."

These prohibitions reminded all the people of Israel—and judges in particular—to deal quickly with any exploitation of the vulnerable and to remain free from lust for multiplied possessions or human approval. Later, when King Jehoshaphat brought the people "back to the LORD," one of his first acts would be to appoint judges and to echo this text by warning them that there is "no injustice or partiality or taking bribes with the LORD our God" (2 Chr 19:4–7).

The wording of these prohibitions was grounded in Moses's earlier description of the Lord God as an "awesome God, showing no partiality and taking no bribes" (Deut 10:17). By grounding the prohibitions in the nature of God, Moses reminded the nation that God's character formed the foundation for any truly righteous judgments. Even in the pursuit of justice, the God of Israel was a God who went before his people, preparing their way by means of his own mighty works and character. This revelation of God's character would eventually be contained in the words of the Torah—the first five books of the Hebrew Scriptures, written and preserved for the purpose of guiding the people toward covenant faithfulness and wholehearted love for God.[12]

The centrality of the Torah in every judicial decision reminded Israel that, although the people and their leaders would appoint human judges, God alone remained "Judge of all the earth" (Gen 18:25; Judg 11:27; see also Ps 50:6; 75:7; 94:2; Isa 33:22). Human judges issued judicial decisions to maintain justice in Israel, yet neither their power nor their positions ever became their own property. The judges led the people in the pursuit of justice by living first and foremost as followers of God's way. Any power they possessed was delegated by God's will and subservient to God's Word. Inasmuch as the judges derived their judgments from God's written revelation, their judgments were God's judgments, and the truths they proclaimed were treated as God's truth (Deut 1:17; compare John 5:30).[13] Even in the regulations given for the judges of Israel, the God of Israel was a God who went before his people; God did this for the judges of Israel by revealing himself as the model judge and by providing an objective standard for righteous judgments in his written Word.

If Israel had persisted in their pursuit of righteousness, the result would have been long and prosperous possession of the land (Deut 16:20)—and yet Israel fell far short of this goal. During the centuries that stood between Moses and the monarchy, "everyone did what was right in his own eyes," and justice degenerated into horrific cycles of violence and civil war (Judg 17:6; 18:1; 19:1; 21:25 NASB). The flaw was not, however, in the God-ordained office of judge but in the hearts of the people and their judges. What Israel's failure to cultivate justice in the land revealed was the people's need for a single ruler who would mediate God's reign in his own generation and who would raise up sons to sustain covenant faithfulness in the future.[14]

The Demand for a King and the Longing to Be "Like All the Other Nations"

God had promised to provide everything his people might need to flourish in the land if only they would remain faithful to his covenant. And yet a time would come when the people would no longer be satisfied with what their God offered. They would demand a king to represent them, to fight for them, and to judge them so they could become "like all the other nations" (1 Sam 8:20; see also 12:12). The people's desire for a king was not a problem. Kingship had been part of God's design from the beginning (Gen 17:6, 16; 35:11; Num 24:17).[15] The difficulty with Israel's demand would be their desire to become "like all the other nations" (Deut 17:14).

A sovereign protector and judge who ruled like the kings of other nations would have the capacity to stand above the laws that bound his people. If the law of Israel had been nothing more than a corpus of human statutes, such a pattern would not have been problematic—but Israel's law was the Torah, the perfect revelation of God's will for his people. Any king who tried to stand above this law would be attempting to elevate himself to the place of God. The people's demand to have a king like other nations, "while specifically anticipated in the Law, [would be] a direct challenge to the Law. The elders [would be] asking, in effect, to opt out of their covenant . . . and to adopt a pagan model of being a nation."[16] The problem with Israel's request for a king wasn't their desire for a king but their desire for a sovereign man instead of a sovereign God.

Foreseeing the people's future request for a king, Moses mapped out a clear manifesto for Israel's monarchy. This God-inspired design would provide Israel with a much-needed king—but the monarchy that God described would, in fact, accomplish the opposite of what Israel demanded! In God's design, kingship would not be a status to be seized or a goal to be achieved for one's own benefit. Kingship would be a gift given in God's time by God's grace for the good of God's people. The result would be a monarchy that would make Israel unlike any other nation under heaven.

In God's plan for kingship, a clear line of continuity connected the judges and the kings.[17] The king was, in some sense, intended to function as a judge who pursued justice not merely for a single city but for the whole nation. When Moses described judges and kings in Deuteronomy, he was inspired by the Holy Spirit to structure these descriptions so that they paralleled one another (16:18–20; 17:14–20; see table "Right Judgments, Right Offerings, Right Testimony"). One of the primary purposes of Israel's kings would be to judge the people in a way that would establish justice. The kings, no less than the judges, were called to deliver righteous verdicts and to defend the oppressed. "A king who judges the poor with fairness," one ruler of Israel would later declare, "his throne will be established forever" (Prov 29:14; see also 1 Sam 8:5–6, 20; 2 Sam 8:15; 2 Chr 1:11; Ps 72:1–2, 12–14; Prov 20:8; Jer 22:1–3). Still later, when the prophet Isaiah described a future perfect king, he depicted this king as a righteous judge (Isa 16:5; see also Isa 11:1–5). And so the king of Israel functioned, in some sense, as a judge with a responsibility to seek justice not merely for a single city but for the entire nation.

The king was also, however, far more than a judge. The king was expected, above all, to serve as a model of covenant faithfulness and as a representative—an exemplar and incarnation, in some sense—of and for the people. As the exemplar of God's design for his people, the king was called to rule as God's son and God's servant in submission to God's commands, fulfilling the primeval mandate that Adam and Eve had failed to maintain.

In the classic novel *The Once and Future King*, the citizens of England looked at King Arthur and "saw no man at all, but England."[18] When the people of Israel and the nations around them looked at the king of Israel, what they ought to have seen was a living incarnation of all that God had created their nation to be. The king's status as a son of God was a representative status by which the faithful sonship of all Israel was exemplified in a single individual.[19] The priest represented the people of Israel in the presence of God (Exod 28:9–12), but it was the king who exemplified to the world Israel's faithfulness to God's covenant. In Moses's depiction of the ideal king, he placed the exemplary obedience of the king in conscious contrast to the arrogance of any Israelite who ignored God's commands (Deut 17:11–13; 18–20; see "Right Judgments, Right Offerings, Right Testimony").[20]

Right Judgments, Right Offerings, Right Testimony

In his address on the plains of Moab, Moses connected the central themes of covenant faithfulness in judgments, worship, and witness to the roles of judge, priest, king, and prophet (Deut 16:18–18:22).

Key Theme	Deuteronomy 16:18–17:13 Judges and Priests	Deuteronomy 17:14–18:22 Kings, Priests, and Prophets
Right Judgments	"Appoint judges and officials . . . in **all the towns the LORD your God is giving you.** . . .Pursue justice and justice alone so that you will **live and possess the land**" (16:18–20).	"When you enter **the land the LORD your God is giving you, take possession of it, live in it**" (17:14).
	Three prohibitions: "Do not deny justice or show partiality to anyone. Do not accept a bribe" (16:19).	*Three prohibitions:* "He must not acquire many horses. . . . He must not acquire many wives. . . . He must not acquire very large amounts of silver and gold" (17:16–17).
		Instructions for the king in contrast to "the man who acts arrogantly" (17:11–13): "He is to write a copy of this **instruction** . . . so that he may learn to **fear** the LORD his God, to observe all the words of this **instruction**. . . . He will not **turn** from this command **to the right or the left**" (17:18–20).

Right Offerings	"Do not sacrifice to the LORD your God an ox or sheep with a defect or any serious flaw" (17:1).	"This is the priests' share from the people who offer a **sacrifice**, whether it is **an ox, a sheep**" (18:3)
Right Testimony	"If a man or woman among you in one of **your towns that the LORD your God will give you** . . . has gone to worship other gods . . . , you must investigate. . . . If the report turns out to be true that this **detestable** thing has happened in Israel . . . stone them to death" (17:2–5). "According to the terms of the **law** which they teach, . . . you shall do; you shall not **turn aside** from the **word** which they declare to you, **to the right or the left**" (17:11 NASB). "The man who acts [**arrogantly**] . . . **shall die.** . . . Then all the people will hear and **be afraid**, and will not act [**arrogantly**] again" (17:12–13 NASB).	"When you enter **the land the LORD your God is giving you,** do not imitate the **detestable** customs of those nations. . . . Everyone who does these things is **detestable** to the LORD" (18:9, 12). "The prophet who [**arrogantly speaks**] . . . — that prophet must **die.** . . . When . . . the [**word**] does not come true, . . . the prophet has spoken it [**arrogantly**]. Do not **be afraid** of him" (18:20–22).

A Son Selected from among His Brothers

The king of Israel would be—Moses declared—chosen by God "from among [his] brothers"; this king would remain a brother even after becoming king (Deut 17:15, 20). The point of this restriction of kingship to fellow

Israelites was not racial or ethnic but covenantal. The nation of Israel had been forged not primarily through familial kinship but by means of a God-initiated relationship that was available to anyone who would embrace the signs and stipulations of the covenant.[21] To declare that the king was to be selected from among his brothers was to declare that there could be no kingship in Israel separate from God's covenant with Israel.

God had adopted the nation of Israel as his firstborn son on the basis of his covenant with Abraham, and he had confirmed his people's status of sonship through a covenant at Mount Sinai (Exod 4:22–23; 6:3–9).[22] In other nations, a king or priest might be seen as the son of a deity, divinely elevated above his subjects.[23] In Israel, however, the entire nation was God's son corporately, and every person in Israel—including the king—was a brother. The king's responsibilities as a brother within the covenant community would always supersede any power he might enjoy as a monarch over the covenant community. The position to which God called the king was not sovereignty above or separation from the community of Israel but stewardship within the community in submission to the Word of God.[24]

A Servant Dependent on God's Power

The priority of this covenantal relationship is particularly clear in the prohibitions that Moses placed on future kings. The purpose of these prohibitions was to drive Israel to entrust their security to God's faithfulness rather than relying on their own prosperity or political power.[25] The prohibitions given to kings in Deuteronomy 17 were threefold, just as the prohibitions given in connection with judges had been:

1. The king "must not acquire many horses for himself." Horses and chariots formed the foundation for military might in the ancient Near East. No king could hope to turn his kingdom into a superpower without amassing warhorses. Yet the Spirit of God declared through Moses that Israel's future king must "not multiply horses" (Deut 17:16 NASB).[26]

2. The king "must not acquire many wives for himself." This prohibition probably had less to do with the precise number of women in the king's palace and more to do with the king marrying the royal daughters of pagan rulers.[27] Kings in other nations manipulated

marriage alliances to secure protection for their people. Such alliances did not merely mingle two powerful families. They introduced the religious practices of one nation into another nation. If a king of Israel chose to "multiply wives" to solidify political alliances with pagan nations, the orientation of his life ("his heart") was likely to drift from wholehearted devotion to God's covenant (Deut 17:17 NASB; see also Deut 7:3–4; 1 Kgs 3:1; 9:24; 11:1–13).

3. The king *"must not acquire very large amounts of silver and gold for himself."* A royal stockpile of precious metals would require not only trade but also tribute from subjugated peoples and perhaps excessive taxation of Israelite households (1 Kgs 4:21; 10:14–25; 12:9–14).[28] One reason for a king to multiply such wealth would be to purchase his people's safety by bribing rival kings (see, e.g., 1 Kgs 15:18–19; 2 Kgs 16:8–9; 18:14–16; 23:33–35). And yet the wealth of Israel was never meant to be hoarded by a royal family or stashed in a storehouse to bribe other nations. If Israel remained faithful, all the people would enjoy silver and gold, houses and herds, full stomachs and plentiful flocks (Deut 8:12–13). For a king of Israel to "multiply to himself silver and gold" would be to stockpile for himself gifts that had been provided for the sake of the nation (Deut 17:17 KJV).

These prohibitions removed every human resource on which a king might rely to keep his people secure. God's purpose in these prohibitions was to forge a nation that—unlike any other nation—relied on the presence, provision, and protection of their God for their security (see also Pss 33:16–18; 146:3–7; Prov 21:31). These prohibitions reminded the king that any power he possessed was not his own, to be used for his benefit; his power was delegated by God's will for the good of God's people.

A Student of God's Word, Submitted to God's Way

The future king of Israel was forbidden to multiply warhorses, wives, or wealth "for himself"—but there was one item that he was specifically commanded to make "for himself." The king would "write for himself a copy of this law on a scroll in the presence of the Levitical priests" (Deut 17:18 NASB). By copying the covenant anew, each king of Israel was called to engage in a sacred act that would produce a sacred artifact. Through this act and artifact, every king of Israel would participate anew in God's covenant with Israel.[29] The king's personal copy of the covenant would serve as a working document to direct every judgment that the king handed down. The same words that once thundered from the peak of Mount Sinai would rest at the king's fingertips to mold his life and his leadership. The result would be a leader who feared God, submitted to God's instruction, enacted God's statutes, and taught his sons to do the same (17:19–20).

In the nations surrounding Israel, kings possessed absolute power to decree what was right and wrong, and the kings themselves could live above these laws.[30] The privileges of kingship in such contexts were much like what the lion cub Simba expected to enjoy as the monarch of his father's pride in the Disney musical *The Lion King*. In the song "I Just Can't Wait to Be King," the reason that Simba "just can't wait" is because he views kingship as an opportunity to do whatever he pleases whenever he pleases wherever he pleases.[31] But this was not God's vision for the kings of Israel! No king of Israel would stand as a successor to the gods, living above the law with freedom to follow his own way. For the king to be exalted above his fellow citizens or to establish his own statutes separate from God's Torah would be to usurp a role that belonged to God alone.

When Samuel anointed Israel's first true king, the uniqueness of Israel's king was made particularly clear. Neither Samuel nor the Lord initially used the Hebrew word for "king" to refer to Saul. The Lord said instead that Saul would be Israel's "ruler" or "prince" (1 Sam 9:16; 10:1 CSB, NASB). Later, the Lord God applied the same terminology to David (1 Sam 13:14; 2 Sam 5:2). This subtle substitution of "ruler" or "prince" for "king" in the appointments of both Saul and David emphasized the subservient nature of Israel's king. The king of Israel was to be a leader who saw his power as "a sovereign and inviolable devolvement from Yahweh, who acted strictly under the orders of Yahweh for the benefit of Yahweh's people, and held himself as no more than the willing subject of the divine monarch."[32]

The king of Israel was never meant to possess power that was unchallengeable or absolute. Priests superintended the covenant documents that kings were commanded to copy,[33] and God raised up prophets to call rebellious kings to return to these covenant documents.[34] No one in Israel—not even the king—was exempt from faithful obedience to this law.[35] The king's responsibility to live by the same covenant as his people preceded any power he possessed as their leader. Such a restriction was radically ahead of its time in the ancient Near East. It is not "until the thirteenth-century Magna Carta . . . in England" that we find any "comparable notion that royal power should be limited."[36]

The Rise and Fall of Israel's Kings

Israel's first true monarch was Saul the son of Kish.[37] Saul was a tall and handsome warrior from a wealthy family (1 Sam 9:1–2), but this impressive ruler repeatedly claimed sovereignty instead of stewardship by bypassing faithfulness to God's commands. Saul was not a villain from the moment he entered the story, like Cain or Esau. The arc that Saul followed was more like Anakin Skywalker in the *Star Wars* saga, beginning with innocence and promise before stumbling little by little into darkness—except that Saul's story lacks the repentance and sacrifice that characterize Anakin's demise in the closing moments of *Episode VI: Return of the Jedi*. Each time the prophet of God confronted Saul's rebellion, the monarch's initial response was not repentance but self-justification (1 Sam 13:8–15; 15:1–21).[38]

It did not take long for God to raise up a shepherd king to take Saul's place on the throne. King David and his descendants would become "the true successors of the judges."[39] This new king stole the hearts of his people and became a man after God's own heart (1 Sam 13:14; 1 Chr 12:38). His reign set the standard for every future monarchy, and God promised an endless dynasty for one of his descendants (2 Sam 7:12–16; 1 Kgs 15:3–5, 11; 2 Kgs 14:3; 16:2; 18:3; 22:2). Yet David also multiplied wives for himself and stole the spouse of one of his most loyal subjects (1 Sam 25:42–44; 2 Sam 5:13–16; 11:1–21; 1 Chr 3:1–9). David, unlike Saul, repented without hesitation when confronted (2 Sam 12:7–15; Psalm 51)—but not even a king's heartfelt repentance could keep his sons from following in his footsteps. One of David's sons raped his own half-sister (2 Sam 13:1–22). Another son tried to steal his father's kingdom and, in the process, stole his concubines as well (2 Sam 15:1–6; 16:15–23).

Solomon, the appointed heir of David's throne, became known far and wide as the wisest judge and king in his day (1 Kgs 3:9, 16–28; 7:7). Yet King Solomon also defied God's design for kingship. He flaunted all three of the prohibitions that Moses had spoken. He hoarded silver and gold, entered into marriage alliances that resulted in hundreds of wives, and traded for horses from Egypt and Kue (Cilicia) (1 Kgs 3:1–2; 4:26–28; 10:14–11:3).[40] The result was a heart that wandered from God's commands and a burden of taxation and labor that his people could not bear (1 Kgs 11:4–8; 12:4).

Solomon's body had barely stiffened in the tomb before his kingdom was torn in two (1 Kgs 12:12–20). In the centuries that followed Solomon's demise, neither kings nor judges were able to maintain lasting justice (Isa 1:23; Jer 5:28; Ezek 45:9; Mic 3:1, 9; 7:3). In the southern kingdom, only eight kings attempted to follow the God of Israel, and only two of these kings received unqualified commendations (2 Kgs 18:3–7; 22:2). Still, God allowed the descendants of David to maintain their reign in the southern kingdom until the sixth century BC, when the Babylonians gouged out the eyes of the last king of Judah (2 Kgs 25:7). Conquered by Babylon, the people of Judah were exiled, and kingship came to an end. Like Adam at the beginning of time, each king had the opportunity to reign in righteousness as a servant and a son of God. Also like Adam, nearly all of these kings failed in their faithfulness to God's covenant.

What the world needed was a judge and king who would stand as a model of life lived in covenant with God. Yet such a monarchy seemed to stand beyond any human capacity. Every human judge and king thus far had failed. And still, the people and their prophets never stopped hoping for a king whose every verdict was faithful and true.

The Return of the King

In the seventh century BC, one prophet—a skilled poet, writing before the fall and exile of the southern kingdom—saw a new possibility for judges and kings. The Spirit of God revealed a future day when God himself would reign as his people's supreme judge and king. On that day, the people would say, "The LORD is our Judge, the LORD is our Lawgiver, the LORD is our King" (Isa 33:22). God himself would "settle disputes among the nations and provide arbitration for many peoples" (Isa 2:4).[41] What's more, this divine king would be—by some means that Isaiah did not explicitly reveal—"a son" who would sit on David's throne (Isa 9:6–7; see also Hos 3:5).

Human judges were not forgotten in this kingly vision of the future. Through Isaiah, God declared his plan to raise up righteous judges even as he himself would remain the perfect judge,[42] redeeming his people through the very righteousness that their earlier judges had failed to sustain (Isa 1:26–27; 33:22).[43] This promise was fulfilled in part—but only in part— when Ezra appointed "judges to judge all the people" after the exile (Ezra 7:25). The justice of these judges was, however, fleeting and far from perfect. During this era, the people still lived as "slaves in the land" of their ancestors (Neh 9:36–37), and it was not long until God's people found themselves groaning for justice yet again.[44]

It was in the virgin womb of a girl from Galilee that the consummate fulfillment of these prophecies began to blossom (Luke 1:32–33). God himself entered the cosmos in the flesh of Jesus Christ to do what no previous king or judge had done or could do: he upheld every covenant of God and inaugurated a "kingdom not of this world" to provide a foretaste of perfect justice on the face of a fallen earth (John 18:36). This divine descendant of David laid a foundation for lasting justice not by judging humanity but by submitting himself to God's judgment on humanity (John 3:17–18; 8:15–16). Through this sacrificial submission to the Father's judgment, God in Christ established a new covenant and embraced the death that each of us deserves for our failures to pursue perfect justice. Through his empty tomb, Jesus Christ guaranteed a future day when he would reign and "judge the world in righteousness" (Acts 17:31; see also Acts 10:42–43). Now, in this present era that stands between the empty tomb and the judgment throne, God is in the business of uniting unrighteous sinners with the risen King, counting the unjust as just on the basis of the Son's sacrifice and resurrection life.[45]

The kings of Israel had been called to live as protectors and judges who mediated God's reign and modeled faithfulness to God's covenant. From the womb of Mary to the garden tomb and beyond, Jesus Christ modeled this faithfulness at every turn. He submitted to his Father's Word, rejected every trapping of earthly power, and refused to exalt himself above his brothers (John 5:19–20; 8:54; 18:36). He was a king who came proclaiming a kingdom, but he did not bring the full revelation of this kingdom at his first coming (Matt 4:23; Mark 1:15; Luke 4:43). Instead, he promised to come again to multiply this kingdom around the globe until the earth is "filled with the knowledge of the LORD's glory, as the waters cover the sea" (Hab 2:14).

Kingly Leadership in the New Covenant

In light of what this chapter has explored about kings and judges in the old covenant, how should these offices shape the leadership of God's new covenant people today?

According to those who treat kingship as a typology for a particular kind of church leader, kingly leaders are visionary builders who develop organizational strategies and take responsibility for the church's direction. "Ultimately"—one proponent of this typological approach claims—"large ministry areas must be led by a king" because kingly leaders are the ones who actually get jobs done.[46] Another proponent of this approach specifically urges "upper-echelon leaders of complex organizations" to live as kingly leaders, emulating the template for Old Testament kings.[47] Leadership scholars who add judgeship to their typology typically treat the judging leader as a mediator and arbitrator between other types of leadership.[48]

In stark contrast to these understandings of kingship and leadership, Scripture does not describe kingship in terms of visionary leadership or strategic skill. Neither in Moses's description of God's design nor in later depictions of the ideal king is there any hint that visionary organizational strategies were part of the job description for kings in Israel. As such, even if we supposed that kingship might be a type of leadership that is conveyed to particular individuals in the church, the definition of a kingly leader as a dominant visionary strategist is unbalanced at best and fundamentally flawed at worst. Treating kingly leadership as visionary strategy imports a very modern and Western concept of leadership into old covenant kingship and, in the process, skews our understanding of church leadership in the new covenant.

This is not to suggest that visionary strategies are utterly unhelpful or unnecessary for leaders! The point being made here is that Scripture never links such capacities to the office of king. Kingship in the old covenant was focused primarily on modeling covenant faithfulness and on judging the people in righteousness, not on visionary leadership or strategic planning.

Even more problematic for the claim that kingly leadership is conveyed to particular individuals in the church is the fact that new covenant kingliness is never identified as the property of any human individual in Scripture. Kingliness in the kingdom of God is ascribed to God in Christ and to the whole people of God in union with Christ. Jesus promised his first followers that they would reign alongside him (Matt 19:28; Luke 22:30). But this glorious privilege did not stop with those first apostles. "If we endure, we"—Paul wrote to Timothy, referring to all of God's people—"will also reign with him" (2 Tim 2:12; see also 1 Pet 2:9; Rev 20:4–6). Through union with Christ, every believer in Christ participates in the kingship of Christ—and this participation is corporate and communal, not individual. None of us has the right to reign individually or independently in a kingly manner in the church of Jesus Christ. Godly leadership is not kingly dominance but followership exercised with biblical wisdom to guide a community for which God has given us responsibility.

In the first century AD, when a few Christians in Corinth began to act like royalty in a manner that separated them from their fellow believers, Paul did not celebrate their practices of kingly privilege. Instead, he demanded that they return to unity with the body. "You have begun to reign as kings without us," Paul declared with a generous dollop of sarcasm, "and I wish you did reign, so that we could also reign with you!" (1 Cor 4:8). Instead of affirming these kingly claims or claiming a kingly role for himself over the Corinthians, Paul called the Corinthians to imitate his way of life as a servant of Christ and as a manager of God's mysteries (1 Cor 4:1, 16).[49]

Proleptic

From Greek *prolepsis*, "anticipation"

Describing a present action or event that anticipates an action or event that is yet to come

Kingship as Proleptic Participation in Judgment That Is Yet to Come

If kingly leadership is not an individual capacity for organizational effectiveness and strategic vision, what is it? Notice the following biblical patterns:

- The ideal king in the Old Testament was an exemplar of covenant faithfulness who judged the people according to God's Word (1 Sam 8:5–6, 20; 2 Sam 8:15; 2 Chr 1:11; Ps 72:1–2; Prov 20:8; 29:14).

- When Jesus told the apostles that those who remained with him would also reign with him, he tied this reign to participation in the judgment of God's people (Matt 19:28; Luke 22:28–30).
- When the saints were enthroned as a priestly kingdom in John's heavenly vision, they were "given authority to judge" (Rev 20:4).

From these texts and others, it seems that one of the primary expressions of our union with Christ as King will be our participation in his judgments that will be handed down at the end of time. And yet our participation in these future judgments will not wait until the end of time. The church's participation in this judgment begins in the present. How? *When God's people join together in the holy work of church discipline, we participate together in the very judgments of God.*

When Christ returns and reigns at the end of the age, all those united with him will join him in judging the cosmos (1 Cor 6:1–11; Rev 20:4).[50] Whenever a local congregation of believers engages in church discipline, we rehearse this future promise by staging a small play that pictures in a small way the great judgment that is yet to come.[51] In this process, we are participating together in God's vision for judgeship and kingship. This proleptic participation in God's future judgment is not merely symbolic; neither is it accomplished fully in the church's present pursuits of justice. It is an actual—albeit incomplete—present participation in God's future judgment, made possible through our union with the righteous Judge and King, Jesus Christ.[52]

Church discipline is sometimes misperceived as the expulsion of errant or troublesome members from the congregation—but the goal of church discipline is never removal of anyone. The life of every believer has been joined with Christ, who has already delivered us from death by dying in our place; therefore, the desired consequence of a guilty verdict in the new covenant community is never destruction but deliverance (1 Cor 11:31–32; Gal 6:1–2; Heb 10:1–12:13). God's design for church discipline is to call wayward believers to repentance and to restore them to full fellowship with God's people. In this way, church discipline serves as "God's ongoing work through his living Word and people as they fight the good fight of faith together to exalt Christ and protect the purity of his Bride."[53]

This is not to suggest that new covenant believers possess any sort of independent or individual capacity to pass judgment on anyone (Matt 7:1; Luke 6:37; Rom 14:1–13; Jas 4:11). In the New Testament no less than in the Old, God alone remains the supreme Judge (2 Tim 4:8; Heb 12:23–24; Jas 4:12). He has designated his one and only Son to enact his judgments (Acts 17:31). No believer has the power or the right, therefore, to pass judgment in his or her own power; instead, united with Christ the King, the gathered people of God participate together in the judgments of God.[54]

This process begins with a personal expression of concern from one believer to another. Such confrontation occurs first in a conversation between individuals—not in a group, not from a platform or pulpit, not in an open letter posted on a blog, not on a social media page, but personally and privately. If sin is present but the concern is ignored, the confrontation extends to include one or two other believers so that evidence can be assessed fairly. If it becomes clear that the church member is indeed persisting in sin, the matter then is made public. If the offender still refuses to repent, he or she is treated as someone who needs to hear the gospel and trust Jesus for the first time (Matt 18:15–19). This final, heartbreaking step of separation happens only when a professed believer chooses to persist in behaving or believing like an unbeliever. If a leader is removed because of sin, it is particularly important for the entire congregation to hear this final rebuke, because the leader's sin is a sin against the whole community (1 Tim 5:20).

Church discipline is not a process for removing difficult members from a humanly manufactured crowd or club. Church discipline is the holy work of participating proleptically in God's future judgment for the purpose of preserving and expanding God's present reign in the lives of his people. Whenever we as God's people call one another to repentance, we—united with Christ through faith—join in Christ's final judgment on sin by concurring in the present with a verdict that God in Christ will pronounce in the future.[55] In this foretaste of the final judgment, the repentant sinner's embrace of transforming grace culminates in joy throughout the community. If the sinner persists in his or her rejection of God's goodness, the result for the individual and the community is, however, the bitter but necessary pain of separation.

What about You?

Study Matt 18:15–20 and 1 Tim 5:19–21.

If you are a church leader, when was the last time someone confronted you in any of the ways that Jesus and Paul described in these texts? If no one has done so, it isn't because you're such a sanctified person that you've left every shortcoming behind. Have you, perhaps, insulated yourself in such a way that you are no longer being held accountable in your spiritual life? If someone has corrected you recently, did you react defensively, with excuses or justifications for your actions? Or did you carefully consider their words and respond with humility and grace?

Continuities and Discontinuities in Judgments between the Old Covenant and the New

In continuity with the judges in the old covenant, the new covenant community is called to pursue justice on the basis of God's Word without preference or prejudice. No church member may claim immunity from accountability, regardless of his or her position within the community. The same judgments apply to every individual, whether leader or layperson, young or old, president or preschool teacher, prosperous or poor, without regard for the color of their flesh or the origin of their families.[56] In particular, the church must never show partiality by ignoring the sins of significant financial contributors or by failing to hold powerful members accountable to the same standards as other believers (1 Tim 5:21).[57] In this, there are clear continuities between the old covenant and the new (1 Tim 5:21; cf. Exod 23:3; Lev 19:15; Deut 16:19).[58]

There are, however, discontinuities as well. In the first place, new covenant verdicts—unlike judgments in the Old Testament—are not the unique domain of any particular class of leaders within the community of faith. The role of judge and king has been fulfilled once and for all in Jesus Christ; the calling and the capacity to deliver righteous judgments now extends to the entire local body of believers, gathered together in union with Christ (Acts 10:42; 1 Cor 5:4–5, 12; 6:2–5).[59] Discipline begins with an individual confrontation, but it proceeds beyond that point only through the consensus of a local body of believers, compelled by God's Spirit under the authority of God's Word (Matt 18:15–20; John 20:22–23; 1 Cor 5:3–5; 2 Cor 2:6).[60]

> Under the lordship of Christ and under the authority of divinely given elders who lead, the last and final court of appeals in matters related to the local church is the congregation itself. . . . Everyone is involved in this image-bearing work of ruling, judging, and putting all things under our feet as we live under the lordship of Christ. The whole community's work of governance explains why the entire congregation sits in judgment and exercises authority.[61]

Also unlike the verdicts of judges and kings in the old covenant, the primary purpose of corporate rebuke in the new covenant is not to purge sinners from the body but to call sinners to realign their lives with the Word of God so that judgment gives way to comfort and restored community (2 Cor 2:5–11; Jas 2:12–13; cf. Deut 17:5–7, 12). "Nothing can be more compassionate than the severe rebuke that calls a brother back from the path of sin," Dietrich Bonhoeffer reminded the seminary students that he trained. "It is a ministry of mercy, an ultimate offer of genuine fellowship, when we allow nothing but God's Word to stand between us."[62]

Recovering Righteous Judgments in the New Covenant Community

The merciful ministry of church discipline is, however, in decline. In a culture that boasts "only God can judge me," perhaps this decline should not surprise us—but the decline does reveal the degree to which the world's values have shaped the practices of the church.[63] "The decline of church discipline is," R. Albert Mohler has noted, "perhaps the most visible failure of the contemporary church."[64] There are historical reasons for this decline, but the failure to pursue a biblical pattern of church discipline ultimately represents a failure in the leadership of churches and in the training of the church's leaders.[65]

In some instances, church leaders lack the conviction and courage to confront errant members with gentle boldness. This lack of conviction and courage among pastors may be due to fear of unpopularity, of a decline in attendance, perhaps even of the loss of one's job. Pastors who submit to such fears are leading in their own strength instead of relying on the presence, power, and protection of the God who goes before us. In other instances, church leaders simply don't know how to pursue church discipline. They lack the knowledge and creativity to envision how church discipline serves as God's tool for the transformation of his people. Such leaders need training and mentorship to equip them with the tools and patterns they need to lead their congregations in godly discipline.

Regardless of the reasons why a church fails to participate proleptically in God's future judgment, the result is the same: An undisciplined church allows injustice to flourish. A deacon continues to dehumanize other church members through his angry outbursts. Pornography weakens and perverts the relational bond in a staff member's marriage. The demeaning male leader is never challenged when he squelches or even mocks the input of godly women in the church. A child's report of sexual abuse at the hands of a popular youth leader is left unreported to the appropriate authorities. A pastor's racist comments are ignored—or even smirked at—instead of being confronted as a vile assault on God's creation of a glorious kaleidoscope of colors and cultures. In some cases, sinful patterns may result from spiritual immaturity instead of outright rebellion (1 Thess 5:14), but even these patterns must be confronted with boldness and love.

Whenever a situation calls for discipline and we ignore this opportunity, we—like King Saul ignoring the words of the prophet Samuel—implicitly declare that our ways are better than God's ways. The results of this arrogant declaration are disastrous for the church's witness in the world. "When discipline leaves a church," one nineteenth-century pastor pointed out, "Christ goes with it."[66] In Old Testament terms, justice is denied and the privileged persist in their oppression of the vulnerable and weak (Exod 23:6; Deut 16:19; 24:17; Isa 29:21; Lam 3:35; Mal 3:5). Such a church may still claim the title "church" for itself, but it has ceased to reflect the glorious revelation of God's kingdom through Jesus Christ.

When Moses stood before his people on the plains of Moab, he knew the necessity of righteous judges and he foresaw the people's future demand for a king—but he saw only dimly and from a distance the One in whom God's righteous judgments would be fulfilled. More than a millennium after Moses described Israel's ideal judge and king, God would place Moses on a mountain far north of Moab. There, the mediator of the old covenant would glimpse the mediator of a new covenant gleaming like the sun, swathed in royal robes that shone as white as light (Matt 17:2). This new mediator was God's appointed Judge and King. Today, the whole congregation of new covenant believers participates with this glorious King in judgments that have not yet reached their consummation (1 Cor 12:12–13; 2 Tim 4:1, 8). When we as pastors lead the people of God in these exercises of church discipline, we are following the pattern of a God who goes before us, walking in the path of a righteous Judge and King who has already paved our way.

Ignoring Abuse Damages the Church's Witness

"Evangelical churches are plagued with serious problems related to how we respond to and counsel victims of sexual assault. This is a serious problem that damages the gospel and pushes the most vulnerable away from hope and refuge. *Addressing this issue is not damaging the gospel, it is instead seeking to restore the gospel and Christ to their rightful authority and priority over institutions and mishandled theology.*"[67]

—Rachael Denhollander

Proper practice of church discipline does not allow churches to attempt to handle criminal matters internally instead of reporting accusations to appropriate authorities. One aspect of a Christian's submission to the governing authorities is submission to statutes that mandate reporting of suspected abuse, particularly of children (Rom 13:1). How would your church respond to allegations of abuse of a child by a church leader? Would you try to minimize the accusation because you care more about your church's perceived reputation than about protecting vulnerable children? Would you consider attempting to handle the charges internally instead of reporting possible abuse to the appropriate authorities?

Leadership Definition, Dynamics, and Diagnostics

	Leadership Definition	Leadership Dynamic	Leadership Diagnostics
Union with Christ	*The Christ-following leader— living as a bearer of God's image in union with Christ and his people—*	The position to which the leader is called is not sovereignty above or separation from the community but stewardship within the community in union with Christ.	Have you misused church discipline to flaunt your authority or to challenge persons who have resisted your leadership? How can you rest in the faithfulness of God instead of seeking to seize sovereignty for yourself?
Communion with Christ's People	*develops a diverse community of fellow laborers who are equipped and empowered to pursue shared goals*	The power that the leader exercises is not the leader's but Christ's, and this power must be expressed according to God's design for a diverse community of Spirit-equipped servants.	Do specific people in your local church know enough about your personal life to call you to account? Or have you set yourself apart from the people of the church in such a way that you are not held fully accountable? Does your church have a biblically grounded process to call you to repentance if you are leading in ways that are ungodly or unhealthy? When you become aware of a grievous or persistent sin in a church member's life, do you view church discipline as a repugnant duty to be endured or as a difficult but beautiful opportunity for God to redeem and to restore his repentant children?

Mission in the World	*that fulfill the creation mandate and the Great Commission in submission to the Word of God.*	The truth that the leader is called to proclaim is not the leader's vision but God's revelation.	Are you willing to risk your position or popularity to testify publicly to the power of the gospel through loving and faithful practice of church discipline?

Further Reading

Cheong, Robert. *God Redeeming His Bride.* Ross-Shire, UK: Christian Focus, 2012.

Leithart, Peter. *A Son to Me.* Moscow, ID: Canon, 2003.

White, Thomas, Jason Duesing, and Malcolm Yarnell, eds. *Restoring Integrity in Baptist Churches.* Grand Rapids: Kregel, 2007.

Wills, Gregory. "African American Democracies." In *Democratic Religion*, 67-83. Oxford: Oxford University Press, 1997.

A Devoted Community:
Priesthood and Prophecy in Israel

"If a case is too difficult for you—concerning bloodshed, lawsuits, or assaults—cases disputed at your city gates, then go up to the place the LORD your God chooses. You are to go to the Levitical priests and to the judge who presides at that time. Ask, and they will give you a verdict in the case."

Deuteronomy 17:8–9

"The LORD your God will raise up for you a prophet like me from among your own brothers. You must listen to him. . . . Then the LORD said to me, '. . . But the prophet who presumes to speak a message in my name that I have not commanded him to speak, or who speaks in the name of other gods—that prophet must die.' You may say to yourself, 'How can we recognize a message the LORD has not spoken?' When a prophet speaks in the LORD's name, and the message does not come true or is not fulfilled, that is a message the LORD has not spoken. The prophet has spoken it presumptuously. Do not be afraid of him."

Deuteronomy 18:15–22

▶ Chapter Four Key Point

Not every believer in Jesus is a prophet, but prophecy is accessible and desirable for every believer. United with Christ the great high priest, every believer also participates together in a holy priesthood. As equal participants in this shared priesthood, church leaders are called to equip the people to see themselves and their leaders as the devoted property of God. ◀

O h my goodness! How many priests do they have here?"
      That's what I (Timothy) heard whispered in the row behind me, and I smiled because the woman who uttered these words spoke more truth than she knew.

The church where I served at the time had moved into a building that previously housed a Roman Catholic congregation. From time to time, someone who once attended the Catholic church would show up without knowing the building was under new management. By the time they reached the sanctuary, most of these individuals had recognized this was no longer a Roman Catholic gathering—but, somehow, the middle-aged couple sitting behind me made it into the worship service still thinking that the church was operating under the oversight of priests and a pope.

When the worship service began, the woman and her husband caviled back and forth about the strangeness of the songs. They were clearly surprised when the "priest" stepped behind the pulpit and preached a sermon while wearing a plaid shirt and jeans. Their greatest shock came near the end of the service, however, when we began to celebrate the Lord's Supper. After the pastor made it clear that this meal was only for believers, more than a dozen deacons and church members stood in a row in front of the platform, holding out the bread and the cups for the people who were now filing to the front to partake in this holy meal.

That's when the woman in the row behind me whispered, rather loudly, "Oh my goodness! How many priests do they have here?" Her perception was apparently that every church member administering the bread and the cup was a priest.[1] I smiled because, in one sense, this unwitting visitor was wrong—but, in another sense, she was far more right than she knew. She was incorrect, because she assumed that each of those serving Communion had been ordained into the priesthood of the Roman Catholic Church. At the same time, she was quite correct, because every believer in Jesus Christ *is* a member of a "holy priesthood" (1 Pet 2:5). Through union with Christ, every believer participates in the priesthood of the "great high priest who has passed through the heavens" (Heb 4:14).

And yet if every believer in Jesus Christ is part of a holy priesthood, what does this mean for leaders in the church? Does the priesthood of all believers eliminate the need for strong church leadership? If church members are priests in the same sense as church leaders, what possible relevance does priesthood have for church leadership?

Priesthood and Prophecy as a Leadership Typology

Scholars and pastors who treat the offices of Christ as a typology for church leadership typically link priesthood with caregiving and prophecy with teaching. According to this categorization, priestly leaders provide personal care for God's people, in contrast to prophets, who proclaim the Scriptures. Priests focus on resolving conflicts and caring for the vulnerable.[2] Prophets, on the other hand, are masters of "vision, study, preaching, teaching, doctrinal truth, refuting error, and calling people to repent."[3] Some have pressed the point further and identified the church's priestly ministry with the work of deacons while assigning prophetic ministry to the church's teaching pastors.[4]

This chapter will suggest that such linkages are severely lacking in scriptural support. In the old covenant, the work of teaching was never consistently tied to prophetic ministry. Furthermore, even if the Old Testament could sustain these connections, priesthood is not to be identified biblically with a set of caregiving capacities implanted in the lives of certain individuals in the new covenant. New covenant priesthood is a communal identity of total devotion, grounded in our shared union with Christ.

Prophecy and priesthood, no less than the offices of judge and king, *are* relevant for new covenant leadership—but not as typological categories that describe particular skill sets in the lives of certain leaders. Every member of the new covenant community participates equally in a single priesthood through union with "a great high priest who has passed through the heavens" (Heb 4:14), and every believer enjoys potential access to the gift of prophecy (Acts 2:17; 1 Cor 14:1, 5, 31, 39). These foundational realities reshape leadership by reminding leaders that they and the people they lead are, together, the devoted property of God.

Priest

Translates Hebrew *kohen* and Greek *hiereus*; English derives from Latin *pres-byter*, "elder," via Old English *preost*[5]

Priests offered sacrifices on behalf of others. Before the law was given through Moses, every head of a household seems to have served as the priest for his own family (Gen 8:20; 12:7; 13:4; 26:25; 31:54). Some heads of household, such as Melchizedek and Jethro, were recognized as priests beyond their clans (Gen 14:18; Exod 2:16). When God constituted Israel as a nation, the sons of Aaron in the tribe of Levi were devoted as Israel's priests (Exodus 28). The Aaronic priests not only offered sacrifices and blessed the people but also taught the Torah and superintended the copying of the Scriptures (Lev 10:11; Deut 17:18; 31:9–13; 33:10). From the time of David, the priesthood was organized into a rotation of twenty-four divisions (1 Chr 24:7–18; Ezra 2:36–39; Neh 7:39–42).

The Justice League of Judges and Priests

The job description for the judge in ancient Israel was simple: "Judge the people with righteous judgment" (Deut 16:18). But what if a judge would not decide what judgment was the most righteous? How could a judge judge with righteous judgment in those cases when he was not certain whether an act had been intentional or unintentional? And what about situations that were not explicitly addressed in the Torah?

Whenever a judge faced a complex legal case, the judicial process passed from a local judge to a judge and priests convened in the place of God's choosing (Deut 17:8). After hearing the details of the difficult case, the judge and priests were to hand down a final verdict (Deut 17:9).[6] The role of the additional judge in such cases seems clear—the judge undertook a careful investigation, weighing evidences anew and analyzing the testimony of the accusers (see Deut 19:18). Such judges seem to have brought together the roles of detective, prosecuting attorney, and defense attorney.

But what about the priests? What was the particular role of priests in delivering final verdicts? And why weren't judges sufficient to determine what decision represented the righteous judgment of God?

Based on the priestly expectations prescribed throughout the rest of the Old Testament, it seems that the primary responsibility of priests in disputed legal cases was to clarify the precepts found in the Torah.[7] Judges investigated evidence and searched for the truth about the crime; priests searched the Torah and declared verdicts on the basis of the Word of God.[8]

Priests as Guardians and Teachers of God's Word

Earlier in the exodus, God had consecrated priests to bless the people, to represent the people, and to offer sacrifices for the people (Exod 28:9–12; Leviticus 4–16; Num 6:22–27).[9] Yet there was another responsibility placed upon priests that was no less significant than these ritual roles.[10] God commanded the priests and Levites to teach the Torah. This responsibility included priestly proclamation of the Torah in difficult legal cases—but it extended far beyond the clarification of verdicts in complicated courtroom situations. From the earliest stages of Israel's history as a nation, the role of teaching "all the statutes that the LORD has given" was central to the priesthood (Lev 10:11).[11] In his address on the plains of Moab, Moses explicitly assigned to the priests the privileges of instructing the people, safeguarding the Torah scrolls, and superintending the copying of these scrolls (Deut 17:18; 31:9–13; 33:10).[12]

Priests were not merely mediators of God's blessings or representatives of God's people. The priests and their Levitical compatriots were also called to be expositors of God's written Word.[13] Any ritual role that a priest possessed was relativized by his precedent identity as a follower and faithful teacher of God's Word.[14] The presentation of difficult cases before a judicial bench of priests and a judge provided not only a courtroom where righteous judgments could be handed down but also a classroom where the people could be reminded anew to remain faithful to the covenant. Because his judgments were grounded in faithful proclamation of God's Word, the verdicts that a priest declared in these cases were never merely the priest's opinions. His verdicts were the truth of God conveyed to the people of God through the exposition and application of the Word of God.[15]

Levite

From Hebrew *levay*, "of Levi"

After God set apart Aaron and his descendants as Israel's priests, the remainder of the tribe of Levi became assistants to the priests. They received this privilege because of their covenant faithfulness in the aftermath of the golden calf incident (Exod 32:26–29). Every firstborn son in Israel was the devoted property of God, but—provided that the parents chose to redeem their offspring—members of the tribe of Levi could take the place of the firstborn son (Exod 34:20; Num 3:41). The tribe of Levi included three primary clans: Kohath, Gershon, and Merari. Aaron's family was part of the Kohathite clan.

The Failure of the Priests and Levites

And yet the priests of Israel did not remain faithful to their calling. "Both prophet and priest are ungodly," the LORD God lamented through Jeremiah, "even in my house I have found their evil" (Jer 23:11). One key evidence of the priests' ungodliness was their neglect and perversion of their responsibility to teach God's Word.

During the reign of King Asa, the prophet Azariah pointed out how the people had endured "many years . . . without a teaching priest, and without instruction" (2 Chr 15:3). In the time of Isaiah, the prophet saw priests who were too drunk to distinguish injustice from justice; Isaiah mocked such priests by asking, "Who is he trying to teach?" (Isa 28:9). Micah prophesied against the priests in his day because they demanded payment for their teaching (Mic 3:11).[16] According to the word of the LORD spoken through Ezekiel, priests had failed to teach the people the difference "between the clean and the unclean" (Ezek 22:26).

Throughout the history of Israel and Judah, whenever spiritual awakenings interrupted the people's downward spiral of rebellion, renewed practices of teaching from priests and Levites seem to have accompanied the people's revived commitments to the covenant (2 Chr 17:9; 35:3; Neh 8:9). It was through the teaching of the priest Jehoiada that God brought revival through King Joash (2 Kgs 12:2).[17] Such renewals were, however, short-lived. After Israel returned from exile, the expectation persisted that priests and Levites should be teachers. And yet the priests continued to spurn their calling to instruct the people of God (Mal 1:6–14; 2:7–8).

Teaching was not, of course, the only responsibility of Israel's priests. Priests were also responsible to offer sacrifices on the people's behalf and to help the people distinguish between what was holy and what was not (Lev 10:10–11). Teaching was, however, central to their divinely ordained vocation. Based on the indictments spoken by the prophets, it seems that a lack of faithful teaching was one of their primary failures.

Rescued from Doom on the Wings of Eagles

These failures in the old covenant priesthood revealed Israel's desperate need for an unfailing priest—for a priest who was "holy, innocent, undefiled, separated from sinners, and exalted above the heavens" (Heb 7:26). No mere human being could ever measure up to such an exalted standard. And so God the Son embraced the frailty of human flesh and became the great high priest in a priesthood more ancient and more holy than Aaron's (Heb 2:14–18; 5:1–10; 7:11–28; 8:7–13). Suspended from a Roman cross, the perfect priest offered his own flesh as a sacrifice (Eph 5:2; Heb 7:27; 9:14, 26; 10:10–12). Bursting alive from a borrowed tomb, Christ the priest and final sacrifice became the firstfruits of God's victory, guaranteeing God's future restoration of his world (1 Cor 15:20–28).

When the Holy Spirit joins believers with Jesus Christ, we become united to him in everything. Joined with this perfect priest and risen sacrifice, every believer becomes a full participant in a royal priesthood and living sacrifice (Rom 12:1; 1 Pet 2:5, 9; Rev 1:6; 5:10). And yet because this priesthood is not our own accomplishment, neither our priesthood nor our sacrifice adds anything to Christ's completed work. All is accomplished in him, and no portion of our priesthood is separable from his priesthood.[18] "Where he is, there we are too, in the incarnation, on the cross, and in his resurrection. We belong to him because we are in him."[19] His story becomes our story, and our story is now interpreted in light of his story.[20]

This participation in a perfect priesthood was not a postscript or afterthought in God's plan. Before he established the Levitical priesthood, the God of Israel had already promised his people that, through their participation in his covenant, they would become a "kingdom of priests" and a "holy nation" (Exod 19:4–6).[21] Like Frodo and Samwise snatched by eagles from the fires of Mount Doom in *The Lord of the Rings*, Israel had been lifted "on eagles' wings" from the doom of slavery for the purpose of being formed into a priesthood that would extend far beyond the tribe of Levi.[22] The people of Israel had been rescued so that they would become "a kingdom marked by priesthood; that is, service of God on behalf of people and *vice versa*. . . . Israel will thus redefine the meaning of dominion—[as] service."[23]

In the end, however, only one Israelite—the Messiah himself—kept God's covenant with Israel. As a result, this long-expected holy priesthood was constituted not through human effort (2 Cor 3:7–11; Heb 8:7–13) but through our union with the one Israelite who upheld the old covenant and established a new covenant.[24] Through him, every believer becomes part of "a chosen race, a royal priesthood, a holy nation" (1 Pet 2:9). Through his incarnation and priesthood, "Christ has taken our nature into heaven, to represent us," pastor and hymnodist John Newton once pointed out, "and has left us on earth, with his nature, to represent him."[25]

Priestly and Prophetic Leadership in the Old Covenant

So what about the claim that prophecy and priesthood provide a typology for leadership in the new covenant community? According to this leadership typology, those who are skilled in caregiving should be considered priestly leaders, while teachers and preachers should be seen as prophetic leaders.[26] According to this reconstruction of Israel's leadership structures, old covenant priests cared for the people through "symbols of substitutionary sacrifice and reconciliation," while prophets provided the people with instruction in God's Word.[27]

When it comes to biblical and theological support, the links that sustain this typology fall short in at least three ways:

1. In the first place, *teaching in the old covenant was linked far more frequently to priests than to prophets.* Yes, the old covenant priests were representatives and intercessors. Yet the intercessory responsibilities of priests and Levites must never eclipse the instructional responsibility to which the Old Testament repeatedly testifies (Lev 10:10–11; 2 Kgs 12:2; 2 Chr 15:3; 17:7–9; 35:3; Ezra 7:6, 10; Neh

8:7–9; Isa 28:7–10; Jer 18:18; Ezek 7:26; 22:26; Mic 3:11; Mal 2:3–9).[28] When Jesus taught the people during his time on earth, he was fulfilling the old covenant office of priest no less than the office of prophet.

2. *Prophets were not primarily teachers of written revelation; they were recipients of direct divine revelation, and their oracles were tested against previous revelation and against events that succeeded their prophetic proclamations.* The words of the prophets were received through immediate revelation and then proclaimed to divinely designated recipients (Num 12:6–8). If a prophet's proclamation contradicted God's previous revelation or if the prophet's predictions did not come to pass, that individual was to be rejected as a prophet (Deut 18:19–22). Prophets were not raised up by the community like judges were; neither was their position hereditary, as was the case with priests and kings. Prophets were called by God, anointed by his Spirit, and filled with his oracles. Their words were not expositions of written revelation but proclamations in response to direct, divine revelation. As recipients of God's message for a particular people at a particular moment in time, prophets frequently functioned as the public consciences of those in power, rebuking Israel's leaders whenever they began to embrace the delusion that their authority freed them from accountability.[29] The gift of prophecy persisted among the first followers of Jesus. It was possible for a single individual in the early church to function both as a prophet and as a teacher in the New Testament churches (Acts 13:1), but the two gifts were still seen as distinct (1 Cor 12:28–29; 14:6; Eph 4:11).[30] Furthermore, the New Testament authors never listed the gift of prophecy among the requirements for elders in the church (1 Tim 3:2–5; Titus 1:6–9). What then is the role of prophets in the church today? Prophets speak God's truth among God's people and apply these truths to specific circumstances as the Spirit leads them. The church can be a prophetic voice today by encouraging those who possess the gift of prophecy to speak against systemic injustices both within and beyond the community of faith. This could include confronting church leaders with gracious resolve when these leaders have fostered environments where abuse has been hidden. In other instances, it may mean speaking with prophetic clarity

against political leaders when their rhetoric enflames racist ideologies, for example, or when they use their influence to support the injustice of abortion. The church cannot, Karl Barth commented in the context of Adolph Hitler's rise to power, "remain 'neutral' in things great or small where justice is at stake."[31] Today, no less than in the Old Testament, such a prophetic voice will not line up neatly with any particular political party; instead, it will point out patterns of injustice both on the political right and on the left.

3.   Finally, *priestliness in the new covenant is primarily communal, not individual.* In the new covenant community, priestliness is not an individualized quality but a communal identity given to every believer in Jesus Christ.[32] Since no part of our priesthood depends on our own gifts or skills, no believer can possess a different essence or degree of priestliness when compared with other believers.[33] Scripture does not support the supposition that new covenant priestliness is a capacity that different individuals exemplify in differing degrees. Laypeople in the new covenant are not Levitical servants who observe and obey a new order of priestly leaders. United with Christ the great high priest, all of God's new covenant people constitute a common priesthood (Heb 7:11–19; 1 Pet 2:4–9; Rev 5:9–10). Paul did mention "priestly duty" in one instance in connection with his unique calling as "a minister . . . to the Gentiles" (Rom 15:16 NIV). Even then, however, Paul never treated priestliness as a capacity that he experienced in a greater degree than other Christians did.[34] Earlier in this same epistle, Paul had already called all believers to participate together in the priestly work of offering themselves "as a living sacrifice, holy and pleasing to God" (Rom 12:1).[35] A few sentences after Paul described his own "priestly duty," the apostle explicitly extended priestly terminology to all believers, using the language of priestly ministry to describe the Gentile Christians' sacrificial gifts for the sake of their Jewish brothers and sisters ("the Gentiles . . . are obligated to minister to them [the Jews]," Rom 15:27).[36] Here and elsewhere, new covenant priesthood is clearly communal, not individual. Through faith in Christ, women and men from every race and nation are being bound together even now into a single priesthood. The priesthood of the whole community provides every believer with direct access

to Christ the great teacher and priest through the presence of his Holy Spirit (John 13:13–14; 16:12–15; see also Jer 31:33).[37] No individual within the body of Christ can become more priestly than anyone else, because every aspect of Christ's priesthood is already ours in him.[38]

Prophet

From Greek, *prophetes*; translates Hebrew *navi*

Also known as "seers" (1 Sam 9:9), prophets prayed with particular power and proclaimed messages received directly from God (see, e.g., Gen 20:7; Exod 7:1–2; Deut 18:18; 1 Kgs 22:14). This proclamation typically called people to repentance in the present and sometimes included predictions of the future. God appointed prophets for Israel in response to the people's request not "to hear the voice of the LORD our God . . . any longer" (Deut 18:16). Since individuals were not to be regarded as prophets unless their claims came to pass (Deut 18:18–22), some may not have been recognized as prophets until some time after their initial prophecies. Unlike kingship and priesthood, prophecy was not assigned by hereditary privilege, human choice, or appointment by the congregation. Prophets were chosen by God and anointed by his Spirit to mediate his message. Prophets could be anointed with oil to confirm their calling (1 Kgs 19:16), but anointing with oil was not necessary for someone to become a Spirit-anointed prophet. In some instances, composers and musicians seem to have been seen as prophets (1 Chr 25:1–2). Particular individuals continued to be gifted as prophets in the New Testament (Acts 11:28; 21:10–11; 1 Cor 12:29; 13:2), and the proclamation of prophetic words was considered to be possible and desirable for every first-century believer (Acts 2:17; 1 Cor 14:1–5, 31–39).[39]

Every Believer Has Access to God's Revelation

"Although degrees of knowledge, maturity, and experience among Christians remain, there is no longer, in regard to knowing revelation, a basic categorical distinction between priests/prophets and the rest of God's people in the new covenant community."[40]

—G. K. Beale

Because God's revelation is available to every believer, any believer may receive a word from God that calls others to deeper faithfulness and holiness. Are you tempted to ignore admonitions from faithful Christians in your church simply because you know more about the Bible and theology than they do? If so, remember Richard Baxter's admonition to pastors who pride themselves in their theological scholarship: "Take heed. . . . The devil is a greater scholar than you."[41] You and every Christian in your congregation are equal participants in a common priesthood, and prophecy is accessible and desirable for every believer in Jesus Christ (Acts 2:17; 1 Cor 14:1–5, 31–39). What can you do to be more open to the reality that God may convey his truth to you through believers who may know far fewer theological facts than you do?

New Covenant Priesthood as the Devoted Property of God

What does it mean to be "a royal priesthood," with priestliness as a shared identity that is broader than caregiving or intercession? Most important for our purposes, how can church leaders lead if pastors and vocational ministers are no more priestly than other members of the church? What will be argued throughout the remainder of this chapter is simply this: *Even when expanded to encompass all of God's people, the primary point of priesthood in both covenants was to highlight the holiness of the community of faith. This holiness is not primarily separation from the world but sacrificial devotion to God as his property and possession.* This truth transforms every aspect of leadership in the church.

To be a priesthood is to be holy. It was God himself who placed the phrase "holy nation" parallel to "kingdom of priests" in his revelation to Moses, establishing an explicit connection between priesthood and holiness (Exod 19:6). Immediately after describing Israel as a priestly kingdom and a holy nation, God commanded both priests and people to be set apart as holy (Exod 19:6, 10, 22).[42] Centuries later, Simon Peter embedded his citation of this passage in the context of a call to holiness: "As the one who called you is holy, you also are to be holy in all your conduct; for it is written, 'Be holy, because I am holy'" (1 Pet 1:15–16). A few sentences later, the apostle specifically identified God's people as "a holy priesthood" in union with Christ

(1 Pet 2:4–5; compare Lev 11:44–45; 19:2; 20:7). Priesthood includes more than holiness, but it never implies anything less than holiness.

This holiness is not, however, separation from the world for the purpose of deeper personal piety.[43] "Purity," Old Testament scholar Peter Gentry points out, "is a result of being holy in the biblical sense, but it is not the meaning of the word."[44] As French biblical scholar Claude-Bernard Costecalde has demonstrated, the fundamental point of "holiness" in Scripture was not "separation" but "devotion."[45] Understood in this way, "holy priesthood" implies the sacrificial devotion of God's people as the particular possession of the living God (1 Pet 2:5). Through faith in Jesus Christ, we are joined with the great high priest who was devoted to God's purposes to the point of death. With him, we are designated as God's possession and consecrated for God's purposes (see Rom 6:1–11).[46] This union not only unites us with the sacrifice of Christ but also devotes us to his sacrificial life.[47] Thus, our holiness is not measured by our distance from sinners but by our closeness to Christ.[48] To be a priesthood is to be the devoted property and possession of God.

So what does it mean practically, in the community of faith, to live as God's devoted property and possession?

For those who are united with Christ, this sacrificial devotion results first in an attitude of generosity toward our brothers and sisters in Christ (Rom 15:24; Heb 13:16)—but this overflow of devotion never stops at the borders of the believing community![49] Our holiness provides the foundation for the proclamation of our hope throughout the world. Whenever we embrace our place as a devoted priesthood, we find ourselves reaching beyond the new covenant community to proclaim the good news of God's reign and to pursue his justice in the world around us. God's holy people are—in the words of Simon Peter—called to declare "the praises of the One who called [us] out of darkness" to the people around us who do not yet believe; our praise opens the door for people from every social and ethnic background to "glorify God" (1 Pet 2:9, 12). This recognition of God's glory will happen in this life for those who turn to Christ now; it will happen at the end of time for those who do not (1 Pet 2:12).[50]

When we embrace this identity as a sacrificial priesthood united with Christ, we are able to live with confidence and freedom. The worst that can be said about us has already been said about him; the most that we can suffer for him has already been suffered by him; and the most that we can lose has already been lost in his death and regained through his resurrection. We can be both vulnerable and bold, taking risks in our love for others, because—even in suffering—Jesus Christ is the God who has gone before us.[51] This sort of holiness is not marked by a life withdrawn from the world but by a life sacrificially devoted to God's purposes in the world, fully engaged in the proclamation of his Word and in the pursuit of his justice for the flourishing of our communities and the glory of God.

In the old covenant, the priesthood was devoted not only to offering sacrifices but also to teaching and guarding the Scriptures. In the new covenant, the entire community of faith participates in this priestly work of proclaiming and preserving truth that has been not only inscribed in words but also etched in our hearts (Jer 31:33). As we proclaim and pursue these patterns of life, God reveals and deepens our identity as his own devoted possession. This devotion reshapes church leadership by freeing leaders from at least two deadly delusions about their role in the church: (1) the delusion that the people are the leader's property and (2) the delusion that the leader is the people's property.

What about You?

Study Exod 19:1–6 and 1 Pet 2:1–10.

In 1932, the University of Southern California started stenciling "Property of USC" on athletic T-shirts for the purpose of preventing theft.[52] Their anti-theft strategy backfired when the stenciled attire became more popular than the original unstenciled T-shirts. USC turned this problem into profit by producing and selling "Property of USC" shirts to students. In the decades that followed, public universities throughout the United States began to stock and sell "Property of" sportswear, emblazoned with the name of their institution. The phrases "kingdom of priests" and "holy priesthood" (Exod 19:6; 1 Pet 2:5) are like "Property of" T-shirts that God places on everyone he has chosen and purchased as his own. When he referred to Israel as a "kingdom of priests," God was declaring his people to be "Property of God." The apostle Peter applied this terminology to the church, identifying new covenant believers as a chosen community devoted to God's purposes.

The people in your church are God's treasured possession. Do you treat them as the property of God or as your own? In what ways are you tempted to respond to the people as if they are your property, gathered together to implement your vision and plans? In what ways do you fall short in seeing your leadership role as a sacred stewardship of a community that has been purchased by the blood of Christ?

The Delusion That the People Are the Leader's Property

It is a privilege to lead the people of God—but leadership in the kingdom of God should result in humble stewardship, not prideful ownership. The people we lead are our responsibility (Heb 13:17), but they never become our property. That is why Peter commanded his fellow elders to "shepherd God's flock among you . . . not lording it over those entrusted to you" (1 Pet 5:2–3). Church leaders are never called to tower above the congregation as if the purpose of these people is to fulfill their own dreams and visions. God has called the leaders of the church to serve as shepherds in the midst of a flock that has been wholly devoted to God's purposes.

And yet the delusion that the people are our property remains a persistent temptation.

Some expressions of this delusion are obvious. There is the dictatorial pastor who is driven to anger when people do not measure up to his expectations, the bullying elder who silences dissent by abusing the gift of church discipline, the unaccountable pastor who demands control over the church's finances. Such leaders may rack up charges on the church's credit card that do not clearly contribute to the purposes of the church, or they may leverage their influence over the people of the church to obtain personal favors for themselves or their families.[53] In each of these instances, the people and their resources are being treated as if they are the leader's property instead of God's property.

This delusion also manifests itself in more subtle ways—in ways that may be hidden, accepted, or even applauded among church leaders. It's seen when a church is leveraged as the pastor's platform for book sales, business deals, or a spot on the main stage of massive parachurch conferences. It's seen when a pastor treats a small congregation or an associate ministry role as a passing inconvenience until a more prominent position becomes available. It's any action or attitude that sees the church as a tool to be manipulated for our benefit instead of a holy communion in which we share a sacred stewardship. In an age of social media platforms and high-profit conferences with rosters full of celebrity pastors, the temptation to use the church in this way is perhaps stronger than it has ever been. Paul House describes the struggle well:

> Pastors whose goal is to brand their ministries, build their reputations, manage a complex organization, become popular enough or singular enough to have off-site video churches, command six-figure book contracts for products mainly ghostwritten, and have thousands of followers on social media outlets don't match anything in the pastoral epistles. They match the "super-apostles" who opposed Paul in Corinth.[54]

Dietrich Bonhoeffer eloquently described the despairing results of expecting the church to serve as a platform to advance our own vision when he wrote this:

> The man who fashions a visionary ideal of community . . . enters the community of Christians with his demands, sets up his own law, and judges the brethren and God himself accordingly. . . . He acts as if he is the creator of the Christian community, as if his dream binds men together. When his ideal picture is destroyed, he sees the community going to smash. So he becomes first an accuser of his brethren, then an accuser of God, and finally the despairing accuser of himself.[55]

The people of the church must never be treated as a launching pad whose purpose is to send our visionary ideals into orbit around our own wishful dreams. Neither is the church meant to serve as the source of our social stature or emotional well-being. The people of God are the property of God, a holy priesthood purchased by the blood of Christ and devoted to his purposes. To treat the people as if they are our property is an act of treasonous theft; it is stealing for ourselves that which Christ our great high priest has bought at the cost of his own blood. "If we take on Christian service and think of such service as the vehicle that will make us central," D. A. Carson has pointed out, "we have paganized Christian service, we have domesticated Christian living and set it to servitude in a pagan cause."[56] Far too many pastors over the past decade have used their churches as platforms for obtaining book deals, conference opportunities, and personal profit. In almost every instance, we have watched these pastors move from using the church as their platform to treating the church as their property and then to abusing their position when the people fail to live up to their expectations.

Leaders are indeed permitted to make a living through the church's giving (1 Cor 9:7–14; Gal 6:6; 1 Tim 5:17–18), but this benefit does not turn the people or their resources into our property to be used as we choose. That was, after all, the presumptuous sin of Eli's sons that was so "very severe in the presence of the LORD" (1 Sam 2:17)! Leaders and laity together are God's property devoted to God's purposes for God's glory. Like the land that was allotted to Israel but remained the property of God, the people of God are apportioned to godly stewards without ever becoming the possession of any of these stewards (1 Pet 5:3).[57] Precisely because the people are God's property and not our own, we as church leaders will "give an account" for the ways that we lead these people and use their resources (Heb 13:17).

The Church as the Property of Christ

"The Christian church is the congregation of brothers in which Jesus Christ, by Word and Sacrament, acts presently as Lord by the Holy Spirit. As the church of pardoned sinners, it has to testify in the midst of a sinful world . . . that it is solely his property."[58]

—Barmen Declaration, thesis 3

The Delusion That the Leader Is the Property of the People

"Let me tell you something, Dr. T." The deacon leaned over the lunch table to make certain I (Timothy) didn't miss a single word he had to say. "If your wife ever has to call me about this again, I will personally take over your calendar so that you're home when you need to be." More than a decade in retrospect, I realize that this threat from a deacon who loved me probably saved my ministry.

I had served four years as the church's associate pastor when the senior pastor left to lead a nearby church plant. A few months later, the congregation asked me to take his place and I accepted the call. But there was a problem: Even after calling an additional staff member to replace my previous role, I didn't let go of the roles I'd had as associate pastor. And so, in addition to leading the staff and preparing multiple messages each week, I was still overseeing monthly trainings for Sunday school teachers, attending every youth and children's ministry meeting, playing guitar in the youth worship band, and helping with the logistics for three upcoming mission trips. The result was that my wife was spending far too many evenings at home alone with our first daughter.

My wife tried to talk to me about releasing some of my previous responsibilities, but I was unwilling to see the problems that she was seeing. So Rayann called a faithful deacon named Mark and described what was happening in our household. And that is how I ended up being interrogated over lunch at Applebee's about why I was spending so many evenings enmeshed in church leadership instead of heading home.

That afternoon, I began the process of delegating and reassigning a long list of responsibilities, but I found the release to be much more of a struggle than I thought it would be. After an hour or so of wrestling with the list, I came to a painful recognition: I was living under the delusion that the people of the church could not accomplish any of these tasks without my direct involvement. Without me, they could do nothing—or so I thought. One result of this delusion was that I was living as if I belonged to the people and programs of the church instead of grounding my identity in my union with Christ.

In some ways, the notion of being constantly engaged in church work seemed noble and sacrificial. When I was a young pastor, I recall having heard older pastors boast about spending all their evenings at church and admonishing younger pastors, "You take care of the church, and God will take care of your family." Scripture never, however, supports such a dualistic split in responsibilities. According to the apostle Paul, our integrity as leaders in the church is grounded in our habits of leadership in our homes (1 Tim 3:4–5). A pastor who neglects his family and functions as if he is the church's property isn't demonstrating sacrificial love for the church. What he is revealing instead is his own unwillingness to develop and to deploy the people of God for the work of God (Eph 4:12).

Leaders who live as if the church depends on them frequently live behind a mask of strength, never revealing their weaknesses. They cannot afford to disappoint or disillusion anyone, because they are the essential property without which the church cannot function—or so they believe.[59] They have little time for the unseen aspects of pastoral ministry—prayer, meditation on the Scriptures, personal discipleship and accountability—that provide the power to pursue the public practices of ministry.[60] The problem with this pattern is that none of us can perpetually separate our interior life from our exterior life.[61] That is why leaders must submit to accountability processes and possess a deep commitment to take their own personal and family development seriously.[62]

Whenever we neglect the unseen aspects of ministry in our personal formation and in our homes, we eventually find ourselves unable to engage in the visible practices of ministry in the power of Christ. "We are the nurses of Christ's little ones," Richard Baxter admonished pastors in the seventeenth century. "If we forbear taking food ourselves, we shall famish them."[63] What makes matters worse today is that too many churches celebrate leaders who are overly busy and who fail to delegate responsibilities. What these churches may not recognize is that, by enabling leaders to live as the congregation's indispensable property, they are not only destroying their leaders but they are also causing themselves to miss opportunities to use the gifts that the Spirit has given them.

One part of the answer to this struggle is for the church's leaders to see themselves not as the property of the church but, together with the people, as the devoted property of God. The pastor is the church's servant, but the church is never the pastor's master.[64] What this means practically is that pastors must learn to see their central identity not as leaders of God's people but, first and foremost, as children of God and followers of God's Son. Whenever our identity becomes tied to our performance as leaders, we find ourselves constantly ranking roles and seeking to situate ourselves in positions that provide us with the greatest leverage over others. In the process, we miss the joy of flourishing in covenant with God and others through union with Christ. But that is not the way of Christ-honoring leadership. "Godly leadership," civil rights leader John M. Perkins once pointed out, "is not about attaining recognition or glory; it's about serving others."[65] When we rest in the truth that our identity has been settled once and for all through our union with Christ, we become able to rejoice in others' gifts and to be satisfied with whatever gifts God has placed within us.[66] Only then can we stop gnawing and clawing to gain recognition for ourselves and begin serving with joy as members of Christ's body, awed by the glorious grace that has grafted us into this union in the first place.

When a pastor's position as a leader eclipses the pastor's identity as a follower of Jesus Christ, one tendency is for pastors to begin studying

God's Word solely for the purpose of proclaiming truth to others instead of feeding on God's Word for the nourishment of their own souls as well. Eighteenth-century Baptist pastor Andrew Fuller described this dilemma well when he wrote these words:

> The studying of divine truth as preachers rather than as Christians, or, in other words, studying it for the sake of finding out something to say to others, without so much as thinking of profiting our own souls, is a temptation to which we are more than ordinarily exposed. If we studied Divine truths as Christians, our being constantly engaged in the service of God would be friendly to our growth in grace. . . . But if we study it only as preachers, it will be the reverse. Our being conversant with the Bible will be like surgeons and soldiers being conversant with the shedding of human blood, till they lose all sensibility concerning it.[67]

Together, leaders and laity constitute a holy priesthood, the property of the living God. Pastors and their people do not differ in their essence or even in the degree to which they are God's priesthood.[68] The distinction between them is solely in the way in which they are called to live out their common identity as followers of Jesus Christ. Godly leadership is followership of Jesus Christ exercised with biblical wisdom in the context of this holy priesthood.

Have you slipped into a pattern of being more concerned with people's perception of your sermon than with how the text applies to your own life? Your fellowship with Christ matters far more than any church member's impressions of your performance on Sunday. Your identity in Christ precedes your calling as a leader. United with Christ, you and the people you serve are a holy priesthood; this priesthood is God's property, devoted to his purposes—not yours.

Do you become embittered when church members fail to notice—or, even worse, when they criticize—your labors? Your identity has already been settled in Jesus, and your popularity with the people neither increases nor decreases the Father's love for you in Christ. Humbly consider critiques that may be true; respond with grace to those that aren't. Refuse to lick your wounds by responding to criticism with criticism. You are part of a holy priesthood, and this priesthood is God's property—not yours.

Do you find yourself convinced that, if only you were serving a different church, everything would be better? Your identity has already been settled in Jesus, and God has placed you in this particular local expression of his holy priesthood at this particular time for a purpose that you may never know in this lifetime. Love this place and these people; they are God's property, devoted to his purposes—not yours.

What about You?

Study Deut 6:4–9 and 1 Tim 3:2–7.

Dayton Moore, general manager of the Kansas City Royals, had a friend who asked him from time to time how his team was doing. Moore would begin talking about his baseball team and the friend would respond, "No, you idiot . . . your team at home"—reminding Moore that his faithfulness as a husband and father mattered more than any wins or losses on the baseball diamond.[69] When the apostle Paul summed up God's requirements for the church's pastoral leaders, part of his message to would-be pastors seems to have been the same: "No, you idiot . . . your team at home." Paul wrote a single extended sentence—six verses in English translations—listing the qualifications for a pastor (1 Tim 3:2–7).[70] He spent two of those six verses spelling out specific expectations related to the leader's household (1 Tim 3:4–5). Think about that structure for a moment: Paul plowed through administrative and teaching skills in only a few words, yet he devoted about one-third of his text to the issue of a pastor's home life.

Why such a focus on the pastor's family? The apostle's Spirit-inspired response is that if leaders can't lead their own households, how can they possibly guide God's household? (1 Tim 3:5). What we as Christian leaders accomplish for God beyond our homes will typically never be greater than what we practice with God within our homes. This does not mean that we should turn our children or spouses into perfectly arranged pawns in our own personal publicity campaigns. Even in the homes of the church's best leaders, words are spoken that should never even have been thought, and choices are made that are far from cherubic. And yet even with these challenges and more, every Christian household can become a context in which parents and children alike confess their failures and learn to return again and again to the gospel. Particularly in the families of church leaders, parents must be deeply engaged in guiding their children toward gospel godliness.

What do you do to disciple your spouse and children? Do your children, in particular, sense that you and your spouse are shaping them to become more like Jesus? If someone asked your children, "What do your parents do to help you to learn about Jesus and to love him more?" what would your children say?

The Neglected Acts of a Pastor

"Three pastoral acts are so basic, so critical, that they determine the shape of everything else. The acts are praying, reading Scripture, and giving spiritual direction. . . . None of these acts is public. . . . Since almost never does anyone notice whether we do these things or not, and only occasionally does someone ask that we do them, these three acts of ministry suffer widespread neglect."[71]

—Eugene Peterson

Your calendar creates your culture, both personally and corporately. Develop a long-term plan to make consistent space in your calendar for prayer, Scripture, and discipleship. Discuss these priorities with your congregation. Begin the process of developing other leaders and volunteers so that you can deploy them in the work of ministry and delegate tasks to them. Shape them not only as doers of ministry but also as individuals who also make space in their own lives for prayer, Scripture, and discipleship.

If Everyone Is a Holy Priesthood, Why Do We Still Need Leaders?

"Everyone in the entire community is holy, and the LORD is among them," a band of rebels from the tribes of Reuben and Levi declared when they revolted against Moses and Aaron. "Why then do you exalt yourselves above the LORD's assembly?" (Num 16:3). The rebels were consumed by earth and fire the next day, strongly suggesting that God did not share their sentiments. And yet their question made some sense. God had, after all, designated all of Israel as his holy priesthood (Exod 19:6; 22:31; Lev 20:7, 26). If all the people participated together in this single priesthood, why were leaders needed at all? The problem with the rebels' question was not their recognition of the holiness of the whole congregation. It was their insolent attempt to exalt themselves, coupled with their presumption that the holiness of the whole community eliminated any need for distinct leadership roles within the community (Num 16:3–7).

The reality of a holy priesthood that includes all God's people has never negated the need for God-called leaders among these people.[72] Leadership and followership were, after all, part of God's plan before humanity's fall. Even before sin entered the world, Adam and Eve together constituted a royal priesthood that included both a leader and a follower living in complementary union with one another. The primeval sin perverted the practices of leadership, but God's design for a comprehensive priesthood persisted alongside humanity's need for leadership.

In the Old Testament, God reminded Israel of this truth by slaughtering the rebel sons of Israel and causing a wooden staff to flower with life and fruit (Num 16:31–35; 17:8–11). In the New Testament, God created a new community by slaughtering the one and only righteous Son on a wooden stake and causing life to blossom anew in the dark death of a borrowed tomb. Through union with this Son, we find our life in Jesus Christ, our devoted priest and sacrifice (Rom 12:1; 15:27). In the church today, the shared devotion of everyone in the community frees us to find our identity not in any position we hold—regardless of how exalted or abased that role may seem—but in the covenant relationship by which God has bound the community to himself. Within this new covenant community, God has designed a diversity of roles, and he situates each one according to his will (1 Cor 12:11). This diversity of roles includes leaders, but these leaders are not a new priesthood that is exalted above the people.

The new covenant community needs no priestly leaders; this community exists only because the "great high priest" has already come (Heb 4:14). What the church needs are leaders who equip their people to see themselves, with their leaders, as "a holy priesthood"—a divinely devoted, covenant-constituted community that shares sacrificially with one another and models God's ways in the world (1 Pet 2:5–12). Through his perfect high priesthood, Jesus Christ has paved the way and provided an example for this priesthood. When the people of God—leaders included—live as followers of God with their identities secure in Christ the great high priest, there is no contradiction between strong leaders and the equal priesthood of all believers (1 Pet 2:5–9; 5:5). Those who lead can lead without dominating or manipulating, and those who follow can follow without fear, because leaders and followers together are pursuing the God who goes before them.

Leadership Definition, Dynamics, and Diagnostics

	Leadership Definition	*Leadership Dynamic*	*Leadership Diagnostics*
Union with Christ	*The Christ-following leader— living as a bearer of God's image in union with Christ and his people—*	The position to which the leader is called is not sovereignty above or separation from the community but stewardship within the community in union with Christ.	Do you see yourself first and foremost as God's property or as the church's property? Do the rhythms of your daily life consistently reflect a reliance on God's power by making space for prayer and meditation on the Scriptures? Are you receiving spiritual direction from a godly mentor who holds you accountable to maintain faithfulness in your family life as well as in your church leadership?
Communion with Christ's People	*develops a diverse community of fellow laborers who are equipped and empowered to pursue shared goals*	The power that the leader exercises is not the leader's but Christ's, and this power must be expressed according to God's design for a diverse community of Spirit-equipped servants.	Do you perceive the people in your congregation as God's treasured property and possession? How does your perception of them as God's property impact your patience with them and your expectations about how they should respond to your leadership?

| Mission in the World | *that fulfill the creation mandate and the Great Commission in submission to the Word of God.* | The truth that the leader is called to proclaim is not the leader's vision but God's revelation. | In a holy priesthood, all the members enjoy the privilege of teaching and learning from one another. If you are an elder or a pastor, you have the privilege not only of teaching and learning but also of safeguarding the church's teachings. How are you actively and compassionately guarding what is taught in your congregation? Are you watching your doctrine closely, centering your teaching and preaching not on your skills or experiences but on the Word of God that points to the grace of God in Christ? |

Further Reading

Hughes, R. Kent, and Barbara Hughes. *Liberating Ministry from the Success Syndrome.* Wheaton: Crossway, 2008.

Massey, James Earl. *Stewards of the Story.* Louisville: WJK, 2006.

Nouwen, Henri J. M. *In the Name of Jesus.* Chestnut Ridge, NY: Crossroad, 1989.

Peterson, Eugene. *Working the Angles.* Grand Rapids: Eerdmans, 1989.

The Shepherd Leader: A Protector and Provider Who Is Present with His People

"This is what the Lord of Armies says: I took you from the pasture, from tending the flock to be ruler over my people Israel. I have been with you wherever you have gone, and I have destroyed all your enemies before you. I will make a great name for you like that of the greatest on the earth. I will designate a place for my people Israel and plant them, so that they may live there and not be disturbed again. Evildoers will not continue to oppress them as they have done ever since the day I ordered judges to be over my people Israel. I will give you rest from all your enemies."

2 Samuel 7:8–11

"For this is what the Lord God says: See, I myself will search for my flock and look for them. As a shepherd looks for his sheep on the day he is among his scattered flock, so I will look for my flock. I will rescue them from all the places where they have been scattered on a day of clouds and total darkness."

Ezekiel 34:11–12

▶ Chapter Five Key Point

Following the example of Christ the shepherd, church leaders are called to be present with the people in their churches, to provide for them, and to rescue those who stray. ◀

109

A few years ago, an individual who claimed that he was called to pastoral ministry informed me, "I love to teach, and I want to preach—but I really can't stand spending time with people." He went on to describe his dream position: to provide a polished exposition of Scripture every Sunday morning, to decide a church's vision and direction, but never to deal directly with the people in the congregation. I (Timothy) did my best to dash his dreams against the rocks of reality by pointing out a fatal flaw in his projected job description: No such position exists in the very Scriptures that he claimed he wanted to proclaim.

What this young man needed was not merely an improvement in his people skills—though, frankly, he could have used that too. What he needed was to learn the difference between cattle and sheep. In the Scriptures, cattle might meander among the oaks of Bashan or find themselves being fattened in pens for slaughter (Amos 4:1; 6:4). Either way, their tending never required their keepers to live among them. Sheep, however, always need a shepherd, and shepherds live among their sheep. The presence of a shepherd is essential to the survival of the flock. If sheep find themselves "without a shepherd," the flock quickly becomes fragmented and fragile (Num 27:17; 1 Kgs 22:17; 2 Chr 18:16; see also Zech 10:2).

Despite the fact that our heavenly Father has claimed sole proprietorship of the "cattle on a thousand hills" (Ps 50:10), he has never indicated that the leaders of his people should live as ranchers or cowboys. Instead, God refers to his people as sheep and to their leaders as shepherds—a metaphor that places leaders among the people, personally sustaining and safeguarding the flock (Num 27:15–18; 2 Sam 5:2; 1 Kgs 22:17; Ps 77:20).

That's why I challenged this would-be pastor who wanted to remain separated from the people with the difficult truth that he was contradicting himself. He wanted to be a rancher instead of a shepherd, ruling over God's people from a distance instead of living and leading among them. But a true shepherd can never lead from a safe and comfortable distance. It is inconceivable to be a shepherd without living among the sheep.

All God's People Are Sheep—but Not All of Them Are Shepherds

So far in this book, we have seen that the offices of the old covenant have not been conveyed in unique or exclusive ways to particular new covenant leaders. The offices of judge, king, prophet, and priest are communicated to the whole body of believers in union with Christ. The church custodian who has spent her entire life in Title V housing, the teaching pastor of a multicampus megachurch, and the newly baptized son of a bank president are all equal participants in the same judgeship, kingship, and royal priesthood. And, if the Spirit of God should so move, any one of them could participate in the gift of prophecy as well.

The authors of the New Testament *do*, however, apply the metaphor of the shepherd in a unique sense to those who serve as elders or overseers in the church (John 21:15–19; Eph 4:11; 1 Pet 5:1–4).[1] United with Christ the perfect shepherd and sacrificial lamb, all of God's people become sheep—but not all of God's people are called to become shepherds. The elders of the church are specifically and distinctly designated as shepherds who join in the work of the chief Shepherd (1 Pet 5:4). Although helpful for understanding the relationship between old covenant and new covenant leadership, the roles of prophet, priest, judge, and king are not offices that are conveyed to those who lead the people of God today.[2] It is the image of shepherd that the authors of Scripture uniquely and specifically apply to the overseers of God's new covenant people.

But what does it mean, to live as a shepherd leader among God's new covenant people? And what should we make of the unique application of the shepherding metaphor to the leaders of the church? How specifically should this metaphor from the Old Testament shape our habits as leaders today?

The call to serve as a shepherd among God's new covenant people is a gracious designation from God that none of us deserves, and anyone who senses a calling to serve in this capacity "desires a noble work" (1 Tim 3:1). Precisely because the role of a shepherd is such a high calling and noble work, it is crucial to explore what it meant to be a shepherd in the old covenant so that we may understand better what shepherd leadership should look like among God's new covenant people today.

Shepherd Leaders before and beyond Israel

Long before God constituted Israel as a nation, shepherding already functioned as a metaphor for the roles of gods and kings. Depictions of rulers as shepherds can, in fact, be traced as far back as written history.[3] The

Mesopotamian deity Enlil was known by the epithet "reliable shepherd,"[4] and Hammurabi, the law-giving king of Babylon, referred to himself as a shepherd as well.[5]

Shepherds were seen as "abhorrent" by some Egyptians during the New Kingdom era (Gen 46:34). Yet this abhorrence seems to have been limited to wandering shepherds from other lands and nations.[6] Within Egypt, a shepherd's crook served as a symbol of the pharaoh's authority as well as a hieroglyph for the word "rule."[7] Centuries before the exodus, an Egyptian poet criticized one of the pharaohs of the Middle Kingdom because this ruler was behaving like a distant lord who allowed the people's leaders to behave "like a herd running at random." The latter stanzas of the poem expressed hope for a future pharaoh who might rule more like a shepherd, with the poet envisioning a day when the people of Egypt would say regarding their pharaoh, "Though his herds are few, he spends a day to collect them."[8] For people in the ancient Near East, shepherding provided a fitting metaphor for the lifestyle of the leader who worked for the well-being of his realm.

Shepherd Leadership among the Patriarchs

For the patriarchal predecessors of the nation of Israel, shepherding was, however, far more than a mere metaphor. Shepherding was the means by which Abraham and his offspring survived and thrived as they awaited the place that God was preparing for them. Abraham and his sheep-herding descendants were sojourners and strangers in other people's lands, seeking the fulfillment of God's promise of permanence.[9] Not surprisingly, long before they became a nation with judges and kings, these sojourners already saw their God as their shepherd. When Jacob blessed his grandsons, the ancient patriarch referred to his God as "the God who has been my shepherd" (Gen 48:15). On his deathbed, Jacob declared that Joseph's life had been preserved "by the name of the Shepherd" (Gen 49:24).[10]

Shepherd Leadership from the Exodus to the Kings

By the time the nation of Israel entered the Promised Land, an entire generation had lived and died as shepherds in the wilderness (Num 14:33). In the process, the shepherding metaphor had expanded to include the rule not only of God himself but also of God's appointed rulers. When the people drew near to the land of promise, Moses asked God to replace him with a faithful leader "so that the LORD's community won't be like sheep without a shepherd" (Num 27:16–17). Later generations clearly viewed Moses and Aaron as Israel's shepherds in the wilderness. "You led your people like a flock," Asaph sang, "by the hand of Moses and Aaron" (Ps 77:20; see also Isa 63:11; Hos 12:13).

The shepherd that God provided in response to Moses's request was Joshua the son of Nun. It was Joshua who shepherded the first generation of Israelites in the Promised Land (Num 27:17–23).[11] Throughout this generation, the people persisted in faithfulness to God's covenant (Judg 2:17)—but their faithfulness did not last. Soon after the leaders of Joshua's generation were laid in their graves, God's kingdom of priests began to turn from God's ways. During those dark decades, "there was no king in Israel; everyone did whatever seemed right to him" (Judg 17:6; 21:25). God commanded the tribal judges to serve as the people's shepherds in this time of chaos, but the judges faltered and the sheep scattered (1 Chr 17:6; compare 2 Sam 7:7). The people saw no hope for justice in the heirs of the priests or prophets (1 Sam 2:12–25; 3:10–14; 8:1–5), so they sought the same security they saw in other nations. They demanded a king.

The Quest for a Shepherd King

The first ruler of Israel was impressive, but he was no shepherd. He was a chaser of donkeys and a driver of oxen whose reign began in glory but ended in tragedy. When the prophet Samuel first met Saul, the man who would be king had spent three days seeking a lost drove of his father's donkeys (1 Sam 9:20). Saul had climbed the highest mountains and run through the fields, but he still had not found what he was looking for—and he never did (1 Sam 9:4). While he was being escorted to his coronation banquet, Saul received word that someone else had found the wayward donkeys (1 Sam 9:20–24).

After being anointed and acclaimed as the ruler of Israel, Saul heard the news that would result in his first battle while he was driving a yoke of oxen. He responded to the news by chopping the beasts into pieces and sending the bloodied fragments throughout the land to strike fear in his subjects' hearts (1 Sam 11:5–7). Saul did indeed win a series of military victories, but this hacker of oxen and hero of the battlefield never developed into a shepherd of the flock.[12]

After the fall of Saul, God raised a new ruler. This king was a shepherd from beginning to end. From his introduction in the fields of Bethlehem all the way to his deathbed in Jerusalem, shepherding metaphors and motifs are entwined with David's story.

When the prophet Samuel showed up on Jesse's front porch in search of a new king, David was left in the field to watch his family's flock—a young man so unimpressive that he was not even invited to join the parade of potential princes (1 Sam 16:11). On the eve of his first battle, David was back in the pasture again. Before heading to the battlefield, the young shepherd ensured the safety of his father's sheep by entrusting them to another caregiver—quite a contrast when compared to Saul's choice to launch his first crusade by chopping up his oxen (1 Sam 11:5–7; 17:20).[13] When asked why he should be allowed to face the Philistine giant, the only résumé that David could provide was a recitation of how he had safeguarded his flock (1 Sam 17:32–35). These scenes reveal a crucial difference between David and Saul: David guarded his father's lambs, protected them from wild beasts, and even risked his life to rescue them, whereas Saul hacked his oxen to death before his first battle and could not even keep track of his father's donkeys.

The Practices of an Ideal Shepherd

After settling into a cedar-paneled palace, King David concluded that the ark of God's covenant should dwell in a temple instead of a tent.[14] God's denial of David's request provided the context for one of the most significant scenes in David's life. After covering an entire decade of David's life in a mere six chapters, the second book of Samuel suddenly slows to a crawl, with a carefully crafted message from the Lord followed by a lengthy response from David (2 Samuel 7).[15] This single chapter stands as the "cornerstone of the biblical view of kingship."[16]

After rejecting David's plan to build a temple, God established an everlasting covenant with David and his descendants. The Lord God began his response by reminding David that he had taken him "from the pasture and from tending the flock" (2 Sam 7:8). Then God related the ways that he himself had shepherded David during his rise to power:[17]

- The Lord had remained present with David ("I have been with you," 7:9).
- The Lord had rescued David ("I have destroyed all your enemies," 7:9).
- The Lord promised to provide a name for David and a place for the people of Israel ("I will make a great name for you. . . . I will designate a place," 7:9–10).[18]

This threefold description of God's care for David provides a helpful snapshot of the practices of an ideal shepherd: Shepherds remain with the sheep, rescue them from danger, and provide them with a place where they receive what they need to be secure. One result of God's shepherding would be peace for David and for the people ("so that they may . . . not be disturbed. . . . I will give you rest," 7:10–11). If any future king of Israel became a beast who preyed on the people, David's covenant-keeping God would "discipline" this king with a shepherd's rod (7:14).[19]

This covenant with David is far from the last place where provision, presence, and protection appear in connection with sheep and shepherds, however. In his most famous psalm, David recognized the Lord as his shepherd (Ps 23:1). According to David, his shepherd God was

- present to guide him ("he leads me," "you are with me," 23:3–4)
- powerful to rescue him ("I fear no danger," "in the presence of my enemies," 23:4–5; see also Ps 28:7–9)[20]
- faithful to provide for him ("I have what I need," "green pastures," "quiet waters," "he prepares a table," 23:1–2, 5)

Once again, the leadership of the Lord God led to peace and rest in a place that God himself had prepared ("he lets me lie down," "I will dwell in the house of the LORD," 23:2, 6).[21]

Practices of presence, protection, and provision are entwined in descriptions of the ideal shepherd in Scripture because no sheep can survive long without a shepherd who is present, powerful, and faithful to provide. A few years ago in Turkey, a single sheep leaped over the edge of a cliff, and more than a thousand of his fellow sheep followed. According to the news report,

One sheep jumped to its death. Then stunned Turkish shepherds, who had left the herd to graze while they had breakfast, watched as nearly 1,500 others followed, each leaping off the same cliff, Turkish media reported.

In the end, 450 dead animals lay on top of one another in a billowy white pile. . . . Those who jumped later were saved as the pile got higher and the fall more cushioned. . . . "There's nothing we can do. They're all wasted," Nevzat Bayhan, a member of one of twenty-six families whose sheep were grazing together in the herd, was quoted as saying.[22]

In a more recent incident, a sheep tumbled to its death along the coast of Sussex after being frightened by an unleashed dog—but, considering a sheep's disadvantages in close combat, it's no wonder that a sheep might prefer a deadly plunge to a dogfight.[23] Without antlers or claws or fangs, sheep are hard pressed to strike back at predators. Lacking the capacity to climb or to run at high speeds, they cannot escape easily either. Simply put, an independent sheep is a dead sheep.

Because they are so vulnerable, sheep do not typically rest unless they feel safe and secure.[24] For sheep, "rest is not only a function of being well provided for. It is a state of security that comes from the shepherd's protective presence."[25] That is why the authors of Scripture repeatedly described people who were leaderless as "sheep without a shepherd" (Num 27:17; 1 Kgs 22:17; 2 Chr 18:16; Isa 13:14; Matt 9:36; Mark 6:34). That is also why God called for leaders who would not only lead his people but also shepherd them. Every sheep needs a shepherd and a flock.

The God Who Goes before Us Is Already in the Tomorrows

"The . . . shepherd was always ahead of his sheep. He was in front. Any attempt upon them had to take him into account. Now, God is down in front. He is in the tomorrows. It is tomorrow that fills [us] with dread. But God is there already, and all tomorrows of our life have to pass before him before they can get to us."[26]

—F. B. Meyer

What fills you with dread as a leader? What worries keep you awake at night? How should the recognition that God "is in the tomorrows" reshape your daily practices of leadership?

Shepherd Leadership as a Way of Leading

When God raised up human leaders as shepherds, he was calling them to participate in his work of rescuing his people, remaining with them, and providing for them. This calling did not elevate leaders to positions of sovereign lordship over the people; instead, it placed them in positions of sacrificial stewardship among the people of Israel. God alone remained the supreme shepherd of his people, because only a sovereign God is capable of perfect provision, protection, and presence (Ps 80:1; Isa 40:11; Jer 31:10; Micah 7:14). The position of the God-called shepherd leader is one of service and obedience, guiding and guarding the people under the authority of the supreme shepherd.

When applied to human leaders in the old covenant, the title "shepherd"—unlike judge, king, prophet, or priest—did not describe a particular office or position. Kings could be described as shepherds (2 Sam 5:2; 1 Chr 11:2; Ps 78:71–72; Isa 44:28)—but so could judges and a variety of other political and religious leaders (Num 27:17; 2 Sam 7:7; 1 Chr 17:6; Jer 10:21; Zech 10:2–3).[27] What this breadth of applications suggests is that *shepherd leadership was not a particular office of leadership in the Old Testament but a calling to lead in a particular way.* The way of the ideal shepherd was a way of provision, presence, and rescue that guided the people toward a place of rest. In the early church, this way of leading would become so closely tied to the work of the church's leaders that the word "pastor"—which means "shepherd"—developed into a title for new covenant elders and overseers.

Pastor

Latin, "shepherd"; translates Greek *poimen*

Pastoral ministry is a spiritual gift closely associated with teaching (Eph 4:11). Although the gift of shepherding may be broader than the office of elder, the capacity to teach and to shepherd the people of God is essential for the church's elders (Acts 20:28–31; 1 Pet 5:1–4; see also 1 Tim 3:2; 2 Tim 2:24; Titus 1:9).

The Rise and Fall of Israel's Shepherds

It was the example of King David that set the standard for shepherd leadership in the Old Testament. Even before he was recognized as king, David was the one who remained present with God's flock, leading them out and bringing them in (2 Sam 5:2). As king, he rescued his people from their enemies (8:1–3) and gave them provision and rest (6:19; 7:1). When David failed, even his failure could be described as a failure in shepherding. Instead of being present with his "flock," David had remained in Jerusalem (11:1). Instead of protecting his flock, he took one of them—Bathsheba, the wife of Uriah—and exploited her for his own pleasure (11:2–5, 14). When Nathan confronted David, the prophet did so by telling him a parable about sheep (12:1–7). Later, when David repented of another act of rebellion, his confession revealed the heart of a shepherd: "I, the shepherd, have done wrong. These are but sheep. What have they done?" (2 Sam 24:17 NIV).

In the decades that followed David's death, political and religious leaders drove the people like domineering sovereigns instead of shepherds. As a result, the kingdom was broken, and God's flock became "scattered on the hills" (1 Kgs 22:17; 2 Chr 18:16). The people turned to other nations, desperate for human saviors, but none of these supposed saviors was able to save. "Like sheep without a shepherd," Don Henley and the Eagles sang two decades ago, quoting the New Testament Gospels (Matthew 9:36; Mark 6:34), "we wander 'round this desert and wind up following the wrong gods home."[28] The Eagles intended these lyrics to describe Western society near the end of the twentieth century, but their words provide an apt description of the divided kingdom of Judah and Israel as well. Without a shepherd to guide them, the Israelites wound up following all the wrong gods home. The result was exile.

What the Prophets Had to Say to Israel's Shepherds

Both the shepherds and the sheep were unfaithful to their covenant with God. And so, in time, God raised up other nations to relieve Israel's shepherds of their positions and to remove his flock from their pastures. Soon after the Babylonians pillaged Jerusalem in the early sixth century BC, Jeremiah spoke this oracle regarding the leaders of Judah: "This is what the LORD, the God of Israel, says about the shepherds who tend my people: 'You have scattered my flock, banished them, and have not attended to them'" (Jer 23:2).

Because the shepherds of Judah had abandoned and abused the flock of God, God planned a storm of judgment that would, according to Jeremiah, "shepherd all your shepherds away" (Jer 22:22, author's translation). A decade after Jeremiah spoke these words, Jerusalem was destroyed and the dynasty of David was interrupted, just as Jeremiah had predicted (Jer 25:1–14).

When a deported priest named Ezekiel heard the horrible news, he drew from the oracles of Jeremiah to declare God's truth to his fellow exiles in Babylon (Ezek 1:3; 33:22).[29] According to Ezekiel, the people had become prey for "every wild animal"—probably a reference to the beastliness of their Babylonian conquerors and captors (34:5–6).[30] And what was the cause of this beastly state of affairs? According to Ezekiel, it was a lack of godly rulers. Ezekiel laid responsibility for Judah's deportation squarely at the doors of the palace and the temple.[31] The shepherd leaders of Judah had sheared and slaughtered God's flock to enrich themselves (Ezek 34:2–3; see also Zech 10:3–12). Instead of rescuing the lost and straying sheep, royal and religious leaders had abandoned the people and consumed their corpses,[32] governing them "with violence and cruelty" like Pharaoh in the days of Moses (Ezek 34:3–4; compare Exod 1:13–14).

God's solution to this failure of leadership would require something far more radical than a slight tweak in the current shepherding situation in Israel. God would dismiss his people's current shepherds and raise up a new shepherd who would be, at the same time, both Davidic and divine. The Spirit of God inspired Ezekiel to arrange this dismissal so that it appeared squarely in the center of the first part of his prophecy against the shepherds of Judah (Ezek 34:9; see "The Structure of Ezekiel's Oracle").

The Day That God Dismissed His Shepherds

Have you ever faced a situation where someone did such a poor job on a project that you declared, "I'll just do it myself"? That is not too different from what God did in response to the self-centered shepherd leaders of Judah. "I will demand my flock from them and prevent them from shepherding the flock," the God of Israel declared. "I will tend my flock" (Ezek 34:10, 15). Faced with shepherds who had abused and exploited his flock, God declared that he was handing a heavenly pink slip to the leaders of Judah and taking over as the shepherd of his sheep (see also Zechariah 10:3; 11:4–17; 13:7).

Of course, God's decision to dismiss Judah's leaders was not quite identical with our decisions to accomplish a task on our own. When we as human beings declare that we will complete a project without input from others, that declaration almost always represents a failure in our own patterns of leadership. Human leaders usually refuse to delegate either because we arrogantly assume that we alone are capable of completing a task correctly or because we are unwilling to invest the time to train someone else. The problem with our tendency to do it all ourselves is that—because we are finite and frail—none of us is actually able to complete every aspect of a task perfectly.

God, however, is perfectly glorious and infinitely powerful. God's planning never writes a check that his power cannot cash. And so, when God delegates a task to a human leader, it is not because God is unable to accomplish his plan on his own. When God delegates, this decision is a work of grace in which he offers us the gift of participating in a perfect plan that God ordained before time began. What this means practically is that, whenever God decides to accomplish a task without any help from humanity, it is because it is a task that God and God alone can do.

When God dismissed the shepherds of Israel and declared that he would become his people's shepherd, it was because this was a task that he alone could accomplish. God promised to shepherd his people personally because he alone could shepherd them perfectly. A day was coming when the Lord of the flock would live among his sheep, seeking the lost, bringing back the strays, bandaging the broken, and feeding the hungry. God himself would rescue his sheep (Ezek 34:11–13, 16; compare Amos 3:12), provide for them (34:14, 16), and dwell among them (34:15). The result would be rest and peace for God's children (34:14–15; see also Isa 40:10–11; Mic 5:2–6).

According to Ezekiel, some of the oppressors weren't shepherds but fellow sheep. Stronger "sheep . . . , rams and goats" had muddied the still waters and trampled the green pastures until nothing remained to sustain weaker sheep (34:17–19). In response, God would separate the sleek from the weak and fill the feed-troughs of these ovine oppressors with judgment (34:20–22; compare Matt 25:31–46).

After dismissing the shepherds and cleansing the flock, God's plan was to appoint a new shepherd over Israel: "one shepherd, my servant David" (34:23; see also Mic 5:2–4). The intent was not, of course, that David would return from his tomb![33] The point was that a ruler *like David* would one day reign over the nation again. During the reign of this new David, God would establish a "covenant of peace" with his people and rescue them from the oppression of other nations ("eliminate dangerous animals," 34:25). Ezekiel crafted this declaration of a new Davidic ruler so that it stood as the centerpiece of the second half of his prophecy (34:24; see "The Structure of Ezekiel's Oracle against Israel's Shepherds").

But how could this new David serve as the "single shepherd" of God's people if God himself had already promised to be their shepherd? (Ezek 34:13, 23).[34] Some later Israelites saw the fulfillment of this prophecy in Zerubbabel and in the reigns of the Hasmonean kings—but these rulers fell far short of God's promise of a descendant who would "come forth from" David's own flesh and whose reign would be "established forever" (2 Sam 7:12, 16 NASB).[35] Even after Zerubbabel and the Hasmoneans, the Jewish people still clearly anticipated a "shepherd ruler [who] would lead his renewed community in a second exodus, provide for God's flock in their exilic wilderness, and renew his covenant with them there."[36]

The consummate answer to this expectation was far greater than anything Ezekiel probably knew or imagined. God himself would come to earth as a descendant of David (Matt 1:1–6; Luke 3:23–31). He would provide food in the wilderness, rescue the broken and lost, and gather the sheep that were scattered (John 6:1–15; 10:28–29). He would dwell with his flock and remain with them to the end (John 1:14; 13:1). And then he would give his life as a ransom for his lambs (John 10:11–12).

According to Ezekiel's prophecy, barren trees would become fruitful through the work of the coming shepherd, and the earth itself would burst forth with new life (Ezek 34:27)—and, indeed, that is what happened. The shepherd became a lamb, stricken by God for sins that were not his own (Zech 13:9; Matt 26:31–32; Rev 7:9–17). The tree on which the stricken shepherd was hung to die yielded the fruit of forgiveness,[37] and the depths of the earth where he was buried burst forth with new life at his resurrection.[38]

His death established the covenant of peace that Ezekiel had predicted, and his resurrection turned out to be the firstfruits of a new world that is yet to come (Ezek 34:25; 1 Cor 15:20–28; Heb 13:20). Forty days later, the risen shepherd ascended into the heavens. And even then, he did not abandon his sheep. The shepherd sent his Spirit so that he could remain with his flock forever, just as God had promised through Ezekiel (Ezek 34:24, 28–30; Matt 28:20; John 14:16; Acts 1:6–11; 2:1–13).

Ever since he empowered his people through his Spirit, Jesus the good shepherd has been gathering a flock from every nation and making them his own (Matt 28:19; John 10:14–18). As he gathers this flock, God has chosen not only to serve as the supreme shepherd of his people but also to work through human shepherds. In the Gospels, the apostles began as sheep (Matt 10:16) and became shepherds (John 21:15–18) who then recognized other God-appointed leaders as shepherds of the flock (Eph 4:11; 1 Pet 5:1–2).

Those who are privileged to shepherd God's people are never lords over the flock; we are followers of a greater shepherd who alone remains the true owner of the sheep (Heb 13:20; 1 Pet 2:25; 5:4). Godly leadership is followership exercised with biblical wisdom for the good and the guidance of a community for which God has given us responsibility. Any power we possess has been divinely delegated to guide God's flock toward his purposes and his peace.[39]

The Structure of Ezekiel's Oracle against Israel's Shepherds (Ezekiel 34)

A. The unfaithfulness of Israel's shepherds: "This is what the LORD God says to the shepherds: . . . You do not tend the flock. You have not strengthened the weak, healed the sick, bandaged the injured, brought back the strays, or sought the lost" (vv. 2–4).

B. The flock scattered because of the shepherds' unfaithfulness: "My flock went astray on all the mountains. . . . My flock was scattered. . . . There was no one searching for them" (vv. 5–6).

C. The sheep exploited instead of rescued: "Shepherds feed themselves" (vv. 7–8).

X. God's solution, the removal of past shepherds: "Hear the word of the LORD! This is what the LORD God says: Look, I am against the shepherds. I will demand my flock from them and prevent them from shepherding the flock" (vv. 9–10).

C'. Sheep rescued instead of exploited: "Shepherds will no longer feed themselves" (v. 10).

B'. The flock made safe because of the Lord's faithfulness: "I myself will search . . . as a shepherd looks. . . . On the day he is among his scattered flock . . . I will shepherd them on the mountains" (vv. 11–14).[40]

A'. The faithfulness of Israel's God: "This is the declaration of the LORD God. 'I will seek the lost, bring back the strays, bandage the injured, and strengthen the weak, but I will destroy the fat and the strong. I will shepherd them with justice'" (vv. 15–16).[41]

A. God's declaration of ownership: "The LORD God says . . . 'My flock'" (v. 17).

B. God's promise of rescue from fellow Israelites: "I myself will judge between the fat sheep and the lean. . . . They will no longer be prey" (vv. 20–22).

C. Provision for rescue from fellow Israelites: "I will establish over them one shepherd. . . . He will tend them" (v. 23).

X. God's solution, the provision of a new shepherd: "I, the LORD, will be their God. . . . My servant David will be a prince. . . . I, the LORD, have spoken" (v. 24).

C'. Provision for rescue from exile among the nations: "I will make a covenant of peace. . . . They will know I am the LORD when I . . . rescue them" (vv. 25–27).

B'. God's promise of rescue from the nations: "They will no longer be prey for the nations. . . . I will establish for them a place renowned for its agriculture" (vv. 28–29).

A'. God's declaration of ownership: "This is the declaration of the LORD God. You are my flock" (vv. 30–31).

The Presence, Provision, and Protection
of the Shepherd Leader

To be a shepherd leader is to be present with the people we lead. In the world's way of thinking, successful leadership correlates with inaccessibility; the most successful leaders are protected by layers of security, staff, and secretaries. Mere mortals might gain, at best, a brief audience with such a leader—usually in the form of a moment of fawning adoration over the leader's latest book or conference presentation.

Unfortunately, church leaders can easily fall into similar patterns. Among pastors however, such inaccessibility should be seen not as a badge of honor but as a shameful signpost of capitulation to the world's values. If shepherds cease to be available to the sheep, they cease to behave as shepherds. "If it seems necessary to you to surround yourself with assistants and delegates so that you are inaccessible to the people," Steve Timmis writes, "you need to consider carefully whether you can, at the same time, remain a foot-washing servant."[42]

> Somehow we have come to believe that good leadership requires a
> safe distance from those we are called to lead. Medicine, psychiatry,
> and social work all offer us models in which "service" takes place in
> a one-way direction. Someone serves, someone else is being served,
> and be sure not to mix up the roles! But how can we lay down our
> life for those with whom we are not even allowed to enter into a
> deep personal relationship?[43]

This is not to suggest that a pastor must be leashed to every member's passing whim or present at every church function. "If a pastor sees his role in terms of meeting every need and responding to every demand, he will end up becoming a follower of the sheep rather than their leader."[44] Pastors must schedule consistent times for the purposes of study, prayer, and spiritual refreshment (Luke 5:16; Acts 6:2, 4), as well as making space for rest and recreation and time for family. And yet pastors must also prioritize patterns of presence with their flock.

In these patterns of presence, it must not be the world's values that decide where the shepherd invests time with the flock. The world's way would be to prioritize the people who are most powerful or most popular, or those whose bank accounts are most likely to multiply the church's budget.

Shepherds, however, are called to "seek the lost, bring back the strays, bandage the injured, and strengthen the weak" (Ezek 34:16)—which sounds like the shepherd's priorities should be shaped not by people's high positions but by their brokenness and need.

The more time pastors spend with their flock, the better they will understand how people view the world, in what areas they struggle most, and how the gospel can best be applied to their lives. When one pastor was asked about the most important steps in his weekly preparation to preach, he replied,

> For two hours every Tuesday and Thursday afternoon, I walk through the neighborhood and make some home visits. There is no way I can preach the gospel to these people if I don't know how they are living, what they are thinking and talking about.[45]

In some communities, being present with the people may require setting aside one day each week to work alongside a farmer or rancher. In other places, the presence of the shepherd might mean spending the afternoon walking the city square in a small town. It could entail playing baseball with some youth in an inner-city park, volunteering at a community center, or participating in weekly tutoring programs with recently released prisoners. The precise approach to pastoral presence will differ from one context to the next. What matters is not the specific pattern of presence. The priority is that every member of the flock has a clear sense that they have a shepherd who knows them, who feels compassion for them, and who will risk his own well-being to bring them back if they stray.[46] "If I do not show concern for the one sheep that strays and gets lost," Augustine remarked in the fifth century regarding his congregation in the city of Hippo, "even a sheep who is strong will think it's nothing more than a joke to stray and to be lost. I do indeed desire outward gains, but I'm more afraid of inward losses."[47]

Because people's lives are marked by suffering and sorrow, persistent presence with the flock will inevitably lead to pain for the shepherd—but it is through suffering alongside the flock that we become most like Jesus, the chief shepherd. "Great leaders for social change enter into the pain of the people who have the pain," civil rights leader John M. Perkins once pointed out. "And they bear that pain with the people, in the pain."[48] That's as true for leadership in the church as it is for leaders of social change. "Leaders in the church," D. A. Carson writes, "should suffer most. They are not like generals in the military who stay behind the lines. They are the assault troops, . . . who lead by example as much as by word."[49] It is impossible to heal pain from a safe and sterile distance. The call of a pastor is a call to be present even in people's brokenness and pain.

This presence with the people, even in times of suffering, provides the foundation for our capacity to protect them and to provide for them. After all, if we are not present with the flock to know their needs, how can we provide for these needs? And if we do not know what threatens them, how can we rescue them from harm? Adequate protection for the flock of God cannot be accomplished if the appointed shepherds do not keep watch over the church for the sake of those entrusted to their care.[50]

One key aspect of protection and provision has to do with faithfully proclaiming God's Word to the people and guarding against doctrinal error. But provision and protection entail far more than proclamation. When the Word of God is proclaimed in its fullness and when pastors live out this proclamation among the people, our patterns of shepherding contribute to the formation of communities where people sense the safety of knowing that they will never go physically or spiritually hungry; where every person is valued regardless of the hue of their skin or the status of their citizenship; where the church's leadership renounces every hint of racial supremacy and stands with those who lament the systemic injustices against African Americans and Native Americans in which so many of our churches and denominations have been complicit; where abuse is never excused or ignored; and where church discipline is pursued for the purpose of rescuing those who stray. Clearly, no team of church leaders can accomplish all of these tasks on their own![51] The church's shepherds can and must, however, take the lead in modeling and cultivating this culture of protection and provision.

Shepherds as Spiritual Fathers

"Today, in our fatherless culture, shepherds in the church function as spiritual fathers to those who lack a godly image of a man in the home and world."[52]

—Eric Mason

Paul called pastors to train young men "to be self-controlled" and to serve as an example through "good works" (Titus 2:6). Particularly if you are a pastor, are you investing in the lives of young men who lack a godly father? If not, how can you prioritize personal time with at least one young man who does not have a godly father?

We Are Sheep before We Are Shepherds

When the sheep are secure in their shepherd's care, the flock is able to rest. For the flock of God in union with Christ, this rest does not mean inactivity. It means contentment and peace. It means cultivating the capacity for consistent times of sabbath. It means recognizing that—because we have been made right with God in Christ—we can pause our busyness and work. God is not a workaholic; his rest on the seventh day reveals that the well-being of his creation does not depend on endless work.[53]

This brings us as church leaders to a handful of difficult questions: Do we drive the people in our congregation to be constantly busy, always rushing from one event to another? Do we model life without margins, or do our schedules demonstrate healthy rhythms of hard work and peaceful rest that draw life from our union with Christ? Do we pride ourselves on our overpacked church calendars? If the shepherds are always on the go, their sheep will never learn to rest.

If we as shepherds cannot bring ourselves to slow down, we have lost sight of a crucial truth about our pastoral role: Our identity in Christ precedes our calling as leaders in Christ's church. We are sheep before we are shepherds; we are members of the body of Christ before we are overseers of the body; we are disciples of God's way before we are teachers of God's Word.[54] Whenever we neglect these truths, we have lost sight of our union with Christ. When that happens, we begin to base our value not on our identity in Christ but on our performance as shepherds. We say yes to far too many tasks, scrambling after the slightest hints of praise in the faces around us. When we fall short of others' expectations, we replay our failures again and again. In the end, we are left with a calendar that is full but a soul that feels empty, one more captive of the deadly delusion that our deeds determine our value. But our value is not determined by our visible successes as shepherds of God's people! Our value and our identity have been decided once and for all by our union with a greater shepherd—Jesus Christ, the chief shepherd and overseer of our souls (1 Pet 2:25; 5:4). He assesses our success not by our busyness but by our faithfulness. For leaders in the church of Jesus Christ, this faithfulness is defined by our conformity to the example of the shepherd God who has gone before us.

Because we do not cease to be sheep when we become shepherds, our status as shepherds will never negate our need for presence, provision, and protection both from the chief shepherd and from our brothers and sisters in Christ. We are called to be both models for the sheep and imitators of the shepherd God. With these truths in mind, let's turn together to the implications of the shepherd imagery in the New Testament.

What about You?

"It is essential that people should also be instructed, taught, and led on in Christ individually in their homes."[55]

—Martin Bucer

"I have found by experience, that some ignorant persons, who have been so long unprofitable hearers, have got more knowledge and remorse in half an hour's close discourse, than they did from ten years' public preaching."[56]

—Richard Baxter

"Personal catechizing and counseling, over and above preaching, is every minister's duty."[57]

—J. I. Packer

Do you and your fellow pastors prioritize personal presence with the people in your congregation? Or have you isolated yourselves from direct participation in the people's lives? How can you develop more effective practices of personal discipleship and counseling among the pastors in your church?

Leadership Definition, Dynamics, and Diagnostics

	Leadership Definition	*Leadership Dynamic*	*Leadership Diagnostics*
Union with Christ	*The Christ-following leader— living as a bearer of God's image in union with Christ and his people—*	The position to which the leader is called is not sovereignty above or separation from the community but stewardship within the community in union with Christ. The shepherd is a follower of God's way who is present among the sheep.	Do you see yourself not only as a leader of the community but also, more importantly, as a member of the community? When church members meet with you, are you distracted or rushed, always looking at your watch or your telephone, or are you truly present with them? Who holds you accountable to develop Christ-honoring rhythms of work and rest?

Communion with Christ's People	*develops a diverse community of fellow laborers who are equipped and empowered to pursue shared goals*	The power that the leader exercises is not the leader's but Christ's, and this power must be expressed according to God's design for a diverse community of Spirit-equipped servants. The shepherd uses this power to provide for the sheep.	How have you cultivated a culture of compassionate provision for physical and emotional needs in your congregation? Or are people in your church ashamed to admit financial or emotional struggles? Do you consistently spend time with a diverse range of people in this Christ-formed community—different ages, different socioeconomic backgrounds, different ethnicities?
Mission in the World	*that fulfill the creation mandate and the Great Commission in submission to the Word of God.*	The truth that the leader is called to proclaim is not the leader's vision but God's revelation. The shepherd is willing to take personal risks to protect and to rescue the sheep.	When a member of the church strays doctrinally or morally, are you willing to take risks to rescue the straying sheep with gentle boldness? Do you seek to provide for people's spiritual needs by boldly proclaiming all of God's Word, not merely the palatable portions of the text?

Further Reading

Anyabwile, Thabiti. *Finding Faithful Elders and Deacons*. Wheaton: Crossway, 2012.

———. *What Is a Healthy Church Member?* Wheaton: Crossway, 2008.

Laniak, Timothy. *Shepherds after My Own Heart*. Downers Grove: InterVarsity, 2006.

Reju, Deepak. *On Guard*. Greensboro: New Growth, 2014.

Worshiping the God Who Goes before Us

Savior, like a shepherd lead us, much we need Thy tender care;
In Thy pleasant pastures feed us, for our use Thy folds prepare.
Blessed Jesus, blessed Jesus! Thou hast bought us, Thine we are.
Blessed Jesus, blessed Jesus! Thou hast bought us, Thine we are.

We are Thine, Thou dost befriend us, be the Guardian of our way;
Keep Thy flock, from sin defend us, seek us when we go astray.
Blessed Jesus, blessed Jesus! Hear, O hear us when we pray.
Blessed Jesus, blessed Jesus! Hear, O hear us when we pray.
—Dorothy Thrupp, *Hymns for the Young*, 1836

Responding to the God Who Goes before Us

God our Father, you have filled our lives with peace
    by raising your Son the Good Shepherd from the dead and
    by establishing a covenant of peace with your people by means of
        his blood;
Now enable us by your Spirit to do what pleases you
(not in our own feeble power and not as a fool's errand to earn your
        favor)
by means of our union with your Son
so that you may receive glory forever. Amen.
—Adapted from Heb 13:20–21

PART THREE

New Covenant Practices for Leadership through Followership

Michael S. Wilder

What does it mean for pastors to live the life of a shepherd among their people? It certainly is not feasible to ask an urban church planter to build a sheep pen on the back corner of the church property! Neither does the call to shepherding mean that suburban or rural church leaders should sign up for the latest seminar on ovine veterinary medicine. Yet living the life of a shepherd among God's people *does* require a reorientation away from the world's perspective on leadership. Let us review the model of leadership that has emerged from our study of the Scriptures:

Definition of Leadership	Nature of Shepherd Leadership	Practice of Shepherd Leadership
The Christ-following leader— living as a bearer of God's image in union with Christ and his people—	The position to which the leader is called is not sovereignty above or separation from the community but stewardship within the community in union with Christ.	The shepherd is a follower of God's way who is present among the sheep.
develops a diverse community of fellow laborers who are equipped and empowered to pursue shared goals	The power that the leader exercises is not the leader's but Christ's, and this power must be expressed according to God's design for a diverse community of Spirit-equipped servants.	The shepherd uses his power to provide for the sheep.
that fulfill the creation mandate and the Great Commission in submission to the Word of God.	The truth that the leader is called to proclaim is not the leader's vision but God's revelation.	The shepherd is willing to take personal risks to protect and to rescue the sheep.

Shepherding is a way of leadership in which a leader is present among the people, leveraging his power to provide for the people and taking risks whenever necessary to protect the people. For a leader among the people of God, shepherd leadership means followership in submission to the one who has purchased the sheep at the cost of his own blood. "To be a shepherd is to be both *responsible for* (the flock) and *responsible to* (the Owner)."[1] Shepherds who conform their lives to this pattern "will not be content for the flock to remain as they are, nor even to manage them more efficiently." Instead,

> They will seek the growth of the flock numerically. They will also seek their progress, individually and corporately, toward maturity. They will not be managers, for managers deal in seen realities, but leaders, for leaders deal in unseen potentials.[2]

The starting point for such leadership is to become a leader who fears and follows God. There is no better place to begin an exploration of this process than the Gospels, where Jesus Christ himself shaped the church's first shepherds. When he called his first followers, Jesus perfectly exemplified leadership that protects and provides for the people in a manner that recognizes potential that is presently unseen.

In this exploration of leadership in the New Testament, we will look first at the patterns of shepherding that Jesus modeled in the four Gospels. Jesus's example challenged his first followers to imitate their Savior through submission to the Father, dependence on the Spirit, and humble service among the people. After looking at the practices that Jesus modeled for his first followers, we will focus specifically on the commissioning of the apostle Peter on the shore of the Sea of Galilee (John 21:15–23). In this commission, Jesus commanded Simon Peter to follow him, to feed the sheep, and to prepare himself for suffering and sacrifice. In the final chapter of the book, we will see how Simon Peter fulfilled Christ's commission in a community of sojourners and exiles. His leadership among these brothers and sisters provides a roadmap for today's church leaders who still long to lead faithfully during times of suffering and sacrifice. The principles in this section will be applicable in a broad range of contexts; however, the focus will be pastoral leadership in the local church.

The Shepherd's Call:
Fearing and Following God

"He fell facedown and prayed, 'My Father, if it is possible, let this cup pass from me. Yet not as I will, but as you will.'"

Matthew 26:39

"Jesus called them over and said to them, "You know that those who are regarded as rulers of the Gentiles lord it over them, and those in high positions act as tyrants over them. But it is not so among you. On the contrary, whoever wants to become great among you will be your servant, and whoever wants to be first among you will be a slave to all. For even the Son of Man did not come to be served, but to serve, and to give his life as a ransom for many."

Mark 10:42–45

▶ Chapter Six Key Point

Jesus formed the first shepherds of his church by modeling leadership through submission to the Father, dependence on the Spirit, and servanthood among his followers. ◀

As we peer into the Gospels, the goal is to consider how the Lord Jesus Christ—the perfect embodiment of prophet, priest, judge, and king—modeled what it means to be a leader who fears and follows God. Jesus is the supreme exemplar of this disposition. It is wise to approach this process with caution, because no human being can imitate every act of the divine Lord. At the same time, the very genre of the Gospels makes it clear that these texts were penned as theological and historical biographies intended to shape our virtues and values.[1] These four accounts point every Christian leader toward a virtue-rich way of life that clearly displays what it looks like to be a leader who fears and follows God. The Gospels were never meant to be solely informational; they were written to be transformational, and transformation is cultivated through imitation (1 John 2:6).

"Follow me," Jesus said to the men who would become the first leaders in his church, "and I will make you fishers of men" (Mark 1:17).[2] This command to follow was an invitation specifically into (1) a life of submission to the Father, (2) a life of dependence on the Holy Spirit, and (3) a life of humble service. Throughout this chapter, this threefold invitation will be our guide as we unpack what it means to live as leaders who fear and follow God.

Fear of God

To fear God is primarily to obey his words and to do his will. When the Assyrians settled as pagan populations in Israel, wild beasts tormented the new inhabitants of the land until a priest was sent to teach them "how they should fear" the LORD (2 Kgs 17:24–28)—a phrase that suggested obedience to the Torah (see also Deut 6:24; Ps 112:1; 119:63; Eccl 12:13–14). In one sense, believers in Jesus Christ become free from the fear of God's wrath through the gift of God's righteousness in Christ (Rom 8:15; 1 John 4:18). In another sense, every believer is still called to live in the fear of God by following his words and his will (2 Cor 7:1; Eph 5:21).

Fearing and Following God: The Barriers and the Blessings

After his baptism, temptations, and initial miracles and preaching, Jesus called four men to follow him. These men, according to Mark's Gospel, "immediately" left their family businesses and accepted the invitation to a new way of life (Mark 1:18, 20). It is interesting but not surprising that, at the beginning of his ministry, Jesus selected a small group of men into whom he would intentionally pour his life. Jesus clearly intended to develop these individuals as leaders who would follow him completely. Their first step in this process was a choice in response to a call—a choice to leave the life they knew and to venture into a pathway they had never seen. From beginning to end, this invitation was costly.

In many churches, the cost of this invitation seems to be hidden, as church leaders soften what it means for followers of Christ to live obediently. The faith described in the Gospels and exemplified in the early church was anything but easy. It cost many early Christians their lives and continues to do so today. When one would-be follower of Jesus walked away from this costly calling, Simon Peter commented to Jesus, "We've given up everything to follow you" (Mark 10:28). A question was, of course, implied in this statement, and the question was, "What's our reward for leaving behind our family businesses to follow you?" What Jesus promised in response was blessing and life—but he made it clear that these would come "with persecution" (10:30). Following Jesus would be rewarding, but it would require much. Jesus spent three years modeling costly followership for the first leaders of his church. His pattern for followership was a pattern of submission, dependence, and service.

Followership through Submission to the Father

Near the end of his ministry on earth, Jesus made his way to a familiar place on the western face of the Mount of Olives (John 18:2). His intention was to spend time in prayer. Jesus chose to spend his final hours before facing the cross in fellowship with his Father.[3] Jesus was "distressed"—"horrified," "dismayed," even "terrified"—as he approached this moment (Mark 14:33).[4] "My soul is very sorrowful, even to death," he said to his disciples. "Remain here, and watch with me" (Matt 26:38 ESV).

It was not death itself that troubled Jesus. What seems to have troubled him was the forsakenness he would experience as he suffered and died.[5] The Son's eternal fellowship with the Father would be torn for a time as he endured infinite forsakenness and wrath. It was only in connection with this suffering that the Gospel writers described Jesus as sorrowful in his soul (Matt 26:38; John 12:27). Jesus was distressed because God the Father was about to make "him to be sin who knew no sin, so that in him we might become the righteousness of God" (2 Cor 5:21 ESV). The weight of the world's sin would be upon him as the Father unleashed his righteous rage against sin.

Jesus invited the future leaders of his church to be part of these final moments with his Father before the cross: "Remain here, and watch with me" (Matt 26:38 ESV). Then, "going a little farther he fell on his face and prayed, saying, 'My Father, if it be possible, let this cup pass from me; nevertheless, not as I will, but as you will'" (Matt 26:39 ESV). Notice both the posture and the content of his prayer. Falling on his face, Jesus took the lowliest possible posture. In so doing, he acknowledged the Father's authority and expressed his own submission.[6]

Jesus began his prayer with the words "my Father," expressing the intimacy of his relationship with his heavenly Father. "If it be possible," he said, "let this cup pass from me." Then he expressed a truth that must be central in every Christian leader's vocabulary: "nevertheless, not as I will, but as you will." In his second and third prayers, Jesus more explicitly acknowledged that the cross was indeed his Father's will. He recognized the pain but still submitted to the plan.

Imagine this garden scene as it is played out. Jesus has predicted his death and Peter's denial, then he proceeds with a troubled soul to a familiar place with three of his closest friends. He invites them to pray as well, then he lies down flat, with his face buried in the dirt, and begins to speak: "My Father, if it be possible, let this cup pass from me; nevertheless, not as I will, but as you will. . . . My Father, if this cannot pass unless I drink it, your will be done."

The lessons the disciples learned in that garden on that night must have been priceless. They saw their dear friend, Savior, and Lord in agony, yet they also saw him submitting willingly to his Father's will for his Father's glory. They learned that day what it means to follow God and to lead his people. They learned that followership requires submission to the Father's plan. The disciples observed in Christ a disposition toward submission. Jesus was present among his people as their brother and submitted alongside them to the same Father (Heb 2:11).

But the lessons learned ran deeper than this disposition toward submission. The disciples also saw the stark contrast between Simon Peter's arrogant assertions of strength (Matt 26:34–35) and their Savior's admission of his frailty.[7] The pleas of Jesus that night were real and filled with emotion. Jesus did not hide his troubled spirit from his closest followers. Instead, he invited them to join him. This scene in the garden challenges leaders in the church today to consider their disposition toward submission, their willingness to be honest about their frailty, and their deep need for strength not only from God himself but also from God's people.

This passage prominently reveals Jesus as a leader who fears and follows his heavenly Father. He deliberately submitted to his Father's will. Through this act of submission, the first followers of Jesus saw their leader lead by following. But Christ's followership was not merely about submission; it was also about dependence.

What about You?

Study Matt 26:26–36.

How should this text transform your perspective on prayer as a leader? In this passage, Jesus (1) recognized his need for intimacy with the Father, (2) prayed with a predetermined disposition of submission to the Father's will, (3) was fully aware of his own frailty and weakness, and (4) sought strength for obedience through prayer and community. Name one specific way that these truths should reshape your present practices of leadership.

The Power of Prayer in the Life of the Leader

"When we depend upon organizations, we get what organizations can do; when we depend upon education, we get what education can do; . . . but when we depend upon prayer, we get what God can do."[8]

—A. C. Dixon

What consumes more of your time—organizational management or prayer? On what do you depend to sustain your ministry—your own processes of planning or the power of God's Spirit? How can you reorient your daily agenda to prioritize time for seeking the power of God's Spirit through prayer?

Followership through Dependence on the Spirit

Jesus was dependent on the Holy Spirit, and he modeled for his disciples what it means to live a life of dependence upon the Spirit's power. Before and after his crucifixion, Jesus promised his followers that they would receive a helper who would lead them, teach them, convict them, comfort them, and empower them to advance his kingdom (John 14:15–31; 16:7–14; Acts 1:8).[9] The dependence of Jesus on the Holy Spirit is a key theme in the Gospel of Luke.[10]

Luke states, "Jesus returned to Galilee in the power of the Spirit" after his temptations in the desert (Luke 4:14). This is the fourth time that Luke noted the role of the Holy Spirit in the earthly life of Jesus (see Luke 1:35; 3:22; 4:1). But what could the Holy Spirit add that Jesus as God the Son did not already possess? The obvious answer is *nothing*! Why, then, did Luke highlight the presence and power of the Holy Spirit in the life of Jesus? One key reason is that Luke wanted his readers to recognize Jesus as the prophesied Messiah, dependent upon the Spirit's power. What, then, did the Holy Spirit contribute to the ministry of the man Christ Jesus? The Holy Spirit provided

> everything of supernatural power and enablement that he, in his human nature, would lack. . . . Jesus relied on the Spirit to provide the power, grace, knowledge, wisdom, direction, and enablement he needed, moment by moment and day by day, to fulfill the mission the Father sent him to accomplish.[11]

In his human nature, Jesus depended on the power of the Holy Spirit. It was through the Spirit that he experienced "wisdom and understanding," "counsel and might," "knowledge," and "the fear of the LORD" (Isa 11:1–2).[12] The Spirit not only led Jesus into the desert to face temptation (Luke 4:1) but also into Galilee to teach, to heal, to enlist his first followers, and to face opposition from religious authorities.[13] It was in Nazareth of Galilee that Jesus entered the synagogue on the Sabbath. He rose to read the scroll of the prophet Isaiah.[14] In that scroll, Jesus found these words in a place of his own choosing:[15]

> The Spirit of the Lord is upon me, because he has anointed me to proclaim good news to the poor. He has sent me to proclaim liberty

to the captives and recovering of sight to the blind, to set at liberty those who are oppressed, to proclaim the year of the Lord's favor. (Luke 4:18–19 ESV)[16]

These words were drawn from two different passages in the prophecies of Isaiah (58:6; 61:1–2).[17] After reading these words, Jesus sat and said simply, "Today this Scripture has been fulfilled in your hearing" (Luke 4:21 ESV).

When Jesus applies the passage to himself, he is saying that the present time is like the message of comfort that Isaiah brought to the nation. In fact, the totality of the deliverance that Isaiah described is now put into motion with Jesus' coming. He is the Servant *par excellence*.[18]

Here, Jesus declared himself to be the Spirit-empowered Messiah.[19] "The Spirit anoints Jesus not only for the preaching of the message as summarized in Isaiah 61 but also for the embodiment of that message. . . . All these Isaianic themes speak of the way that the kingdom comes through the power of the Holy Spirit."[20] Later, in the second volume of Luke's account of the church's origins, Peter would declare to Cornelius that "God anointed [Jesus] with the Holy Spirit and with power" (Acts 10:38). Jesus lived a life of perfect dependence on the Holy Spirit—but this Spirit-dependent life is not limited to Jesus.[21] Jesus made it possible for everyone who trusts in him to live a life empowered by the Holy Spirit. Moments before he ascended into the heavens, Jesus declared to his first followers, "You will receive power when the Holy Spirit has come on you" (Acts 1:8). And that is precisely what happened ten days later, on the day of Pentecost.

Jesus—the perfect shepherd and the incarnate God who goes before us—depended on the Holy Spirit. In this, he exemplified a way of life to which every believer is called. More important for our purposes, he revealed that none of us can lead God's people effectively in our own power. The shepherds of Christ's church must practice not only a disposition of submission to the Father but also an overwhelming dependence on the Spirit as modeled in Christ's ministry. When Paul wrote to a young pastor named Timothy, he reminded him never to forget how the Spirit had gifted him and then declared that it was only through the Spirit that Timothy would be able to guard the truth entrusted to him (1 Tim 4:14; 2 Tim 1:6, 14).

It is not possible to persist as a faithful leader in the church of Jesus Christ without deep dependence on God's empowering Spirit.

The Church, Established through the Work of the Spirit

"A congregation is the coming together of those who belong to Jesus Christ through the Holy Spirit. . . . This takes place when [people] are called by the Holy Spirit to participation in Christ's word and work. . . . Woe to us where we think we can speak of the church without establishing it wholly on the work of the Holy Spirit."[22]

—Karl Barth

Recall a specific time when you have tried to do the work of the church without depending "wholly on the work of the Holy Spirit." What would you have done differently if you had been more sensitive to the workings of God's Spirit?

What about You?

Here are a few biblically grounded patterns that characterize Spirit-empowered leaders:

1. Spirit-empowered leaders trust the Spirit-inspired Scriptures (2 Pet 1:20–21).
2. Spirit-empowered leaders recall and rely on the teachings of Jesus (John 14:26).
3. Spirit-empowered leaders are growing in holiness (2 Thess 2:13).
4. Spirit-empowered leaders seek the guidance of the Holy Spirit in their decisions (Acts 13:2–4; 16:6–10; 20:23; 21:4, 11).
5. Spirit-empowered leaders lead the people of God toward faithful unity (1 Cor 12:4–13; Eph 4:4–6).

Read the biblical texts listed above. Which of these patterns do you see most strongly in your own life? In which of these areas is God calling you to grow? What characteristics of Spirit-empowered leadership would you add to this list?

Followership through Service

True followership results in gospel-motivated servanthood. The apostle John explicitly expressed this truth when he described Jesus taking on the identity of a slave in the upper room—a story that, while familiar, is nothing short of astonishing. What makes the story even more amazing is that it specifically calls the people of God to follow the example of Jesus: "For I have given you an example, that you also should do just as I have done for you" (John 13:15). Every believer in Jesus—and particularly every God-called leader in the church—should live every part of their life as a servant of the Most High King. In this God is not asking anything from us that he has not already done for us. Even when embracing the place of a slave, Jesus is the God who goes before us.

This passage begins by mentioning the love of Jesus for his followers all the way "to the end" (John 13:1).[23] This points toward the nature of God's love for his people, grounded in covenant faithfulness to his people.[24] Later in the chapter, we see the opposite of covenant faithfulness: the faithless imposter Judas rejecting the covenant and betraying the King who kept every covenant from beginning to end.

Jesus expressed his loyal love through an act of humble service. The ever-faithful King embraced the place of the lowest slave. "He laid aside his outer garments, and taking a towel, tied it around his waist" (John 13:4 ESV). At a banquet such as this one, a slave might have served the guests by bowing as they arrived, untying and removing their sandals, and washing the filth from their feet.

> This responsibility was considered so degrading that a Hebrew slave could not be compelled to perform it. . . . Washing feet and untying sandals were jointly considered the exclusive domain of a Gentile slave because the task was so humiliating.[25]

By performing this task, Jesus willingly chose for himself the role of the lowest and least-honored slave.[26] The theme of servanthood that is present throughout John's Gospel comes through powerfully in this passage—but this servanthood is of a particular type that is deeply grounded in the Old Testament. It is "not merely servanthood in itself, but sacrificial, suffering servanthood exemplified in the Suffering Servant passages" in the prophecies of Isaiah (42:1–9; 49:1–13; 50:4–11; 52:13–53:12).[27]

Imagine the scene for a moment: The incarnate God, Creator of all things, including you, chooses to wipe the filth from your feet. Nowhere else in ancient Jewish or Greco-Roman literature does a superior wash the feet of an inferior.[28] Through this act of self-sacrificial service, Jesus modeled leadership that was grounded in an unprecedented expression of service. In this way, he corrected his disciples' desire to exalt themselves (see also Mark 10:35–45). Jesus clearly understood that love for the Father and for those given to him by his Father would require deep suffering and humility.

After washing the disciples' feet, Jesus asked them,

> Do you understand what I have done to you? You call me Teacher and Lord, and you are right, for so I am. If I then, your Lord and Teacher, have washed your feet, you also ought to wash one another's feet. For I have given you an example, that you also should do just as I have done to you. Truly, truly, I say to you, a servant is not greater than his master, nor is a messenger greater than the one who sent him. If you know these things, blessed are you if you do them. (John 13:12–17 ESV)

Servanthood is part of the identity that we share as the people of God, and leaders are not exempt from this calling. Paul, Timothy, Peter, James, Jude, and John were all very different leaders, but each one saw himself as a slave of Christ (Rom 1:1; Phil 1:1; Titus 1:1; 2 Pet 1:1; Jas 1:1; Jude 1:1; Rev 1:1). Even the demons recognized that Paul and Silas were "slaves of the Most High God" (Acts 16:17). As we consider this imagery, it is important to recognize that, in the world of the New Testament, "a slave no longer belonged to himself and therefore he had no autonomy of will or action."

> The slave [did] not have the freedom to choose which of the master's commands he [would] obey for the master's will [was] binding on the slave. . . . Slaves lived to please the master without any expectation of compensation or reward. Romans highly prized slaves who had internalized the will of the master sufficiently so that they could carry out the will of the master and demonstrate the master's character. This was especially important on rural estates when the master was absent and a slave overseer was given stewardship of the master's resources. The most faithful slaves did not

simply heed the master's will; they internalized it so that they could more effectively serve as an extension of the master.[29]

An understanding of the distinct characteristics of slavery in the first century AD can deepen our understanding of how this metaphor should shape Christian leaders today. The following patterns characterized Greco-Roman slavery:

1. *A slave was owned by the master.* A leader who lives as God's slave is "God's purchased possession, redeemed by God and under his absolute authority."

2. *A slave's identity was derived from the master.* The close identification of slaves with their master "meant that they were his representatives in society and commerce, acting as an extension of the master himself."

3. *A slave exercised representative authority.* The leader who sees himself as God's slave claims no power or authority of his own but serves solely in the name of Jesus.

4. *A slave was subject to the will of his master.* The slave was expected to "internalize the will of the master sufficiently so as to act in accordance with his will even in the absence of explicit commands."

5. *A slave was called to a life of unconditional obedience.* "The Christian leader is not free to withdraw from serving others."

6. *A slave lived in complete dependence on the master.* God will equip his slaves with everything they need in order to fulfill his will (Heb 13:21).

7. *A slave was vulnerable to mistreatment.* "Because physical slaves were considered an extension of their master, they could conduct business with the master's authority. However, in that role, they could also endure abuse or mistreatment on the master's behalf."[30]

When Jesus modeled this way of leading in the presence of his followers, Simon Peter saw his Savior's leadership role as a status too exalted to include the washing of feet. The apostle's rejection of this act of service revealed Peter's flawed perspective on what it meant to be a leader. In Peter's mind, strong leadership excluded humble servanthood. Jesus disagreed. "If I do not wash you, you have no share with me," was the reply that Peter received (John 13:8 ESV). Simon Peter's rejection of this act of service revealed that he did not yet comprehend the nature either of servanthood or of salvation. In the kingdom of Christ, the Sovereign King has chosen to lead his people by means of humble service, and the path that this King calls his people to follow will lead them through the valley of humility (Phil 2:3–8).

The Gospel of Mark highlights a similar theme of leadership that embraces the role of a slave. At one point in Mark's Gospel, James and John asked to sit to the right and to the left of Jesus in the kingdom to come (10:37). This was not the first time that the disciples had jockeyed for leadership roles in the kingdom. As a matter of fact, this is the second time such a struggle is recorded in Mark's Gospel. Both times, this conflict occurred after Jesus predicted his impending death (Mark 8:31; 9:31; 10:33–34). Each time, it seems that the disciples were keenly aware that Jesus was the Messiah and his kingdom was near—but the disciples mistakenly thought this required the imminent restoration of an earthly kingdom coupled with positions of power for the Messiah's followers.

Perhaps this ambitious request from James and John was driven by the promise of honor in the kingdom to come (Matt 19:28). Maybe it was because of their present places in Jesus's inner circle of disciples (Mark 5:37). Perhaps it was due to their mother's desire for them to possess a special place of leadership (Matt 20:20–28). Regardless of their motivations, James and John clearly displayed unholy ambition. Unholy ambition seeks personal fame and is rooted in a desire for self-advancement; holy ambition seeks God's fame and is rooted in a yearning for God's reign.

Jesus first replied with a question: "Are you able to drink the cup that I drink, or to be baptized with the baptism with which I am baptized?" (Mark 10:38 ESV). In the Old Testament, the metaphor of a cup could point to suffering (Ps 75:8; Isa 51:17–22; Jer 25:15–28; Ezek 23:31–33) or to salvation (Pss 16:5; 23:5; 116:13). The imagery of baptism here most likely implies being engulfed with calamity. Both James and John experienced suffering. James was martyred at the hand of Herod Agrippa I (Acts 12:1–2), and John suffered exile (Rev 1:9). Part of what Jesus was teaching his disciples was that the way of his kingdom was not one of seeking power but of submitting to the cross.

Jesus drove home the lesson with this declaration:

> You know that those who are considered rulers of the Gentiles lord
> it over them, and their great ones exercise authority over them.

But it shall not be so among you. But whoever would be great among you must be your servant, and whoever would be first among you must be slave of all. For even the Son of Man came not to be served but to serve, and to give his life as a ransom for many. (Mark 10:42–45 ESV)

Jesus was not providing a principle for leadership when he declared that he came to serve; he was providing a pattern for the leader's life. By identifying greatness as servanthood and by presenting himself as the slave who gives himself for others, Jesus described a pattern that sees the leader first and foremost as a follower of the God who goes before us.

Christ-following servanthood is not condescension. Condescending leaders serve with an inward sense that they are doing their followers a favor by serving. Such leaders are not serving because they are servants; they serve because they want to be seen as servants by those that they view as servants.[31] This is not the way of authentic servanthood. Christ-centered servanthood is followership exercised with biblical wisdom in the context of a community for which God has given us responsibility.

Christ-following leaders serve even when no one will ever know about their service, and they do not see their service as a favor that they perform for the people they lead. They are not servants because they serve; they serve because they are servants. In this Jesus Christ asks no more of us than he himself has already done. This path that Jesus calls us to follow is a path that he has already pioneered, and he has gifted us with the same Spirit that empowered him.

Servant Leadership and Scripture

Robert Greenleaf is credited for introducing the concept of servant leadership into corporate America. He used the phrase "servant leader" to describe the individual whose desire to lead "begins with the natural feeling that one wants to serve, to serve first. Then conscious choice brings one to aspire to lead. That person is sharply different from one who is leader first."[32] Some aspects of Greenleaf's theory seem compatible with Christian leadership, but others clearly are not. Leaders in the church are called to lead as slaves of God. Timothy Cochrell has described ten characteristics that distinguish New Testament leadership from Greenleaf's model of servant leadership.

	Robert Greenleaf's Model of Servant Leadership	Timothy Cochrell's Biblical Model of Leadership as a Slave of God
1. Fundamental Qualification of the Leader	Altruism and innate desire to serve	Divine calling and empowerment
2. Fundamental Basis of the Leader's Identity	Personal choice to be an altruistic and moral person; natural inclination to serve others	Union with Christ; character and will of Christ
3. Moral Qualifications of the Leader	Humility, empathy, integrity, selflessness	Humility, obedience, selflessness, faithfulness to God in service of others
4. Locus of the Leader's Accountability	Leader is accountable to self and to those served	Leader is ultimately accountable to his Master and secondarily to those he serves

	Robert Greenleaf's Model of Servant Leadership	Timothy Cochrell's Biblical Model of Leadership as a Slave of God
5. Source of the Leader's Authority	Authority granted by followers on the basis of leader's servanthood; authority exercised through persuasion	Authority granted by the Master on the basis of leader's calling; authority exercised through proclamation
6. Source of the Leader's Direction	Directed by follower's highest priority needs and by the leader's own intuition	Directed by God's Word and God's character, empowered by God's Spirit
7. Leader's Goal for the Organization	To make followers wiser, freer, and more autonomous	To obey the Master's will by serving his people so that God's kingdom will advance in their hearts and in the world
8. Leader's Goal as an Individual	To autonomously serve others and lead them to do the same	To dependently serve Christ and lead others to do the same
9. Leader's Relationship to Followers	Demonstrates empathy and acceptance to make the follower autonomous and self-directed	Demonstrates Christlike character and sacrifices to make followers more like Christ
10. Cost of Leadership	Unspecified	Persecution and mistreatment by those who oppose Christ

Adapted from Timothy Cochrell, "Slaves of the Most High God: A Biblical Model of Servant Leadership in the Slave Imagery of Luke-Acts" (PhD diss., SBTS, 2015), 294–295.

The Slave Metaphor

Particularly in North American contexts, the metaphor of slavery can call to mind the system by which men and women were stolen from Africa, reduced to the status of property, and sold for profit. The Greco-Roman system of slavery should, however, be sharply distinguished from the practice of race-based, lifelong chattel slavery that has so deeply infected American history.[33]

Greco-Roman slavery could be an undesirable status, and Christian slaves were encouraged to gain their freedom if at all possible (1 Cor 7:21). Yet this form of slavery was not necessarily permanent, and the system was certainly not race based. Any individual from any race could become a slave for a set period of time in order to work off debts; after working off his or her debt, such a slave became free.[34] By contrast, the African slave trade was made possible through the theft of human beings on the basis of race for the purpose of profit.

The Spirit-inspired authors of Scripture explicitly condemned the theft and sale of human beings as "manstealing" (1 Tim 1:10 KJV; see also Exod 21:16).[35] The iniquitous trade in African slaves that stained Western societies from the seventeenth through the nineteenth centuries was analogous to the practice of manstealing condemned by the apostle Paul, *not* to Hebrew or Greco-Roman slavery.

Christian Leaders as Examples

The words and works of Jesus shaped the lives of those who led the earliest churches. His teaching and example were characterized by an attitude of humble service toward God's people, dependence on God's Spirit, and a disposition of submission to God the Father. These patterns should, of course, characterize the lives not only of Christian leaders but also of every follower of Jesus Christ. Leaders in the church are, however, particularly responsible to imitate Jesus in such a way that younger believers recognize in them an example to imitate (see 1 Cor 4:16; 11:1; Phil 3:17; Titus 2:7; Heb 13:7; 1 Pet 5:3). The apostle Paul described himself as someone who was "not seeking [his] own benefit, but the benefit of many, so that they may be saved" (1 Cor 10:33). As a result, he could urge the wayward

Corinthian church, "Imitate me, as I also imitate Christ" (1 Cor 11:1). To imitate Christ as a leader is to recognize in him the God who has gone before us and to submit every aspect of our leadership to his example of service, dependence, and submission.

Leadership Definition, Dynamics, and Diagnostics

	Leadership Definition	Leadership Dynamic	Leadership Diagnostics
Union with Christ	*The Christ-following leader—living as a bearer of God's image in union with Christ and his people—*	The shepherd is a follower of God's way who is present among the sheep. The leader's imitation of Christ through submission to the Father evidences a right understanding of derived authority.	Do your patterns of leadership reveal to those around you that the greatest place to be as a leader is within God's will, operating in submission to his authority? Or do you direct attention to your own authority, trying to make certain that people are aware of the position that you have attained?
Communion with Christ's People	*develops a diverse community of fellow laborers who are equipped and empowered to pursue shared goals*	The shepherd uses his power to provide for the sheep. The leader's imitation of Christ through authentic servanthood fosters an environment in which fellow laborers are increasingly motivated to serve others, without concern for who gets the credit.	Carefully assess the leadership environment you have created. Is it marked by humility, love, and service for the sake of others? Or is it marked by groups or individuals who feel compelled to make certain that they get credit for their efforts?

	Leadership Definition	Leadership Dynamic	Leadership Diagnostics
Mission in the World	*that fulfill the creation mandate and the Great Commission in submission to the Word of God.*	The shepherd is willing to take personal risks to protect and to rescue the sheep. The leader's willingness to depend on the Holy Spirit empowers the leader and provides a model for the church as they seek to fulfill God's mission in the world.	Do you recognize and admit to those around you that you do not have the knowledge, wisdom, skills, or insight to accomplish the mission apart from the work of the Holy Spirit? Do you actively seek the power and guidance of the Holy Spirit in your planning and decisions? Are you willing to follow where he leads regardless of the cost?

Further Reading

Cochrell, Timothy. *Slaves of the Most High God: A Biblical Model of Servant Leadership in the Slave Imagery of Luke-Acts.* Nashville: B&H Academic, 2018.

Hawthorne, Gerald. *The Presence and the Power.* Eugene: Wipf & Stock, 2003.

Tidball, Derek. *Ministry by the Book.* Downers Grove: InterVarsity, 2009.

Ware, Bruce A. *The Man Christ Jesus.* Wheaton: Crossway, 2012.

The Shepherd's Commission: Living as a Leader Who Follows, Feeds, and Dies

"John saw Jesus coming toward him and said, 'Here is the Lamb of God, who takes away the sin of the world!'"

John 1:29

"Jesus told them, . . . 'I am the good shepherd. The good shepherd lays down his life for the sheep.'"

John 9:41; 10:11

"'Feed my sheep,' Jesus said."

John 21:17

▶ Chapter Seven Key Point

Jesus, the model shepherd, knew his sheep, led his sheep, and suffered for his sheep. Shepherd leaders who follow the example of Jesus are commissioned to follow, feed, and die as they nourish the sheep, guard the sheep, and follow the model shepherd. ◀

As children, we begin the learning process by watching others. That is how we gain an initial concept of how to ride a bike, how to respond to adults, or how to succeed in a particular sport. This observation goes a long way, but our learning does not end there. Typically, observation must be accompanied by specific instruction from a mentor or coach. This instruction then leads to an opportunity to try the new practice for ourselves. And when we try the new practice, we usually imitate our instructor—whether we are riding a bike, learning to be well-mannered, or tossing a baseball.

Observation. Instruction. Imitation. It is what we do to learn new skills.

That pattern is as true in leadership as it is in every other area of life. We watch, we learn, we imitate—it is how we learn to lead.

It is this pattern that we described in the previous chapter. The Gospels portray Jesus as a God-fearing, God-following leader who demonstrated submission to the Father, dependence on the Spirit, and willingness to serve. As he pursued these patterns, he instructed his disciples how to live and how to lead. Jesus then called his disciples to imitate his life of submission, dependence, and service. These patterns should characterize the life of every believer in Jesus Christ, and leaders in particular.

There is another pattern and identity that was a distinct mark of those entrusted to lead the church of Jesus Christ—that of a shepherd. Even in shepherding, God is the one who goes before us. He was a shepherd of his people long before any of us were called to be shepherds. When Jacob extended a blessing to Ephraim and Manasseh, he did so in the name of "the God before whom my fathers Abraham and Isaac walked, the God who has been my shepherd all my life to this day" (Gen 48:15).

This shepherd imagery blossoms throughout the Old Testament as God continues to make himself known as the shepherd of Israel. The imagery of a shepherd is applied to God himself, to the leaders of Israel and Judah, and to the coming Messiah.[1] As we move into the New Testament, the authors of the Gospels utilize shepherding imagery at least a dozen times.[2] Some of these include descriptions of Jesus's compassion for the people who were "like sheep without a shepherd" as well as the comforting words of Jesus for his "little flock" and his parables of straying sheep, lost sheep, and searching shepherds (Matt 9:36; 18:12–14; Mark 6:34; Luke 12:32; 15:4–7).

John's Gospel includes three primary references to the motifs of sheep and shepherding (John 1:29–36; 10:1–30; 21:15–17).[3] In the first chapter of this Gospel, John the Baptist identifies Jesus as the "Lamb of

God who takes away the sins of the world" (1:29). The Gospel closes with the restoration and commissioning of Peter; in this passage, Peter is called to embrace a life of suffering and sacrifice as a shepherd of the sheep (John 21:15–17). Between these two texts, Jesus declares himself to be "the good shepherd" (John 10:11), identifying himself as the long-anticipated shepherd and king predicted by Jeremiah, Ezekiel, and Zechariah (John 10:11).[4]

"The good shepherd" is a declaration that calls for imitation. The adjective translated "good" implied "an attractive quality, something noble or ideal. 'Model' captures these connotations, but also implies a second nuance that is important in this context: Jesus should be emulated."[5] To refer to Jesus as the "good shepherd" was not primarily to recognize him as righteous. It was to identify him as the model for shepherding. Jesus was the model leader who suffered in order to purchase salvation and security for his flock.

When Jesus identified himself as the model shepherd, he was flinging a stinging rebuke into the faces of the religious leaders of his own day.[6] Much like their predecessors whose practices were condemned by the prophets Ezekiel and Jeremiah, the religious leaders of Israel were far from model shepherds; they had abandoned their God-given role as the people's protectors and providers (compare Ezekiel 34; Jeremiah 23).[7] John portrays Jesus Christ as the good shepherd who gives abundant life and demonstrates sacrificial love for his sheep.

According to John's Gospel, "the door of the sheep" (John 10:7 ESV) and "the good shepherd" (10:11) were "figures of speech" (sometimes translated "illustrations") (10:6)—an unusual and much debated term.[8] Whatever the precise nuance of this term, it highlights this text as a "symbol-laden discourse."[9] By using this figure of speech, Jesus wove together several biblical motifs and applied them in his context.[10] His discourse blends the shepherd imagery from the prophecies of Ezekiel and Jeremiah with threads from Isaiah's descriptions of a suffering servant.[11] In this way, Jesus revealed himself as a righteous, suffering shepherd who comes to bring new life for his flock at the cost of his own life. By his own sinless life and sacrificial death, he filled "the shepherd-vacuum that existed among God's people in a way that prior shepherds—Moses, Joshua, David—were unable to fill because of sin and death."[12]

Jesus, the Suffering Shepherd

It is the sacrificial suffering of Jesus that made him a *good* shepherd.[13] Over and over in this passage, Jesus described how he would lay down his life to rescue his sheep (John 10:9–10, 11, 15, 17–18, 28–29).[14] John the Baptist had identified him as the sacrificial lamb (John 1:29); in this discourse, Jesus echoed the prophecies of Isaiah (Isa 53:4–7) and identified himself both as suffering shepherd and sacrificial lamb. This righteous, suffering shepherd stands in stark contrast to the thieves, robbers, and hirelings—the religious leaders of Israel who sought their own interests instead of the well-being of the flock.[15] These pseudo-shepherds were acting much like their Old Testament counterparts and deserved the same indictment: "Thus says the Lord . . . I am against the shepherds. . . . I will rescue my sheep from their mouths" (Ezek 34:10).

King David had been the iconic shepherd of Israel who literally and figuratively risked his life to protect the flocks both of his earthly father and of his heavenly Father (1 Sam 17:34–37). By declaring himself to be the model shepherd, Jesus identified himself as the long-awaited Davidic ruler. Like David, he would risk his life to rescue his Father's flock; unlike David, he would live a perfect life and sacrifice that life for the sake of that flock.

Following the Example of the Suffering Shepherd

Of course, Jesus alone fulfilled the role of the suffering shepherd who gave his life for the sake of his flock.[16] Nevertheless, as the model shepherd, Jesus provided a pattern for the human shepherds who would one day guide and guard his flock. For Christ-following leaders, suffering is not to be avoided; it is to be recognized as a participation in the same patterns that characterized the life of Jesus Christ. A Christ-following leader should expect to face difficulties, even extreme difficulties, when leading the flock of God. "Ministry," Derek Tidball reminds us, "is self-giving sacrifice."[17] As we examine the Scriptures, we see at least four realities that come to fruition in the lives of leaders who follow the example of Jesus by enduring suffering.

1. *Suffering sanctifies the leader.* Suffering has a way of maturing leaders. Suffering in obedience to God's Word while empowered by God's Spirit in the context of God's people sanctifies those who are

called to serve as shepherds (John 16:13; 17:17; Rom 8:13–14; Gal 5:18; Eph 4:11–16). Christ himself entreated his Father to remove the cup of wrath from him, yet he also embraced the Father's will and was obedient to the point of death (Phil 2:8).

2. *Suffering develops the leader's endurance.* "Affliction produces endurance," Paul said to the Christians in Rome, "endurance produces proven character, and proven character produces hope" (Rom 5:3–4). Your status as a child of God and a sheep of the Good Shepherd precedes your place as a leader of God's people. Do not find it remarkable that you, along with the people you lead, experience afflictions in the present that will enable you to endure sufferings as a leader in the future.

3. *Suffering cultivates greater sympathy for the flock.* "Souls still remain in our churches," Charles H. Spurgeon said, "to whose deep and dark experiences we shall never be able to minister till we also have been plunged in the abyss where all Jehovah's waves roll over our heads."[18] As the leader experiences hard times, illnesses, rejection, feelings of isolation, even persecution, the leader will become more sympathetic—even empathetic—toward the flock that he guides and guards. Teaching becomes different. Counseling becomes different. Relationships become different. Though we are mere under-shepherds, we begin to exhibit qualities of the chief shepherd of whom it has been said, "We do not have a high priest who is unable to sympathize with our weaknesses, but one who in every respect has been tempted as we are, yet without sin" (Heb 4:15 ESV).

4. *Suffering deepens the leader's love for the flock.* The shepherd-leader is drawn from the flock itself. He is not an outsider or an interloper. He is a brother in Christ. As such, he has been called to lead and love the people from among the people. That love for others is motivated by the love Christ displayed on the cross. As shepherd-leaders, we are called to follow Christ's example of sacrificial love. Between the two of us, we have experienced more than a half-century of church ministry. Over and over, we have seen in our own lives and the lives of other leaders that suffering deepens the leader's love for the sheep—especially, and oddly enough, for the sheep who seem most difficult to lead.

When the Yoke of Service Becomes a Yoke of Suffering

"It is good for a man to bear the yoke of service, and he is no loser when it is exchanged for the yoke of suffering. May not severe discipline fall to the lot of some to qualify them for their office of under-shepherds? How can we speak with consoling authority to a situation which we have never known? The complete pastor's life will be an epitome of the lives of his people, and they will turn to his preaching as men do to David's psalms, to see themselves and their sorrows, as in a mirror."[19]

—Charles H. Spurgeon

Are you serving in a difficult ministry context? Do not rush to escape this context by giving up on your calling or by quickly sending out résumés in the hope of pursuing your calling elsewhere. You will grow to be a more compassionate shepherd by remaining and loving the place where you are until God's call to leave is unmistakably clear.

What about You?

Study Col 1:24–29 and 1 Pet 4:12–19.

"I rejoice in my sufferings," Paul said, and he was able to do this because God's strength was working powerfully within him (Col 1:24, 29). What these sufferings produced in Paul's life was a pattern of endurance, character, and confidence (Rom 5:3–4). Sufferings can produce the same pattern in our lives today.

I (Michael) pastored a church while completing my doctoral studies, and I began my ministry feeling like most do: joyful, contented, excited. There were new people to meet, Bible studies to be taught, and God's Word to be preached. Eighteen months later, changes I had made were advancing but pockets of resistance were arising, and I was exhausted. My prayers were driven by the opposition I was feeling around me.

One Sunday night as the folks were gathering for worship, I lingered outside the front door. Worship was supposed to begin at 6:00 p.m. It was 6:05, and I could not make myself go inside. Everything within me wanted to quit my ministry in this place—right then. As the next two minutes ticked by, I sensed the Spirit of God strengthening me and telling me to endure. I was given confidence that the chief shepherd was not finished with me or with these people. As I looked up, I saw an amazing sight—in the midst of a summer evening, there was a bright spring-colored, green-leafed branch sticking out some three feet above the rest of the branches on the nearest maple tree. It was out of place to be sure, but God used that sight to give me hope for future growth in the lives of this people whom God had called me to shepherd. It reminded me of those who might confess Christ as Savior in the years to come. That very moment, I chose to remain steadfast in that place. God strengthened me, increased my love for this people, and began a maturation process in me as a leader in a way that I had never experienced before.

The rest of the story is that we saw that small country church grow spiritually and numerically, with some thirty-five new believers baptized over the next eighteen months. I look back now and recognize that I would have missed so much growth in myself and in that church if I had not remained there. God works through suffering and opposition to mature us as leaders.

In what areas of ministry are you tempted to quit right now? How might God be developing empathy and endurance in you through this difficult season? Envision what the future could look like if you remain faithful where you are.

The God Who Goes before Us Knows His Sheep

Jesus's rebuke of the religious leaders of his day went beyond their unwillingness to sacrifice and suffer for the well-being of the whole flock. It included a condemnation of their lack of care for the individual members of the flock (John 9:24–34). This theme of being concerned with the individual was not new with John's writing. It was also evidenced in the prophecies of Ezekiel:

> The weak you have not strengthened, the sick you have not healed, the injured you have not bound up, the strayed you have not brought back, the lost you have not sought, and with force and harshness you have ruled them. (Ezek 34:4 ESV)

Here the terms that describe the status of the sheep are all singular, suggesting that part of the problem may have been a lack of individualized concern for members of the flock. In this regard, we think immediately of the New Testament parables of straying and lost sheep that entail a search for a single member of the flock (Matt 18:12–14; Luke 15:4–7).

According to Jesus, a sheep recognizes its shepherd's voice: "He calls his own sheep by name and leads them out" (John 10:3).[20] Calling animals by name seems perfectly normal if these animals happen to be our pets. It seems a bit odd—at least to the Western mind—to call animals by a nickname if they are being raised as a commodity, to provide wool or meat. This seems, however, to have been typical for Semitic shepherds in the first century AD.[21] Such naming suggests that shepherds developed personal knowledge of the sheep—of each creature's markings, tendencies, quirks, patterns of life. A good shepherd knew his sheep, and his sheep knew him (John 10:14). "This intimacy of a shepherd and his flock provides a beautiful illustration of the trust, familiarity, and bond existing between Jesus and his followers."[22]

For Jesus, knowledge of the sheep extended beyond those presently in the flock to include those who were not yet his followers (John 10:16; see also John 6:37; Luke 15:1–4; Eph 1:3–5). Relationships with Jesus the shepherd would not be limited to any particular language or hue of melanin; from the beginning, God's plan was to draw together a diverse flock that included men and women from every ethnicity and culture. During the Feast of Dedication that followed these encounters with the religious leaders (John 10:22), Jesus returned to this shepherd motif as he spoke to the Jews. He said, "My sheep hear my voice, and I know them" (John 10:27).

All of this imagery reveals at least three truths about our model shepherd: (1) Jesus knows each sheep intimately; (2) Jesus cares about each sheep individually; and (3) the love of Jesus for each sheep is rooted in his relationship with his Father. "I know my own and my own know me, just as the Father knows me and I know the Father," Jesus said (John 10:14–15). The Son's love for his sheep was born from his relationship with the Father. So it is with shepherd leaders in the church today. Our love for the sheep who have been entrusted to our earthly care arises from our relationship with the Father through our union with the Son.

Following the Example of the Shepherd Who Knows His Sheep

Some people in our congregations are very private, while some tend to share a bit too much information about themselves. Some are joyful, and some are cantankerous. Some are responsive to correction, and some are resistant. But all of them are gifts to be treasured, entrusted to our care (Heb 13:17). When people are seen as gifts, pastoral attitudes change—there is more patience, more care, more valuing of the individual. And there is more love. The pastor's love for the flock is rooted in the pastor's own relationship with the Shepherd. We love as Christ has loved us (John 13:34–35; 15:12). "No one can expect to lead God's people unless this relationship is formed first," Derek Tidball has pointed out. "The pastor needs intimate knowledge of his people and they need to feel confident in his leadership and to be able to trust that he will not lead them into any danger."[23]

Jesus, the Shepherd Whose Sheep Follow Him

The model shepherd "goes before" the sheep, "and the sheep follow him, for they know his voice" (John 10:4). The sheep follow their shepherd. Notice three specific patterns that characterize this followership:

1. *The shepherd goes before his sheep.* The Shepherd leads his flock in "paths of righteousness for his name's sake" (Ps 23:3). All of God's people must follow—but this is particularly crucial for the human leaders who shepherd God's church. The leader's resolve to follow God's way is at the heart of the leader's commitment to lead God's people. This followership requires submission and dependence. It also demands that we as leaders slow down and take the time to fix our attention on the Shepherd. We cannot lead unless we follow, and we cannot follow unless we remain close to the Shepherd.

2. *The sheep follow because they trust the shepherd.* The sheep will not follow a shepherd they do not trust (John 10:5). A sheep's willingness to follow a shepherd is grounded in memories of the shepherd's proven presence, provision, and protection. Pastors cannot be strangers to church members and then expect that these same

members will desire to follow their leadership. Trust takes time because trust is relationally earned, not positionally derived.

3. *The sheep develop discernment.* One role of a shepherd is to equip the sheep to discern and to follow the call of the shepherd. Jesus told his hearers that the sheep know their shepherd's voice (10:4, 16, 27). When it comes to those who follow God, this does not mean training the people to discern the voice of those who are appointed as their human leaders! We are neither the model shepherd nor the source of authority. We are under-shepherds, followers of the God who goes before us; our calling is to equip the flock to follow him. In the Old Testament, this happened primarily through the Scriptures as the Israelites "listened to God's voice by living in conformity with his revealed will."[24] In Jesus's day, this hearing happened as people heeded his words (John 15:10). Today, it occurs as people are equipped by shepherds and teachers to understand the Scriptures and to discern the Spirit's guidance as he applies the Word of God in their lives (Eph 4:11–16; John 16:13–15).

Why Does Trust Take So Much Time?

Trust takes time because trust is relationally earned, not positionally derived.

Carefully consider your past and present ministry contexts. Have you at times expected people to follow your plans even though you had not taken the time to know the people or to understand their concerns?

Leadership Definition, Dynamics, and Diagnostics

	Leadership Definition	*Leadership Dynamic*	*Leadership Diagnostics*
Union with Christ	*The Christ-following leader—living as a bearer of God's image in union with Christ and his people—*	The shepherd is a follower of God's way who is present among the sheep. Jesus rescued his followers and brought them into union with himself by enduring the sufferings of the cross. The Christ-following shepherd who demonstrates a willingness to suffer for the well-being of the people becomes a participant in the afflictions of Jesus, the suffering shepherd.	Evaluate your own disposition toward suffering as a leader in God's church. Do you see your sufferings as one facet of following Christ? Do you draw strength from your union with Christ and your participation in his victory? Are you willing to persevere, trusting that God's grace is sufficient even in your suffering?
Communion with Christ's People	*develops a diverse community of fellow laborers who are equipped and empowered to pursue shared goals*	The shepherd uses his power to provide for the sheep. Jesus knows his followers by name, personally and uniquely. The Christ-following shepherd provides not only knowledge of God's Word but also an awareness among the people that they are known and loved.	How well do you know the people you lead? Develop intentional patterns in your leadership to engage in your people's lives with the goal of greater personal knowledge of each one.

	Leadership Definition	Leadership Dynamic	Leadership Diagnostics
Mission in the World	*that fulfill the creation mandate and the Great Commission in submission to the Word of God.*	The shepherd is willing to take personal risks to protect and to rescue the sheep. Jesus protected his followers from false beliefs by equipping his followers to know his voice. The Christ-following shepherd protects the flock by equipping them to understand the Scriptures and to discern the guidance of the Holy Spirit as the Spirit applies the Word of God in their lives.	In what specific ways could you protect your people by equipping them to grow in their capacity to understand the Scriptures for themselves and to recognize the Spirit's guidance in their lives? As the people grow in their capacity to understand Scripture for themselves, are you willing to take the risk of not being the resident Bible expert to whom people come with all of their questions?

The Shepherd's Commission: Follow, Feed, Die

Early in John's Gospel, Jesus is portrayed as the sacrificial lamb (John 1:29). Later, Jesus is described as the shepherd who will sacrifice his life and suffer for the sake of his sheep (John 10). By the time we arrive at the final chapter of this Gospel, Jesus has become the shepherd who seeks a straying sheep in order to restore him and to commission him as a shepherd leader in the early church (John 21).[25] This commission was threefold:

1. *The commission to follow the Shepherd.* Christ-centered leadership is, first and foremost, followership exercised with biblical wisdom in the context of community for which God has given us responsibility. In the dark night that preceded the crucifixion of Jesus, Simon Peter denied Jesus three times and declared he was not a follower of Jesus (John 18:17–25). In the closing chapter of John's Gospel, the denials of Peter are erased by the command of Jesus: "You follow me!" (21:22). That morning, these became words of grace spoken to a broken but hopeful man. Peter was being restored not to an office but to a person. He was being reminded that, though his own faith had failed, Christ's calling had not.

2. *The commission to feed the flock.* Three times, Simon Peter denied Jesus. Three times, Jesus asked Peter whether Peter loved him. Peter answered in the affirmative, and Jesus drew a clear connection between Peter's love for his Savior and Peter's calling as a shepherd to care for the sheep (John 21:15, 16, 17).[26] Surely this must have been a life-changing experience for Peter.[27] Later, Peter urged pastors, "Be shepherds of God's flock that is under your care . . . because you are willing, as God wants you to be" (1 Pet 5:2 NIV).

3. *The commission to die.* The conversation did not end until Jesus revealed to Simon Peter the high cost of this commission:

   > "Truly, truly, I say to you, when you were young, you used to dress yourself and walk wherever you wanted, but when you are old, you will stretch out your hands, and another will dress you and carry you where you do not want to go." (This he said to show by what kind of death he was to glorify God.) And after saying this he said to him, "Follow me" (John 21:18–19 ESV).

Following would cost Peter his life. Jesus offered no apology for this fact; instead, he simply declared the reality of what it would mean for Peter to live as an under-shepherd who imitated the model shepherd. Jesus also made it clear that the pathway for each leader would look different. For Peter, it would mean an early death; for John, it would mean long life (John 21:22)—but the calling for both of them was to follow Jesus all the way.

Simon Peter was publicly restored and publicly commissioned. The commission—follow me, feed my sheep, and die—must have been forever etched in this shepherd's mind, just as it should be etched in the mind of every Christian leader today. We have been given responsibilities for which we will be held accountable (Heb 13:17). This is a weighty stewardship with eternal consequences.

A Leader Who Was Prepared to Suffer

"Because of jealousy and envy the greatest and most righteous pillars [of the church] were persecuted, and fought to the deaths. . . . There was Peter, who, because of unrighteous jealousy, endured not one or two but many trials, and thus having given his testimony went to his appointed place of glory."[28]

—Clement of Rome

According to Clement of Rome, Peter endured "many trials" before his death. Clement probably spoke these words three decades or so after Simon Peter's martyrdom. After reading these words, how would you describe Peter's preparation and willingness to suffer for the sake of the gospel?

The Shepherd's Practices: Nourish, Guard, Serve

Pastors are not lords over the sheep but servants of the Shepherd and stewards of the flock. This truth should leave an indelible mark on how we lead God's people. It calls us to tend the sheep because we are the means God has chosen (1) to provide for their needs, (2) to guard them, and (3) to serve them. We are called to serve the sheep from among the sheep, and we are never greater than the sheep among whom God has placed us.

1. *Shepherd leadership calls for nourishing the flock.* One primary responsibility of the shepherd is to provide nourishment for the flock (Ezek 34:2). In the church, the pastor's leadership is most strikingly demonstrated through his teaching ministry—not only in public proclamation but also in personal mentoring and discipleship. Jesus, the model shepherd, was known as one who taught with great authority (Matt 7:28–29). Remember when Jesus invited his disciples to retreat to a deserted place? When they arrived, the spot was no longer deserted, because the people had anticipated where Jesus might be headed. Compassion welled up within Jesus when he saw the people, because "they were like sheep without a shepherd," and his immediate response is telling: "he began to teach them many things" (Mark 6:34). He saw shepherdless sheep, and he immediately began to feed them. Peter was told to imitate precisely what Jesus had modeled—"Feed my lambs. . . . Tend my sheep. . . . Feed my sheep" (John 21:15–17 ESV). It was through providing for God's people that Peter was called to demonstrate authentic love for the chief shepherd. True compassion for people and love for God compels the pastoral leader to nourish God's flock. This provision encompasses more than proclamation—it includes, for example, the formation of environments where people are safe from hunger and abuse—but nourishment of the flock never includes less than the sustained teaching of God's Word.

2. *Shepherd leadership calls for guarding the flock.* The rulers of Israel were devouring and abandoning the flock, so God's sheep were scattered and became fodder for wolves (John 10:12; see also Ezek 34:3, 5, 8). The divine shepherd, who would reverse the evils of the leaders, declared that he would rescue his sheep, giving himself for them (John 10:11, 15; see also Ezek 34:12, 14, 15, 22). A mark of divine leadership is protection. So it is with shepherds in Christ's church (Acts 20:29). Spiritual wolves continue to prey on God's people. The shepherd must remain diligent, as the entry points for assault have multiplied through the Internet and social media, as well as through wider media and publishing opportunities. Vast smorgasbords of false doctrine are now available through the mere touch of a screen.

3. *Shepherd leadership calls for sacrificial service among the people.* Jesus, the model shepherd, makes this clear in his words to the Pharisees: "The good shepherd lays down his life for the sheep" (John 10:11). This is exactly what Christ did on our behalf through his finished work on the cross. It is no wonder then that, immediately after calling Peter to feed his sheep, the resurrected Jesus also called Peter to follow him to the point of death (John 21:18–19). For some, this life of sacrifice will culminate in martyrdom. For others, the sacrifice is seen in remaining faithful to the same group of people year after year, tending the flock in good times and in bad, dying to one's own dreams for the sake of the congregation where God has placed us. These sacrifices are less obvious than martyrdom, but they are no less real.

There is much that is glorious in pastoral work, but the congregation, as such, is not glorious. . . . Pastors agree to stay with the people in their communities week in and week out, year in and year out, to proclaim and guide, encourage and instruct as God works his purposes (gloriously, it will eventually turn out) in the meandering and disturbingly inconstant lives of our congregations. . . . Most pastoral work takes place in obscurity: deciphering grace in the shadows, searching out meaning in a difficult text, blowing on the embers of a hard-used life. This is hard work and not conspicuously glamorous.[30]

The difficulty is that there are pastors who choose to live as self-centered shepherds, much like the rulers described in Ezekiel. They are consumed with their own gratification and personal enrichment. Such pastors operate in ways that preserve their power and position rather than serving in ways that demand personal sacrifice. In stark contrast, leaders who understand their role as shepherds live among their people and pay "careful attention . . . to all the flock" (Acts 20:28 ESV). As a pastor, you are neither a sovereign over your church nor a hireling of your church. You are an undershepherd of the living God, and you have been commissioned to follow, feed, and die. Your exemplar in this is Jesus himself, the shepherd who intimately knows his sheep and who has endured affliction to the point of death for their salvation. Even in sacrifice and death, Christ himself is the God who has gone before us.

"Do You Love Me?"

"If there is any focus that the Christian leader of the future will need, it is the discipline of dwelling in the presence of the One who keeps asking, 'Do you love me?' . . . It is not enough for [leaders] of the future to be moral people, well trained, eager to help. . . . The central question is, Are the leaders of the future truly men and women of God, people with an ardent desire to dwell in God's presence, to listen to God's voice, to look at God's beauty, to touch God's incarnate Word, and to taste fully God's infinite goodness?"[29]

—Henri J. M. Nouwen

Do you live with a deep desire to dwell in the presence of the One who called you to love him long before he called you to lead his people? Or has the busyness of your ministry duties choked out your longing simply to love your Savior and to dwell with him? What disciplines of prayer and meditation will you pursue to renew your yearning for his presence?

Leadership Definition, Dynamics, and Diagnostics

	Leadership Definition	Leadership Dynamic	Leadership Diagnostics
Union with Christ	*The Christ-following leader—living as a bearer of God's image in union with Christ and his people—*	The shepherd is a follower of God's way who is present among the sheep. The leader must be a faithful follower of Jesus Christ, the model shepherd. Follow.	The commission to shepherd leadership demands Christ followership. Are you genuinely following Christ's leadership in your life? Are you resting in your union with him? Cultivate spiritual habits that will deepen your followership, including extended seasons of prayer and fasting, spiritual retreats, and consistent patterns of meditation on Scripture.
Communion with Christ's People	*develops a diverse community of fellow laborers who are equipped and empowered to pursue shared goals*	The shepherd uses his power to provide for the sheep. The leader demonstrates love for the chief shepherd by nourishing, guarding, and serving the flock. Feed.	The desire to fulfill your responsibility to teach, develop, and guide your followers must be fueled by a deep love for Christ. Are you making the connection between your love for Jesus and your commitment to love his people? Find in Christ the capacity and the desire to love and to teach even the most difficult followers.

	Leadership Definition	Leadership Dynamic	Leadership Diagnostics
Mission in the World	*that fulfill the creation mandate and the Great Commission in submission to the Word of God.*	The shepherd is willing to take personal risks to protect and to rescue the sheep. The leader is willing to suffer affliction for the sake of fulfilling the mission and remaining faithful to the Word of God. Die.	As a shepherd of God's people, you must be willing to suffer, even to the point of death, for the fulfillment of God's mission in the world. Sometimes afflictions come from within the body of Christ; other times the afflictions come from the flesh, the world, and the devil. Either way, live as a model of patiently enduring affliction for the sake of God's mission as Peter did.

Further Reading

Bailey, Kenneth. *The Good Shepherd*. Downers Grove: InterVarsity, 2014.

Köstenberger, Andreas J. "Shepherds and Shepherding in the Gospels." In *Shepherding God's Flock*. Edited by Benjamin Merkle and Thomas Schreiner. Grand Rapids: Kregel, 2014.

Spurgeon, Charles Haddon. "The Sheep and Their Shepherd," sermon 995, Newington, England, 1871.

Tidball, Derek. *Skillful Shepherds*. Downers Grove: InterVarsity, 2003.

The Shepherd's Identity: Learning to Lead as a Fellow Elder and Brother

"Shepherd God's flock among you."

1 Peter 5:2

"You yourselves, as living stones, a spiritual house, are being built to be a holy priesthood to offer spiritual sacrifices acceptable to God through Jesus Christ."

1 Peter 2:5

"Rejoice as you share in the sufferings of Christ, so that you may also rejoice with great joy when his glory is revealed."

1 Peter 4:13

▶ Chapter Eight Key Point

Pastors are brothers with the members of their congregations, called to cultivate the identities of their brothers and sisters in Christ as redeemed sojourners, living stones, and suffering servants. ◀

Every Sunday morning, I walk to the pulpit and begin that week's message by introducing myself: "Good morning. I'm Pastor Michael, and I'm glad we have the opportunity to open God's Word together." Contained in that greeting is a presentation of my role among those gathered as well as the focal point of my ministry with them. Regarding my role as one of the pastors in the church, I readily acknowledge that I am simply a brother among a family, a brother who has been asked to lead, teach, protect, and pray. That mind-set is more present today than when I first began serving in pastoral ministry nearly three decades ago. I am not detached from or above the community, but a family member within the community who depends on the encouragement and correction offered by my brothers and sisters.

If this is not your ministry mind-set, it is time for a radical change in your thinking. "Why?" you might ask. The answer is simple—*pastors are brothers who have been set aside by a local congregation to shepherd the flock.* They are leaders who have been called to imitate their Savior and commissioned to follow the chief shepherd, to feed his sheep, and perhaps even to die for his name.

A prime New Testament example of this mentality is the apostle Peter. Recall his commissioning in John 21 where his role as an under-shepherd was made clear, his responsibilities clarified, and the cost of his journey made known. Leading to this encounter, Peter spent three years observing Jesus, the righteous suffering shepherd, learning what it would mean for him to fully follow Christ and serve in a similar role among the people of God.

This chapter will explore how Peter fulfilled his commission, with particular attention paid to his leadership among a community of dispersed exiles and sojourners. Peter's leadership among these brothers and sisters in Christ provides a roadmap for today's church leaders who desire to shepherd their people well. In order to accomplish this goal, we will narrow our focus to Peter's first letter,[1] written while he was imprisoned for his witness (1 Pet 5:13).[2] Addressing the churches, he expresses the heart of an apostle and a "fellow elder" for a people who have been born again to a living hope and are facing opposition as they seek to live out the new life they have received.[3]

In this letter, Peter both instructs the elders to shepherd the flock of God (1 Pet 5:2), and provides for them a beautiful model of what it means to lead those placed in their care. Peter demonstrates through his writing how to *shape a people's identity and to equip them for holy living in a world hostile toward their Savior.* He uses language such as "aliens," "exiles," "sojourners," "strangers," "a royal priesthood," and "a holy nation" to describe and to address his readers, pointing toward their identity as God's renewed covenant community.[4] He teaches that God's people are *redeemed sojourners, living stones*, and *suffering servants*. The readers are challenged to live out this identity in the face of increasing opposition. This letter that we call 1 Peter reveals the heart of a pastor who is seeking to root his flock's identity in Christ and prepare them for what it means to live as theological exiles in a foreign land. As shepherds, we are tasked with *protecting* Christ's followers from harm and yet *preparing* them for suffering. In this letter, the apostle Peter pursues this task with the churches in Pontus, Galatia, Cappadocia, Asia, and Bithynia; in the process, he provides us with insight into the role of a pastor in the New Testament church.

Elder

Translates Greek *presbyteros*

Elders are leaders in the church who must be mature in their faith (1 Tim 5:22), blameless in their character (Titus 1:6–8), and able to teach God's truth (2 Tim 2:24; 3:14–17; Titus 1:9). The term "elder" emphasizes the maturity of the individual appointed to this position; "overseer" defines the central responsibility of the role. The elders' placement of their hands on Timothy suggests that the early churches formally recognized appointments to this position (1 Tim 4:14). A plurality of elders seems to have led each local church in the first century. Paul and Barnabas appointed "elders" (plural) in "every church" (singular) (Acts 14:23), and Paul commanded Titus to persist in this practice by appointing "elders in every town" (Titus 1:5). Without exception, each time the New Testament describes the leadership structure of a church, that structure is a plurality of elders.[5]

The Identity and Attitude of the Shepherd Leader

Perhaps the best way to understand Peter's approach to fulfilling his commission is to fast-forward to the end of this letter and hear the directions he gives to the elders who serve locally in the churches to which he is writing.[6] By doing so, we arrive at 1 Pet 5:1–4 and find in verse 2 the imperative, "shepherd the flock of God."

What about You?

Study Acts 20:28 and 1 Pet 5:2.

Notice that both Paul and Peter saw the shepherds of the flock as men who served "in" or "among" the people. If you are a pastor, do you try to lead God's people from "above" them? Or do you lead them from "among" them? If you tend to lead from "above" instead of leading from "among," how might you reorient your practices of ministry to correct this tendency?

This directive to shepherd the flock is situated in an interesting and telling place in the progression of the letter. These four verses are set between two sections that focus on suffering and opposition (4:12–19 and 5:6–11). The first of these passages speaks of opposition from outside the church by those who would deride Christianity and insult those who profess belief in Christ. The second passage sees the opposition arising from the devil himself, whom Peter describes as the adversary who "prowls around like a roaring lion, seeking someone to devour."

Peter tells his readers in the first passage, "Do not be surprised at the fiery trial when it comes upon you to test you" (4:12 ESV). They were to expect the difficulty of opposition, and they were to understand it as a means of sanctification in their lives. This is why Peter states that it is "time for judgment to begin at the household of God" (4:17 ESV). The word "judgment" here is probably best understood as refinement rather than destruction (1 Pet 1:6–7; Mal 3:1–5).[7] Beyond the purpose of shared suffering and formation, we sense a reminder that God's judgment and his refinement always begins with the leaders. Peter's choice of words in 1 Pet 4:17 reminds us of Ezek 9:6: "Begin at my sanctuary. So they began with the elders who were in front of the temple."[8] It would seem that Peter is taking the pattern displayed in the Old Testament of judgment on the leaders first (Ezekiel 22, 34; Jeremiah 23) and using it to prepare the elders for the fact that they must walk rightly before the people as an example of those who endure suffering well for the sake of eternal glory.

The second passage reminds followers of Christ, and especially Christian leaders,[9] that Satan would want nothing more than to bring either fear in the face of persecution or temptation that leads to a cataclysmic failure. Peter understood that in times of persecution, much would depend on the wisdom and faithfulness of the leaders.[10]

Peter's Identity as Fellow Elder, Faithful Witness, and Participant in Future Glory

Between these two mentions of suffering, Peter specifically addresses the elders.[11] He begins in 1 Pet 5:1 by identifying himself as a fellow elder, a witness of the sufferings of Christ, and a partaker of the glory to come.[12] These descriptors give us much insight into how Peter viewed himself and his ministry. It is significant that he uses the label of "fellow elder," since he had already noted his apostleship in 1:1. He is not denying the importance of his apostolic role when he refers to himself as a fellow elder. If anything, he is deepening our understanding of what it meant to be an apostle. We should understand that "the apostolic office included the work of the elder."[13] This is the only occurrence of "fellow elder" in all of ancient literature, including the New Testament.[14] It is similar to Paul's use of terms such as "fellow worker," "fellow soldier," "fellow slave," and "fellow prisoner" to describe the functions of particular Christians, but Peter uses the term to describe the distinct office of a pastor.[15]

Peter's usage of the term "fellow elder" is "consistent with the tendency among the early church leaders to avoid the use of exalted titles."[16] It seems to be a deliberate mind-set and intentional approach to ministry for Peter, as he avoids using language that would elevate himself.[17] His very choice of words creates collegiality between himself and the elders in the churches to which he is writing.[18] Peter writes as an elder to a plurality of fellow elders in each church that received his letter.

> Ideas of "one-man ministry" which are so ingrained in much of our church life could not be further removed from the image of the church as set out in the New Testament, where every member is a minister with gifts which must be exercised if the whole body is to function and grow healthily.[19]

The apostle Peter, who could easily have asserted power over other pastors, chose instead to refer to himself as a "fellow elder" who was serving and suffering with these pastors. The leader's power is never his own, to use as he pleases. Power is shared, for the purpose of equipping the people of the church to pursue God's plan together.

Peter continues by describing himself as "a witness of the sufferings of Christ." This phrase echoes the theme of suffering embedded throughout the letter (1:11; 2:21, 23–24; 3:18; 4:1) and more specifically in 4:12–13. When Peter declares himself to be a witness of the sufferings of Christ, we immediately raise a flag by pointing toward the Gospel accounts of his denial and fearful fleeing during the passion. What does it mean then for Peter to be a witness? The use of "witness" here means that he is one who is bearing witness to something, not just as an eyewitness but as one who personally knows something to be true (see the repeated pattern in Acts 2:14–36; 3:12–26; 4:8–12; 5:30–32; 10:34–43).[20] It was, after all, Peter's preaching on the day of Pentecost that the Holy Spirit used to give birth to the church in Jerusalem. It was Peter's message to Cornelius that expanded the gospel witness to the Gentiles. Earlier still, it was Peter who first confessed that Jesus was the Christ. So Peter's reputation as a witness of Christ's incarnation, life, death, and resurrection was fitting. What Peter faithfully proclaims is not his own personal dream or vision but God's revelation in Jesus Christ (2 Pet 1:16–20).

Not only does Peter point toward his self-identification as a witness (1 Pet 5:1), but he also reminds the elders that they too, along with their flock, will be participants in present sufferings and future glory as they boldly proclaim gospel truths.[21] Peter notes that he is a "partaker in the glory to be revealed" who lives everyday with an expectation that the suffering he is currently enduring will end in glory. Throughout this letter, the theme of suffering preceding glory is prominent (1:11; 4:13). The position to which the leader is called is not sovereignty above or separation from the community but stewardship within the community in union with Christ; the leader is, therefore, never exempt from suffering with the people. Leaders must live as participants with their people in present sufferings; the promise and the result is that both leaders and people will also participate together in future glory. Later, an encouraging promise is made to the leaders who faithfully fulfill their commission: "You will receive the unfading crown of glory" (1 Pet 5:4).

The Unbearable Burden of Individualism

"When you look at today's church, it is easy to see the prevalence of individualism. . . . Not too many of us have a vast repertoire of skills to be proud of, but most of us feel that . . . [leadership] is something that we have to do solo."[22]

—Henri J. M. Nouwen

God did not design his church to be led by isolated individuals. In what areas of your ministry are you attempting to lead on your own? If you're trying to lead by yourself, how might God be working behind the scenes to raise up a team of fellow leaders? What structures and relationships do you need to develop that will hold you accountable to God and to the people you lead?

Your Identity as a Fellow Elder, Faithful Witness, and Participant in Future Glory

Let's be transparent for a moment as we think about how Peter described himself—fellow elder, witness of sufferings, partaker of glory to come. As pastors in the local church, we all carry a sense of personal identity. Unfortunately, our identity in that role is not always akin to how Peter describes himself. Some pastors, particularly senior pastors, do not see themselves as fellow elders; they may instead see themselves as the only elder that matters. Every pastor must, however, see himself as a co-laborer with others in gospel ministry; this requires humility toward fellow elders and accountability to the congregation.

At the core, Peter is a witness. He believes the role of the shepherd includes the necessity of seeking lost sheep (Luke 15). He has confidence, as did Paul, that the gospel is the power of God unto salvation and is a word of hope that must be proclaimed even in the face of opposition and outright persecution. He is not afraid to be bold in his witness. Too often pastors limit their witness to corporate settings and fail to share the gospel with individuals. Consider the number of churches that have not seen one convert in the last year. What an indictment against the shepherds if they are not actively sharing the gospel! Those who aspire to lead the body of Christ should recognize that Peter seems to link the role of elder and witness— "possibly suggesting that one only becomes an elder by taking on the role of witness to the sufferings of Christ."[23]

Peter's witness landed him in a prison, yet he still identifies himself as a believer and leader who will endure momentary sufferings for a glory that is to come. Some pastors fail even to endure church turmoil because it is too much for them. How will such shepherds ever lead a flock to endure the life-ending persecution that may come against the church in the days ahead? Peter lived each day from the time of his restoration and commissioning to his death, knowing that he would suffer for the cause of Christ. It seems this knowledge did not constrain him but freed him. He was confident of what the future held, as there would be a day when he would again behold the glory of his Savior as he had done on the Mount of Transfiguration (Matt 17:1–13).[24] On that day, he would fully participate in God's glory and not just be an observer. Surely Peter longed for that day and for the affirmation that God was pleased with him (Matt 17:5). In a way, Peter's self-description becomes a mirror for us, a means of assessing our faithfulness as pastors. Peter intends to shape the identity of his "fellow elders" in Asia Minor, that they too would serve the body of believers as co-laborers, as bold witnesses, and as leaders who would faithfully endure to the end.

The Attitude of the Shepherd Leader

The responsibility to shepherd the flock was made clear, as was the attitude that each elder must possess. Peter instructs the elders to shepherd, to exercise oversight, to serve as models, to endure, and to anticipate an eternal reward. Accompanying these actions are attitudes of willingness, generosity, eagerness, meekness, and expectancy.[25]

Peter begins with the directive to guard the flock "of God" (1 Pet 5:2), reminding these elders that the sheep are not their property but God's. They are to understand themselves as under-shepherds and stewards of God's possession.[26] As I have suggested in this chapter, this shepherding responsibility can be summed up as protecting and preparing the flock. The elders must guard the flock from heretical influences that will divert the convictions and the affections of the people. They must lead through teaching and correction, always demonstrating a high ethic of care for the wellbeing of both the entire flock and for the individual. This guarding and leading demands the regular presence of the shepherd with the sheep. It is through the ministry of presence and teaching that the shepherd is best able to prepare the flock for any onslaught of opposition (internal and external) and Satanic attack. The shepherd is always attentive to what is happening inside the faith community and sensitive to what the people of God are facing from hostile cultures outside.

Part of shepherding is providing oversight—serving as an overseer—in the church.[27] Watching over the church entails "vigilant attention to threats that can disperse or destroy the flock."[28] Just as Paul connects shepherding and oversight in his farewell address to the Ephesian elders (Acts 20:28), so Peter makes the same connection here in 1 Pet 5:2. He seems convinced that "proper pastoral oversight of the Christian community is crucial if it is to survive external threat."[29]

This oversight is not to be compulsory, but is to be born out of a willing and eager disposition. Too often, elders find themselves leading because they must, or because it is their "job." And yes, there are days in the life of every elder that he must recall God's expectations of him and do what God calls him to do because it is his duty. But the point of caution comes when there are more days of duty than days of delight. This should be a warning sign—either your aspirations to serve as an elder were born out of selfish motives and they are showing, or you are relying on your own strength and you are empty. Either way, repentance is required. To serve as a pastor "simply because it offers a respectable and intellectually stimulating way of gaining a livelihood is to prostitute that sacred work."[30] Peter understood that if church leaders did not guard their own hearts, then a drive toward shameful gain would consume their actions, resulting in the destruction of the flock.

Jesus was clear and so was Peter: The role of elder in the church demands an approach of leading through imitation rather than intimidation. In 1 Pet 5:3, he explicitly rules out domineering over the people (compare Matt 20:25; Mark 10:42); instead, the elders are instructed to be examples to those who have been placed under their care, or in their charge. In using this phase, "those in your charge," Peter is pointing toward a divine assignment of a particular lot or portion of God's flock to a specific group of elders. As we consider this image, our thinking may immediately move to the division of the conquered Promised Land among the tribes of Israel, and if so, that thinking would be correct. "The new 'real estate' in the new community is the people themselves, clustered under caring guardians."[31] It is with this particular allotment of people that the shepherds are expected to live worthy lives.

Peter reminds the elders that if they faithfully endure to the end while shepherding, overseeing, and modeling well, there is an eternal reward awaiting them. He seems to be encouraging an expectant mind-set among these men. He is reminding them that they, like the sheep, are exiles who are sojourning through their earthly lives with an eye toward eternity. They will suffer as elders and will be primary targets of the evil one, but a "crown of unfading glory" is in their future when the chief shepherd appears.[32] The temptation for all of us is to seek momentary glory instead of lasting glory. The shiny allure of stardom draws us to lust after fame rather than to serve the brothers and sisters with humility. When that happens, we have forgotten our role as under-shepherds and attempted to usurp the glory of the chief shepherd.

In light of the directive given by Peter to his fellow elders to "shepherd the flock of God that is among you," we must ask, "But how?" Peter certainly speaks to that in these verses as noted above—willingly and eagerly exercising oversight, not in a domineering manner but in such a way that you prove to be examples to the flock. This is helpful, but let us press this question further. In this letter to these churches, how did Peter fulfill his commission to care for the flock of God?

It seems from the rest of this letter that he sought to do this by *shaping the people's identity* and by *equipping them to live holy lives* in a world that was hostile toward their Savior. He rooted the flock's identity in Christ, teaching them that they were redeemed sojourners, living stones, and suffering servants. He desired to equip them to live out that new identity in a world that would vehemently oppose all attempts. Just as Peter instructed the elders to be an example to the flock, so he becomes one for us as we consider the formation of God's people. In the remainder of this chapter, we will examine just how he went about shaping identity and equipping the saints in the churches in Asia Minor.

Overseer

Translates Greek *episkopos,* also translated as "bishop"

Overseers are church leaders who are appointed to guide the congregation and to guard the church's teachings. Their lives are to be marked by a godly character, a strong reputation outside the church, faithfulness in marriage and parenting, a capacity to teach, avoidance of drunkenness, honesty with finances, and Christian maturity (1 Tim 3:1–7; see also Titus 1:6–9). It is clear that the words "overseer," "elder," and "shepherd" referred to the same office in the New Testament era. Paul "summoned the elders" of the Ephesian church and then reminded them that they were "overseers" who had been appointed "to shepherd the church of God" (Acts 20:18, 28). After the New Testament era, the term "overseer" (or "bishop") very quickly came to describe an elder who guided multiple churches in a particular city or region and who oversaw other elders.

Actions and Attitudes of Shepherd Leaders

	Actions	*Attitudes*
1 Pet 5:2	shepherd the flock exercise oversight	willingness generosity eagerness
1 Pet 5:3	live humbly	meekness
1 Pet 5:4	endure faithfully anticipate a reward	expectancy

Forming the Identity of the Flock

Peter models for his fellow elders what it means to root believers' identity in Christ. He begins by focusing on their identity as redeemed sojourners (1 Pet 1:1–12) with the intent of changing their perspective on earthly life and the trials they will face. He then deepens their identity by pointing toward the truth: They are a royal priesthood who are living stones (2:5–9) expected to reflect this holiness in the normal pathways of life (2:13–3:7). He finishes by exalting Jesus as the righteous suffering shepherd who models what it means to live as suffering servants (3:8–4:19).

Forming the Flock as Redeemed Sojourners

Growing up, I remember my favorite question to ask when we were on our way to the family cabin in the mountains: "When will we get there?" It always felt like it took forever to arrive. I looked forward to hiking, playing in the creek, fishing, sliding down slippery rocks, tubing on the

Chattahoochee, eating fudge, smelling bacon cooking in the morning, and, of course, playing king of the hill (of leaves) in the late fall. I was definitely more worried about arriving at our destination than I was about the journey.

If we think about our lives as a long road trip, we too might be asking, when will we get there? In that case, "there" is our final destination in eternity and heaven. But we do not have to be reminded that, for most of us, it is a long and sometimes treacherous journey from birth to death. From rebirth to life everlasting. The apostle Peter evidences a desire for his brothers and sisters in Asia Minor to not only survive the earthly sojourn but to live it in such a way as to glorify Christ and proclaim his good news to a hostile world. In 1 Peter, we hear a shepherd leading his flock through the twists and turns of life. In his leading, he seeks to ground the flock's identity in the gospel of Jesus Christ, knowing that it is the only foundation that will sustain them in the turbulence ahead.

Peter begins this identity formation process in 1 Pet 1:1–2 by labeling his readers "elect exiles."[33] He is writing to those who make up God's people and are displaced from their true home and awaiting the time when God will bring them to the place for which they now long.[34] As he considers the saving work of the Trinity, he breaks into praise: "Blessed be the God and Father of our Lord Jesus Christ!" (1:3).[35] Peter speaks of a salvation that has been initiated by God himself, displaying his great mercy with the confidence that his power will keep them until that day (1:3–5).[36] Peter wants these people to be convinced when they look in the mirror that they are looking at a redeemed person upon whom God has lavished his love and mercy. But he knows that is not enough. He wants to balance that eternal truth with the momentary reality that Christians still have a life to live between now and then. It is not enough for them to see themselves as the redeemed; they must also see themselves as *redeemed sojourners.*

We would do well to imagine how the road trip called life would be different if we lived every day knowing that this might be the last day before we are martyred for our faith. Peter understood what it meant to have his identity rooted in Christ, but he also equally understood that his journey on earth was just that—a journey on a way to an eternal destiny. So he is impressing on the flock that their identity is that of redeemed sojourners, knowing that this reality should bring a sense of endurance for facing trials and suffering, a sense of hope for eternal relief, a sense of inexpressible joy in the moment, a sense of deep love for Christ, and a sense of urgency for the shared mission.

In light of his readers' identity as redeemed sojourners, Peter instructs them to set their hopes "on the grace to be brought to you at the revelation of Jesus Christ" (1 Pet 1:13). Peter then does what good pastors do: He assures the congregation that the living out of their redeemed identity is powered by nothing less than the grace of God. He positions bookends of grace in 1 Pet 1:3 ("he has caused us to be born again" ESV) and 2:5 ("you . . . are being built up as a spiritual house" ESV) on each side of three imperatives: live holy lives (1:14–16), love your fellow sojourners (1:22–23), and long for the truth of God (2:1–3).[37]

Forming the Flock as Living Stones

Peter continues to form his flock's identity by telling them, "You yourselves like living stones are being built up as a spiritual house, to be a holy priesthood" (1 Pet 2:5 ESV). Coming on the heels of celebrating their redemption, these words emphasize that these believers had been made a part of the most amazing and glorious house ever constructed. It will never fade, it will never lose its glory, it is permanent, it is eternal. It is the church—the very people of God. And God himself is the designer and builder.

The language that is used in 1 Pet 2:4–10 points toward the Jewish temple and the role of the priests there.[38] In the Old Testament, the temple was the place where God promised to meet with his people. Together, the priests and the people were responsible for representing God and his rule to the world. But the Israelites rebelled against God's authority and were exiled as a measure of discipline, with the temple ultimately being destroyed. However, God had promised that one day he would provide a new temple with a sure foundation. Thus, Peter points to Jesus as the cornerstone of this new temple as he quotes Isa 28:16: "For it stands in Scripture: 'Behold, I am laying in Zion a stone, a cornerstone chosen and precious, and whoever believes in him will not be put to shame.'"

Peter tells his readers that Jesus (2:4), chosen and precious in the sight of God, was rejected by humanity and crucified upon a cross but victoriously raised from the dead as a living stone.[39] For those who reject Jesus and his gospel, he has become "a stone of stumbling, and a rock of offense" (2:8). But for those who do believe in Jesus, Peter likens the experience as redeemed children to that of being living stones (2:4–5).[40] They are a part of something much larger and grander than themselves. They are members of the structure that Christ is constructing for his glory (Matt 16:18). As a royal priesthood, believers have the responsibility of displaying God's greatness through devoted lives. Pastors must equip the flock to live differently from the world even as they remain within the world.

Forming the Flock as Suffering Servants

Do you remember being given horrible-tasting medicine as a child? The stuff that parents would virtually have to hold you down to take? Awful! But for parents and children today, that is no longer a struggle. We can walk up to our local pharmacy counter and ask the pharmacists to do the amazing and make bad-tasting medicine taste delicious. If you look on almost any pharmacy website, you will find an advertisement for something akin to the phrase "Fool your taste buds." It will then proceed to explain how parents can be heroes for $2.99—by making a bitter medicine taste like strawberry swirl or chocolate or bubblegum. You can even obtain prescription-flavoring services for your favorite pet, to trick your dog into thinking that the antibiotic prescribed by the veterinarian is really crispy bacon or chicken pot pie.[41]

Just as the pharmaceutical industry has labored to hide harsh medicinal tastes, pastors may be tempted do the same thing in their descriptions of the Christian life. Many churches and pastors either inadvertently or intentionally do this very thing. Even some of the most popular Christian writers and preachers speak as if all things will be smooth sailing if you live right in the Lord. What a distortion of Christianity and the very core of the gospel!

Peter, who identifies himself as a witness of the sufferings of Christ, does just the opposite. He does not sugarcoat the Christian experience. He makes it clear that the Christian journey is marked by suffering and that Jesus himself is the model for how his followers are to endure such suffering. Peter wanted his readers to know that Jesus's suffering provided a pattern for how to imitate God in times of affliction.[42] "For to this you have been called," Peter wrote, "because Christ also suffered for you, leaving you an example, so that you might follow in his steps" (1 Pet 2:21 ESV).

Peter makes no attempt to hide the reality of Christian suffering. Why? In part, it is likely because he knew that some of his readers might be tempted to believe the Christian life should be free from difficulty, sickness, persecution, and suffering. Some of his readers might even have assumed that suffering, especially unjust suffering, demonstrated a failure of God's love.[43] Peter the shepherd refused to allow such ignorance among his people regarding the reality of suffering. That is why he wrote, "Beloved, do not be surprised at the fiery trial when it comes upon you to test you, as though something strange were happening to you" (1 Pet 4:12 ESV). Trials and suffering are a means of testing our faith (1:6–7). They are normative for the Christian's life. Peter went further to point toward the situation in the church as a whole: "The same kind of sufferings are being experienced by your fellow believers throughout the world" (5:9). Suffering is a reality in a fallen world. Then and now, it is happening to Christians around the world and will continue to happen until the end of time (1 Pet 2:21; 5:8).

Peter the fellow elder is concerned that the churches understand that no suffering comes their way except through the hand of their Creator God, according to his will (1 Pet 4:19). Right theology would permit right responses as they encountered suffering due to their strong commitment to the gospel.[44] Peter presses the truth that God uses suffering as a mechanism for sanctification (4:1). He teaches that suffering yields a blessing for the believer, brings glory to God, and purifies the church (4:14–17). Knowing that they will likely doubt God's goodness in the midst of suffering, Peter points them toward God's grace: "And after you have suffered a little while, the God of all grace, who has called you to his eternal glory in Christ, will himself restore, confirm, strengthen, and establish you" (1 Pet 5:10 ESV). Peter wanted these disciples to see that their story was embedded in God's story of suffering, redemption, and glory. Shepherd leaders today must do no less among their flock if these people are to be prepared to endure hostility now and in the future.

What about You?

Christ-centered leadership is followership exercised with biblical wisdom in the context of community for which God has given us responsibility.

- Are you leading as a follower, accountable both to God and to the people you lead?

- Are you actively protecting the flock from false teachings and preparing them to live in a society that may become increasingly hostile toward the Christian faith?
- Are you watching over the particular sheep that God has assigned to you?
- Are you living a life that is worthy of imitation?
- Are you watching over the flock of God with a heart that is willing, generous, eager, meek, and expectant?
- What kind of shepherd do you want to be in five years? What changes do you need to make today to become this kind of shepherd?

Leading a Community of Sojourners, Stones, and Servants

Through this letter written to Christians on the verge of persecution, Peter modeled for his fellow elders how to lead their churches to remain faithful even in a hostile society. Peter seems to have been convinced that the best way to prepare Christians to face persecution was to remind them of their identity in Christ. He celebrated their union with Christ and pointed them toward their identities as redeemed sojourners. It was clear to Peter that these disciples needed to see themselves on an earthly journey for which the indwelling Spirit of God had empowered them. They needed to know that they were part of a larger community of sojourners who together constituted the temple of God, each one of them a living stone. As living stones, they were to represent the holiness of God in the context of a lost and hostile world. As an apostle and elder, Peter desired nothing less than that they evidence their faithfulness as suffering servants of the crucified and resurrected Messiah.

This word that Peter declared is deeply needed today. Western cultures in particular are marked by growing apathy toward religion in general and the Christian faith in particular.[45] The rise of secularism has marginalized orthodox Christian convictions regarding human sexuality, the value of human life, and the very nature of reality. Throughout Europe, Australia, and North America in particular, church leaders are wrestling with the question of how to lead people to live lives filled with grace and truth in increasingly secular contexts.

So how do we do this?

This first letter from Peter provides a place for us to start. As pastors, we must embrace our identities as suffering under-shepherds who live as fellow elders, bold witnesses, and partakers of a glory that is yet to be revealed. By persisting in patterns of presence, provision, and protection, we entrench our people in their identity as redeemed sojourners, living stones, and suffering servants. When we are present among our people to provide for them, we become more deeply aware of the challenges they face. When we are passionate about rescuing and protecting them from harm, we can no longer remain inattentive to the cultural shifts that abound around us, and we become increasingly sensitive to the needs of those who are less privileged.

Each pastor has been providentially assigned a portion of the flock to oversee. With that assignment comes accountability; it was true in Peter's day and it is still remains true today. May we as under-shepherds be found faithful "when the chief Shepherd appears" so that we may receive "the unfading crown of glory" from the King of kings (1 Pet 5:4).

Leadership Definition, Dynamics, and Diagnostics

	Leadership Definition	Leadership Dynamic	Leadership Diagnostics
Union with Christ	*The Christ-following leader—living as a bearer of God's image in union with Christ and his people—*	The shepherd is a follower of God's way who is present among the sheep. The Christ-following shepherd rightly understands the shepherd's identity as one who has been given the responsibility to oversee people purchased by God. This responsibility calls the shepherd to live a life worthy of emulation and marked by endurance. Peter called his fellow elders to shepherd, to oversee, to model faithfulness, and to endure suffering as they awaited the Chief Shepherd's return.	Are you fulfilling your shepherding responsibilities faithfully? Are you doing so with the right attitudes—willingness, generosity, eagerness, meekness, and expectancy? The brothers and sisters among whom you serve are a gift from the Lord. Allow that reality to shape every interaction with them.
Communion with Christ's People	*develops a diverse community of fellow laborers who are equipped and empowered to pursue shared goals*	The shepherd uses his power to provide for the sheep. The Christ-following shepherd seeks to form the identity of fellow believers by aiding their understanding of who they are in Christ as they seek to follow Christ. Peter shaped the identity of the believers in Asia Minor as he taught them to live as redeemed sojourners, living stones, and suffering servants.	As a leader, are you focused primarily on achieving personal or organizational goals? Do you recognize the importance not merely of moving toward goals in front of you but also of empowering the people around you? As a shepherd, do not lose sight of the crucial importance of using your God-given influence to shape your fellow believers' identities in Christ.

	Leadership Definition	Leadership Dynamic	Leadership Diagnostics
Mission in the World	*that fulfill the creation mandate and the Great Commission in submission to the Word of God.*	The shepherd is willing to take personal risks to protect and to rescue the sheep. The Christ-following shepherd serves sacrificially so that fellow believers are equipped to live distinct and devoted lives in a world that is hostile toward their Savior. Peter prepared his fellow believers to proclaim the gospel and to live holy lives in a culture that despised their Savior.	As a shepherd among your flock, are you pressing your people toward personal engagement in gospel proclamation? Are you taking risks that model sacrificial sharing of the gospel? Cast a vision among your people of their shared identity as redeemed sojourners who take risks for the purpose of inviting others to join them on their journey in the kingdom of Christ.

Further Reading

Elliott, John H. "Elders as Leaders in 1 Peter and the Early Church." *HTS* 64 (2008): 681–695.

Hiebert, Edmond. "Counsel for Christ's Under-Shepherds." *BSac* 139 (1982): 330–341.

Laniak, Timothy. *Shepherds after My Own Heart*. Downers Grove, IL: InterVarsity, 2006.

Schreiner, Thomas. "Overseeing and Serving the Church in the General and Pastoral Epistles." In *Shepherding God's Flock*. Edited by Benjamin Merkle and Thomas Schreiner. Grand Rapids: Kregel, 2014.

Worshiping the God Who Goes before Us

"Lead on, O King Eternal,
The day of march has come;

Henceforth in fields of conquest
Thy tents shall be our home.
Through days of preparation
Thy grace has made us strong;
And now, O King Eternal,
We lift our battle song.

"Lead on, O King Eternal,
Till sin's fierce war shall cease,
And holiness shall whisper
The sweet amen of peace.
For not with swords' loud clashing,
Nor roll of stirring drums;
With deeds of love and mercy
The heav'nly kingdom comes.

"Lead on, O King Eternal,
We follow, not with fears,
For gladness breaks like morning
Where'er Thy face appears.
Thy cross is lifted o'er us,
We journey in its light;
The crown awaits the conquest;
Lead on, O God of might."
    —Ernest W. Shurtleff, 1888

Responding to the God Who Goes before Us

O Father of the Suffering Shepherd who has gone before us
    as the sacrifice who opened a path into your presence and
    as the shepherd who has shown us how to lead,
Empower us by your Spirit to exchange
    our feeble visions of the future for your never-failing revelation,
    our delusions of power for your example of servanthood, and
    the ugliness of our self-exaltation for the splendor of participation
        in your sufferings now and
        in your glory forever. Amen.

Conclusion:
Leadership as Followership that Leads to the Cross

From the moment that God formed our primeval parents, his design was for godly leaders to guide others by following God's way in submission to God's Word. The first human being was called to lead the second human being as they ruled a garden temple together in submission to God's greater reign. Their rebellion against their Creator distorted this pattern, but not even the contagion of sin could completely destroy God's good design. The leadership roles that God ordained in the Old Testament—prophets, priests, judges, kings—continued to be characterized by followership of God's ways in the context of communities submitted to God's word.

Each of these old covenant offices was wholly fulfilled in the flesh of Jesus Christ, and every leader among Christ's people today has been called to follow Christ's example. The way to follow Christ as a leader is not, however, by attempting to live among God's people as a prophet, priest, judge, or king. The role of the prophet is accessible to anyone in the church on whom the Holy Spirit may choose to pour out this gift, and the whole people of God in union with Christ participates equally in the offices of judge, king, and priest.

What Jesus modeled for us was not an office of leadership but a way of life that reshapes every aspect of leadership. This way of life pulls us away from striving to situate ourselves in particular offices of leadership. Where it leads us instead is toward the habits of a shepherd, the heart of a servant, and the humble disposition of a fellow participant in the sufferings of Christ.

When that happens, the moral aspect of our leadership becomes grounded in God's vision of justice. Our understanding of power is relativized because any power we possess is recognized as an undeserved gift delegated by God. And our mission is reshaped to fit God's vision for the redemption of his people and the flourishing of his world. This perspective on leadership will not work for those whose lives are not conformed to the cross of Jesus Christ—and it is not supposed to.

A Work of Sabotage

"Christianity," C. S. Lewis explained in *Mere Christianity,* "is the story of how the rightful king has landed, you might say landed in disguise, and is calling us to take part in a great campaign of sabotage."[1] His point was that the world, the flesh, and the devil do possess some power in the cosmos as it currently stands, but their defeat has already been assured by the arrival of the rightful king. Until the King of kings is revealed, those of us who have thrown in our lot with him are called to work out his victory by sabotaging the presuppositions of this present darkness.

This book is meant to be a work of sabotage. The two of us have watched the world's presuppositions about power and visionary leadership wedge their way into too many church leaders' leadership practices—including our own. In some cases, these assumptions have been garbed in biblical and theological language. More often than not, they have been imported with the best of intentions by people who sincerely long to lead like Jesus.

Our goal in this book has been to sabotage these deficient perspectives on leadership not by attacking them directly but by following the pathway proposed by Augustine of Hippo: "to teach, to delight, and to persuade."[2] We have taught by taking a comprehensive look at the whole canon of Scripture.[3] We have worked to cultivate delight by calling attention to the beauty of what God's Word has to say about leadership. Our hope is that, as a result, you have been persuaded to develop a deeper and richer perspective on what it means to lead as a follower of Jesus Christ.

Leading like Jesus Leads to the Cross

There is much to learn about leadership from the life of Jesus—but the vision of leadership that we find in his Word is not likely to earn him top billing on the leadership shelf in your local bookstore. The road to his kingdom did not, after all, land him in an exquisite palace or an oak-paneled boardroom. It took him to a cross—a throne of splintered wood, where his only robes were the flayed ribbons of his own flesh and where the scepter extending from his hand was not a polished staff but a bloodstained spike. Everyone who trusts in him has been called to join him in this suffering and to be united with him in this death. For leaders in particular, the cross means that there is no depth of dereliction or sorrow to which we can be called where our King has not already been. "The way of the Christian leader is not the way of upward mobility in which our world has invested so much," Henri J. M. Nouwen has reminded us, "but the way of downward mobility ending on the cross."[4] That is the path of the one who leads as a follower of the God who goes before us.

ENDNOTES

Foreword

1. This foreword is adapted from R. Albert Mohler, *The Conviction to Lead: Twenty-Five Principles for Leadership That Matters* (Minneapolis: Bethany House, 2012), 133–137. Used by permission. Scripture references are to the NASB.

2. David F. Wells, *God in the Wasteland: The Reality of Truth in a World of Fading Dreams* (Grand Rapids: Eerdmans, 1994), 114.

Chapter One: What If Jesus Didn't Lead like Jesus?

1. Francesco Padoa, "Sopravvive a un ictus e scopre nella risonanza l'immagine di Gesù," *Il Messaggero*, September 22, 2015, https://www.ilmessaggero.it/primopiano/cronaca /ictus_ges_ugrave_risonanza_radiografia_miracolo-1258887.html; Kevin Quinn, "Family Claims to See Image of Jesus in Moldy Shower," ABC.com, May 31, 2012, http://abc13.com /archive/8682378; "Image of Jesus 'Appears in Frying Pan,'" *Telegraph*, March 12, 2010, https://www.telegraph.co.uk/news/newstopics/howaboutthat/7424976/Image-of-Jesus -appears-in-a-frying-pan.html; Tyler White, "Central Texas Man Selling Tortilla He Claims Has Jesus' Face on It," My San Antonio, February 25, 2015, https://www.mysanantonio .com/news/local/article/Tortilla-with-face-of-Jesus-Christ-now-for-sale-6101013.php . Although claims of acheiropoieta have a long history, these particular phenomena seem more likely to be expressions of pareidolia. In pareidolia, individuals perceive and interpret "novel or nonsense" shapes in terms of "familiar real-world objects" that they have observed previously. See Joel Voss, Kara Federmeier, and Ken Paller, "The Potato Chip Really Does Look like Elvis! Neural Hallmarks of Conceptual Processing Associated with Finding Novel Shapes Subjectively Meaningful," *Cerebral Cortex* 22, no. 10 (October 2012): 2364.

2. Bob Briner, *The Management Methods of Jesus* (Nashville: Nelson, 2005), 33–35, 67–68.

3. Ken Blanchard and Phil Hodges, *Lead like Jesus* (Nashville: Nelson, 2008), 13.

4. Laurie Beth Jones, *Jesus, CEO* (New York: Hachette, 1995), Kindle edition, locations 138, 211–259.

5. The leadership principles that form the framework for *Jesus on Leadership* by C. Gene Wilkes (Nashville: LifeWay, 1998) are (1) being humble, (2) being a follower, (3) demonstrating greatness through service, (4) taking risks, (5) finding power through servanthood, (6) sharing responsibility, and (7) building a team—each one of which is paralleled in other popular leadership texts that examine leadership as exemplified in the lives and teachings of Gautama Buddha, Mahatma Gandhi, Confucius, and Kautilya. According to *Being Buddha at Work* by B. J. Gallagher and Franz Metcalf, imitation of the Buddha results in being "humble," choosing "simplicity and service," "taking risks," practicing "servant leadership," sharing

rewards, and building "success teams"—nearly all of the same patterns that Wilkes finds in the Gospels, *Being Buddha at Work* (San Francisco: Berrett-Koehler, 2012), 28, 102–108, 164. According to Nancy Spears's *Buddha 9 to 5*, leading according to the teachings of the Buddha means "balancing your strength and ambition with gentle humility" and vowing not merely to lead but "to serve your employees," *Buddha 9 to 5* (Avon: Adams, 2007), 19, 33, 151. In *A Higher Standard of Leadership*, Keshavan Nair finds in the leadership practices of Gandhi a "spirit of service" that results in the reconciliation of "power with service," *A Higher Standard of Leadership* (San Francisco: Berrett-Koehler, 1994, 1997), 57–94. Further similarities may be found in Kautilya's concept of the king as the upholder of mutual righteous duty and Confucius' teachings regarding social equity, Morgan Witzel, *Leadership from the Masters* (London: Bloomsbury, 2014), 47–56. Both of these include aspects of what Wilkes describes as "Jesus' power—through service," *Jesus on Leadership*, 159–168.

6. The reason that these leadership principles work is because God created a cosmos in which leadership, management, administration, and motivation were present prior to humanity's fall into sin. Although the cosmos is fallen and groans even now for the fulfillment of the kingdom that God guaranteed through the resurrection of Jesus Christ, fragments of the primeval order remain, held together by the power of Christ (Col 1:17). The orderliness of the universe is, in some sense, an anonymous theophany. Because fragments of order remain even in a fallen world, it is possible for an unregenerate person to be unaware of Christ's power—or even to deny his presence completely—and still be an effective leader. Patterns of effective leadership have been distorted because of sin, but portions of these patterns are still present and available by common grace to every human being. There is, therefore, a clear place for the study of leadership principles that are as accessible to unregenerate persons as to the regenerate. The specific difficulty with the "Jesus on leadership" genre is that leadership practices observed in the life of Jesus are distilled into common grace principles that decontextualize these practices and treat Jesus more as a sage than as the incarnate God, crucified and risen Lord, and coming King. The living incarnation of God's redeeming grace is thus reduced to a guru of common grace.

7. The inspiration for this imagery comes from a critical review of Sheryl Sandberg's book *Lean In*, found in Anne Applebaum, "How to Succeed in Business," *New York Review*, June 6, 2013, http://www.nybooks.com/articles/2013/06/06/sheryl-sandberg-how-succeed-business/.

8. Paul House, *Bonhoeffer's Seminary Vision* (Wheaton: Crossway, 2015), 139.

9. John Calvin had this to say about unregenerate philosophers: "Let that admirable light of truth shining in them teach us that the human mind, though fallen and perverted from its wholeness, is nevertheless clothed and ornamented with God's excellent gifts. If we regard the Spirit of God as the sole fountain of truth, we shall neither reject the truth itself, nor despise it wherever it shall appear, unless we wish to dishonor the Spirit of God. . . . Let us, accordingly, learn by their example how many gifts the Lord left to human nature even after its true goodness was plundered," *Institutio Christianae Religionis* 2:2:15. The same could be said regarding researchers in the field of leadership. The human mind after the fall has, however, been epistemically impaired such that human beings are capable of reasoning wrongly about what they observe; furthermore, the phenomena that are observed are fallen from their original good estate as well. For detailed analysis of the noetic effect of the fall, see Timothy Paul Jones, "John Calvin and the Problem of Philosophical Apologetics," *Perspectives on Religious Studies* 23 (1996): 387–403, and Dewey Hoitenga, "The Noetic Effects of Sin," in *Calvin Theological Journal* 38 (2003): 68–102. Deriving leadership principles from the fallen cosmos by means of a fallen intellect—while potentially useful—thus always runs the risk of incorporating patterns of fallenness into leadership. Practices such as

behaviorism and utilitarian management, for example, may work to achieve a leader's objectives, but it is likely that such practices derive more from human fallenness than from God's creation design for creatures formed in his image. A biblical theology of leadership must, therefore, form a foundation for Christian leadership that precedes and directs any quest for usable leadership principles that have persisted in the fallen cosmos.

10. In *The Management Methods of Jesus*, for example, the parable of the landowner who paid one-hour workers the same wages as the laborers that worked all day is presented as proof that each employee should receive what he or she has earned regardless of what anyone else thinks. "Max was being paid all that he had been promised and had not performed as exceptionally as Bill. If we were being fair to Max, we shouldn't worry about what he thinks of Bill's compensation. To do so is to cheat Bill out of his rightful reward," Briner, *The Management Methods of Jesus*, 67. This interpretation stands in stark contrast to the parable's central point, which seems to be that the laborers received what the landowner graciously gave them regardless of what they may or may not have deserved. Contrast Briner's interpretation with New Testament scholar Craig Blomberg's more appropriate presentation of the central point of the parable: "We are fools if we appeal to God for justice rather than grace. . . . All who are truly saved are equally precious in God's sight and equally rewarded," *Matthew* (Nashville: B&H, 1992), 305.

11. Scot McKnight, *The King Jesus Gospel* (Grand Rapids: Zondervan, 2011), 50, 118.

12. Zach Bradley, *The Sending Church Defined* (Knoxville: Upstream Collective, 2015), 15.

13. The authors of *The God Who Goes before You* assume the biblical text as it stands in the sixty-six books of the biblical canon to constitute an inerrant collection of texts that has been copied with sufficient accuracy to preserve its divinely intended meaning, which is centered in Christ and his kingdom. The method followed here has, in general, followed Brian Rosner's definition of biblical theology as "theological interpretation of Scripture in and for the church. It proceeds with historical and literary sensitivity and seeks to analyze and synthesize the Bible's teaching about God and his relations to the world on its own terms, maintaining sight of the Bible's overarching narrative and Christocentric focus," "Biblical Theology," *New Dictionary of Biblical Theology*, ed. T. D. Alexander et al. (Downers Grove, IL: InterVarsity, 2000), 10. Some exegetes have strongly emphasized the necessity of limiting conclusions regarding biblical texts to that which was intended by the original human author. However, what God has providentially bequeathed to us in the Scriptures are not authorial intentions but Spirit-inspired texts that may convey meanings far greater than the initial human authors intended or even imagined. Later meanings that are rightly derived from these words are never incongruent with the text as written by the original authors and conveyed to the original readers, but these later meanings may not necessarily have been envisioned by the initial human authors. This recognition does not allow an ever-evolving breadth of meanings tied together by the continuity of grace as methodologies such as the one proposed, for example, by Richard Hays would seem to allow. See, e.g., *Echoes of Scripture in the Letters of Paul* (New Haven: Yale University Press, 1993), chapter 5. What is possible through careful exegesis in light of the entire canon is the mining of a multilayered ore of meanings from the biblical texts that—though perhaps not intended in every instance by the initial human authors—are clearly congruent with the Spirit-inspired words that these authors wrote and that have been preserved for the church by the power of God.

14. David Prince, "The Necessity of a Christocentric Kingdom-Focused Model of Expository Preaching" (PhD diss., SBTS, 2011), 29.

15. This triad is derived from Richard Lints, *The Fabric of Theology* (Grand Rapids: Eerdmans, 1993), 293. Lints based the triad on three interpretive horizons proposed by

Edmund Clowney: (1) immediate context, (2) context in the particular period of revelation, and (3) context in the entirety of revelation. See also Edmund Clowney, *Preaching and Biblical Theology* (Grand Rapids: Eerdmans, 1961), 16.

16. This approach assumes complementary and progressive intertextuality—that is to say, later meanings do not dethrone earlier meanings and later meanings emerge from faithful exegesis of the initial text. Douglas Moo has suggested the term *sensus praegnans* ("sense of being pregnant," i.e., awareness that meanings may be present in the text that are not fully formed or visible until a later time) to describe this phenomenon, sidestepping the many problems inherent in the term *sensus plenior* ("fuller sense"). See Douglas Moo, "The Problem of *Sensus Plenior*," *Hermeneutics, Authority, and Canon*, ed. D. A. Carson (Grand Rapids: Zondervan, 1986). For further discussion, see G. K. Beale, *A New Testament Biblical Theology* (Grand Rapids: Baker, 2011), 3–15.

17. This approach stands in stark and deliberate contrast to the hermeneutical method proposed by Walter Kaiser, who has argued that "it is a mark of eisegesis, not exegesis, to borrow freight that appears chronologically later in the text and to transport it back and unload it on an earlier passage simply because both or all of the passages involved share the same canon," Walter Kaiser, *Toward an Exegetical Theology* (Grand Rapids: Baker, 1981), 82–83.

18. Augustine of Hippo, *De civitate Dei*, 16:2.

19. The dynamics described here differ from the extracted principles that we have critiqued in the "Jesus on leadership" genre in at least two ways: (1) The dynamics that we describe are grounded in the work of God in Christ in such a way that they cannot be pursued effectively apart from his explicit presence and power, and (2) these dynamics emerge not from isolated acts or events in Scripture but from Scripture read and understood as a coherent whole. For complementary critiques of the misuse of Scripture in popular Christian leadership literature, see, e.g., Lewis Parks and Bruce Birch, *Ducking Spears, Dancing Madly* (Nashville: Abingdon, 2004), 8–10, and Arthur Boers, *Servants and Fools* (Nashville: Abingdon, 2015), Kindle edition, location 947.

20. These three dynamics represent an adaptation of the triad of truth, power, and morals presented by Geerhardus Vos in his lectures on Christology. According to Vos, "There are three spheres in which human beings live and must live: the spheres of truth, of power, and of moral relationship toward God. Because of sin, abnormality has occurred in each of these spheres. . . . In the sphere of truth, [the Mediator] must be a Prophet; in the sphere of power, our King; and in the sphere of moral relationship between God and us, our Priest. One can consider man in three kinds of relationships. First, one can descend from God to man; then one can ascend from man to God; and finally one can conceive of man in relation to his environment. Each of these relationships corresponds to one of the offices of the Mediator. He stands for God before us as Prophet, for us before God as Priest, and to our benefit toward our environment as King," Geerhardus Vos, *Christology*, vol. 3 of *Reformed Dogmatics*, ed. and trans. Richard Gaffin (Bellingham, WA: Lexham, 2015), 86. Jesus as king reveals leadership as right use of power and restores normal relations with our environment; Jesus as prophet reveals leadership as proclamation of truth received directly from God; and Jesus as priest reveals leadership as the pursuit of justice in the context of a covenant community gathered before God. These recognitions from Vos shaped the treatment of kingship, prophecy, and priesthood in chapters 3 and 4 of *The God Who Goes before You*.

21. Daniel Montgomery with Jared Kennedy, *Leadership Mosaic* (Wheaton: Crossway, 2016), ebook, chapter 1.

22. David Prince, "Top 20 Christ-Centered Expository Preaching Checklist," Prince on Preaching, June 18, 2014, www.davidprince.com/2014/06/18/top-20-christ-centered -expository-preaching-checklist; David Prince, "How Does Counseling Help Your Preaching?"

(video), Prince on Preaching, April 25, 2014, www.davidprince.com/2014/04/25/counseling
-help-preaching.

23. Peter Northouse, *Leadership*, 6th ed. (Thousand Oaks, CA: SAGE, 2013), 5.

24. Peter Drucker and Joseph Maciariello, *Management,* revised edition (New York: HarperCollins, 2008), 290.

25. Warren Bennis, *On Becoming a Leader,* revised and updated edition (Sydney: Accessible, 2008), 248.

26. John Maxwell, *The 17 Essential Qualities of a Team Player* (Nashville: Nelson, 2002), 93.

27. Kevin Kruse, "What Is Leadership?" *Forbes*, April 9, 2013, https://www.forbes.com /sites/kevinkruse/2013/04/09/what-is-leadership/#7e4e31595b90.

28. Bernard Bass, *The Bass Handbook of Leadership*, 4th ed. (New York: Free Press, 2008), 23.

29. Joseph Rost, *Leadership for the Twenty-First Century* (London: Praeger, 1993), 7. Rost suggested that practitioners use intuitive skills of perception to determine if the phenomenon they are observing is indeed leadership. In other words, they know leadership when they see it, but they may not be able to articulate clearly the key characteristics by which they are making this judgment. Aubrey Malphurs similarly suggests that when Christian leaders and speakers attempt to define leadership, "definitions are often based more on . . . subjective experiences or anecdotal observations than on Scripture or good research," Aubrey Malphurs, *Being Leaders* (Grand Rapids: Baker, 2003), 10. The difficulty with this approach to defining leadership is, of course, that it lacks a clearly articulated objective base. Definitions may be incomplete, inadequate, and even incorrect, but they are necessary for meaningful communication.

30. John Maxwell, *The 21 Irrefutable Laws of Leadership*, rev. ed. (Nashville: Nelson, 2007), 16; Peter Drucker, "Peter Drucker on Leadership," interview with Rich Karlgaard, *Forbes*, November 19, 2004, https://www.forbes.com/2004/11/19/cz_rk_1119drucker. html#59eed216f484.

31. Peter Northouse, *Leadership*, 5th ed. (Los Angeles: SAGE, 2009), 2. Northouse provides six categories that he understands to be the broad areas of leadership research: group processes; personality; acts of behavior; power relationships; transformational processes; and skills. *The God Who Goes before You* focuses primarily on the personality and power relationship domains.

32. Bass, *The Bass Handbook of Leadership*, 17.

33. For examples of the differentiation between power and roles, see J. R. P. French, "A Formal Theory of Social Power," in *Psychological Review* 63 (1956): 63, 181–194. See also B. H. Rave and J. R. P. French, "Group Support, Legitimate Power, and Social Influence," *Journal of Personality* 26 (1958): 26, 400–409; B. H. Rave and J. R. P. French, "Legitimate Power, Coercive Power, and Observability in Social Influence," *Sociometry* 21 (1958): 83–97.

34. Rost, *Leadership for the Twenty-First Century,* 47. Also see 44–128. In preparation for his 1991 work on leadership, Rost surveyed 587 books, chapters, and journal articles published between 1900 and 1990 and discovered 221 distinct definitions. Equally important is the fact that 366 of these works, some from the most influential writers on leadership, offered no working definition at all.

35. Rost, *Leadership for the Twenty-First Century,* 93–94.

36. "The essential tasks of administration and delegation in the local church cannot be separated from the call to shepherd God's flock. Shepherds must administrate. And administrators should administrate like shepherds. When we administrate, organize, and delegate without an understanding of shepherding, it can become a cold and calculated means to

achieve efficiency. The church is not just an institution that produces results or grows in size; it is the household of God," Brian Croft and Bryce Butler, *Oversee God's People* (Grand Rapids: Zondervan, 2015), 26–27.

37. Simon Western, *Leadership*, 2nd ed. (Thousand Oaks, CA: SAGE, 2013), chapter 2.

38. Rost, *Leadership for the Twenty-First Century,* 102–113. Rost defines leadership as "an influence relationship among leaders and followers who intend real changes that reflect their mutual purposes." See Northouse, *Leadership*, 3. Northouse defines leadership as "a process whereby an individual influences a group of individuals to achieve a common goal." He argues that this definition reflects the common components across most definitions of leadership. See also Bass, who defines leadership as "an interaction between two or more members of a group that often involves a structuring or restructuring of the situation and of the perceptions and expectations of the members. Leaders are agents of change, whose acts affect other people more than other people's acts affect them. Leadership occurs when one group member modifies the motivational competencies of others in the group. Leadership can be conceived as directing the attention of other members to goals and the paths to achieve them. It should be clear that with this broad definition, any member of the group can exhibit some degree of leadership, and the members will vary in this regard," *The Bass Handbook of Leadership*, 25.

39. "Leadership research in the past has been concentrated on white leaders and white followers. . . . Most of the research on leadership on minorities has dealt with blacks as leaders or subordinates. Considerably less has been done with Hispanic, Asian American, and other racial and ethnic minorities," Bass, *The Bass Handbook of Leadership*, 944. According to research from Katya Armistead, African American student leaders tend to focus more on role modeling, building relationships, their own responsibility as leaders, empowering the community, and service when describing leadership when compared with others, Katya Armistead, "How African American Students Define Leadership" (EdD thesis, University of California, Santa Barbara, 2012).

40. One particularly helpful text in this regard has been Bryan Loritts, *Right Color, Wrong Culture* (Chicago: Moody, 2014).

41. Peter Northouse, *Leadership,* 6th ed. (Thousand Oaks, CA: SAGE, 2013), 4–6.

42. R. Albert Mohler, *The Conviction to Lead* (Grand Rapids: Bethany House, 2012), 26.

43. J. Oswald Sanders, *Spiritual Leadership*, 2nd ed. (Chicago: Moody, 1994), 27, 28.

44. Boers, *Servants and Fools*, location 3879.

45. J. Robert Clinton, *The Making of a Leader* (Colorado Springs: NavPress, 1998), 17.

46. Aubrey Malphurs, *Being Leaders* (Grand Rapids: Baker, 2003), 33.

47. John Piper, "The Marks of a Spiritual Leader," Desiring God, January 1, 1995, www.desiringgod.org/articles/the-marks-of-a-spiritual-leader.

48. If a church is effectively reaching people in its context, the church will grow toward being as diverse as its neighborhood. This includes not only racial and ethnic diversity but also socioeconomic and generational diversity. Sadly, a racially diverse church remains more a dream than a reality for most Protestant congregations. More than eight in ten pastors (85 percent) say every church should strive for racial diversity, yet 86 percent say their congregation is predominantly one racial or ethnic group, according to Bob Smietana, "Racial Diversity at Church More a Dream than Reality," LifeWay Research, January 17, 2014, https://lifewayresearch.com/2014/01/17/research-racial-diversity-at-church-more-dream -than-reality/. Neighborhoods in the United States are approximately ten times more racially diverse than the churches in those neighborhoods. See Michael Emerson, *People of the Dream* (Princeton: Princeton University Press, 2008), 39–44. Moving toward authentic diversity at

a local church level in majority-culture congregations will require placing ethnic and cultural minorities in positions of genuine authority; at denominational and organizational levels, it is likely to require the discovery and admission of institutional patterns that have reinforced white supremacy, followed by repentance and reparations. For discussions related to denominational movement toward diversity, see Jarvis Williams and Kevin Jones, eds., *Erasing the Stain of Racism* (Nashville: B&H, 2017).

49. The term "diverse group" is intended to indicate the importance of recognizing and listening to the differing perspectives in a group due to diverse racial, ethnic, socioeconomic, and generational experiences, valuing these perspectives as expressions of a multifaceted array of contexts and cultures that point us toward the "vast multitude from every nation, tribe, people, and language" in John's heavenly vision (Rev 7:9). For a practical introduction to the need for ecclesial diversity as well as a practical guide to leadership in diverse contexts, see Derwin Gray, *The High-Definition Leader* (Nashville: Nelson, 2015).

50. Nancy Pearcey, *Total Truth* (Wheaton: Crossway, 2004), 19.

51. For leaders as personifications of a common purpose, see L. F. Urwick, "Leadership and Morale," address delivered at Ohio State University on March 9, 1953. Urwick stated that the leader is "the personification of common purpose not only to all who work on the undertaking, but to everyone outside of it." See also Malphurs, *Being Leaders*, 13–26.

52. Kevin Vanhoozer, "From 'Blessed in Christ' to 'Being in Christ,'" in *"In Christ" in Paul*, ed. Michael Thate et al. (Tübingen: Mohr-Siebeck, 2014), 28–30.

53. Faith is a condition not only of justification but also of adoption and union with Christ (Gal 3:26; Eph 1:13; 3:17). John Calvin's exegesis led him to the conclusion that union with Christ is a consequence of faith ("Etsi autem verum est, hoc fide nos consequi," "it is true that we obtain this by faith") and that the Holy Spirit is the bond of this union ("Spiritum sanctum vinculum esse, quo nos sibi efficaciter devincit Christus," "the Holy Spirit . . . efficaciously binds us with Christ"), John Calvin, *Institutio Christianae Religionis* 3:1:1).

54. Vanhoozer, "From 'Blessed in Christ' to 'Being in Christ,'" 26. For God the Father regarding and responding to believers as he does Jesus, see, e.g., Robert Letham, *Union with Christ* (Phillipsburg, NJ: P&R, 2011), 51–55; David Broughton Knox, *Justification by Faith* (London: Church Book Room, 1959), 6; Lane Tipton, "Union with Christ and Justification," in *Justified in Christ*, ed. K. S. Oliphint (Fearn, Ross-Shire, UK: Mentor, 2007), 25.

55. "Appreciation of beauty and excellence represents the ability to recognize and appreciate the existence of goodness in the world. Its defining feature is the emotional experience of awe or wonder when the individual is in the presence of beauty and excellence," Armenio Rego et al., *The Virtues of Leadership* (Oxford: Oxford University Press, 2012), 135. Jonathan Pennington, our colleague and friend with whom we labor at Southern Seminary, frequently notes that we must lead with excellence in a manner that is beautiful. He argues rightly that such an attractive means of leadership causes followers to embrace change with eagerness instead of resistance.

56. Annie Dillard, *Pilgrim at Tinker Creek* (New York: Harper, 1974), 138–139.

57. Westminster Shorter Catechism, question 1.

58. Adapted from Montgomery, *Leadership Mosaic*, chapter 7.

59. On the paucity of research into followership, see Mary Uhl-Bien et al., "Followership Theory," in *Leadership Quarterly* 25 (2014): 83. Much so-called followership research has merely been another variation of leadership research, focused on how followers affect and impact leaders; see e.g., Barbara Kellerman, *Followership* (Cambridge: Harvard Business School, 2008). Still less research has examined the role and functions of leaders as followers. This book fills a portion of this gap in the leadership literature by exploring the distinctly Christian dynamic of leading as a fellow follower among the people who are being led.

60. Henri J. M. Nouwen, *In the Name of Jesus*, rev. ed. (Chestnut Ridge, NY: Crossroad, 2002), 73–74.

61. Bruce Ware, "Putting It All Together," in *Shepherding God's Flock*, ed. Thomas Schreiner and Benjamin Merkle (Grand Rapids: Kregel, 2014), 288.

62. *Road to Utopia*, directed by Hal Walker (Paramount, 1946).

63. Daniel Block, "The Burden of Leadership," *Bibliotheca Sacra* (2005): 278.

64. Dietrich Bonhoeffer, "The Führer and the Individual in the Younger Generation," Berlin: 1932–1933, vol. 12 of *Dietrich Bonhoeffer Works*, ed. Larry Rasmussen, trans. Douglas Stott, Isabel Best, and David Higgins (Minneapolis: Fortress, 2009), 273–274.

65. Bart Giamatti, the seventh commissioner of baseball and a former professor at Yale University, frequently pointed out the connections between baseball and the religious notion of Paradise. See Bart Giamatti, "Baseball and the American Character," in *A Great and Glorious Game*, ed. K. S. Robson (Chapel Hill, NC: Algonquin, 1998), 64–65. In the humble opinion of this author (Timothy), baseball is the consummate expression of humanity's divinely designed impulse to organize the created order through sports. "Until baseball appeared, humans were a sad and benighted lot, lost in the labyrinth of matter . . . but, throughout most of the history of the race, no culture was able to produce more than a shadowy sketch of whatever glorious mystery prompted those nameless longings," Thomas Bentley Hart, "A Perfect Game," *First Things*, August 1, 2010, https://www.firstthings.com/article/2010/08/a-perfect-game. Soccer, however, is almost certainly a result of the fall.

66. The church is a particular gathering of believers committed to intentional accountability and fellowship within which "the Word of God [is] sincerely preached and heard" and "the sacraments [are] administered according to the institution of Christ" (John Calvin, *Institutio Christianae Religionis*, 4:1:9; see also Augsburg Confession, article 7). Baptists and others in the Free Church tradition have at times preferred the term "ordinances" over "sacraments" to avoid the Roman Catholic sense of a sacrament as a sacred sign that effects grace in itself (*signum sacro sanctum efficax gratiae*). As used here, however, "sacrament" is intended in the sense of a sign participating in and pointing to saving grace that has already been effected through regeneration and enacted through repentance and faith. "Baptism is . . . a sign of [the Christian's] fellowship with the death and resurrection of Christ, of remission of sins, and of his giving himself up to God, to live and walk in newness of life. . . . The Lord's Supper is an ordinance of Jesus Christ. . . . It is in no sense a sacrifice, but is designed to commemorate his death, to confirm the faith and other graces of Christians, and to be a bond, pledge and renewal of their communion with him, and of their church fellowship" (Basil Manly, "The Abstract of Principles of The Southern Baptist Theological Seminary," articles 15–16). The Belgic Confession and the Scottish Confession added church discipline as a third essential mark of the church. See Philip Schaff, ed., *Creeds of Christendom* (New York: Harper, 1905), 3:419, 461–462. Church discipline may also, however, be seen as an extension or implication of the right proclamation of the Word and the right administration of the sacraments.

67. Gray, *The High-Definition Leader*, 218.

68. Dietrich Bonhoeffer, *Life Together*, trans. J. W. Doberstein (New York: Harper, 1954), 109.

69. David Starling, *Un-Corinthian Leadership* (Eugene, OR: Wipf and Stock, 2014), 25.

Chapter Two: The King Says

1. The game "Simon Says" may have originated in the thirteenth century in response to the capture of King Henry III and Prince Edward by Simon de Montfort, although this is far from certain. See, e.g., J. J. Ferrer, *The Art of Stone Skipping* (Watertown, MA: Charlesbridge,

2012), 152. The Jewish version is also known in some contexts as *Herzl 'Amar* ("Herzl Says," after Theodor Herzl, visionary of modern Zionism). See, e.g., Shoshana Kordova, "Word of the Day / Herzl: Simon Says Found a State," *Haaretz*, November 22, 2013, www.haaretz .com/.premium-word-of-the-day-herzl-1.5293379.

2. Mohler, *The Conviction to Lead*, 134–135.

3. Bob Dylan, "Gotta Serve Somebody," *Slow Train Coming* (Special Rider, 1979).

4. Peter Gentry and Stephen Wellum, *Kingdom through Covenant* (Wheaton: Crossway, 2012), 293–294.

5. Steve Timmis, *Gospel-Centred Leadership* (Surrey, UK: Good Book, 2012), 20.

6. "Ruling is not the essence of the divine image, but rather the result of being made in God's image," Gentry and Wellum, *Kingdom through Covenant*, 188. The recognition of ruling as a result of image and likeness depends in part on understanding that, in a conjunctive-sequential use of *waw* to join clauses, the second clause is temporally or logically consequent to the first. For cohortative followed by imperfect as result, see Bruce Waltke and M. P. O'Conner, *An Introduction to Biblical Hebrew Syntax* (Winona Lake, IN: Eisenbrauns, 1990), 650. Five possible meanings for "image" and "likeness" have been suggested: (1) two separate aspects of human nature, with "image" referring to rational reflection of God and "likeness" to ethical similarity to God; (2) humanity's mental and spiritual faculties; (3) physical resemblance; (4) representative rulership; and (5) relational capacity, most eloquently propounded by Karl Barth. See Gordon Wenham, *Genesis 1–15* (Milton Keynes, UK: Word, 1991), 29–32. Of these, representative rulership is the closest to the view taken here.

7. Gentry and Wellum, *Kingdom through Covenant*, 397–398.

8. Stephen Dempster, *Dominion and Dynasty* (Downers Grove, IL: InterVarsity, 2003), 59.

9. Hans Wolff, *Anthropology of the Old Testament* (Philadelphia: Fortress, 1974), 160–161.

10. Victor Hamilton, *The Book of Genesis: Chapters 1–17* (Grand Rapids: Eerdmans, 1990), 135. רָדָה ("have dominion," Gen 1:26) refers in 1 Kgs 5:4; Pss 72:8; 110:2; Isa 14:6; and Ezek 34:4 to royal dominion. "Without doubt, the terminology employed in Genesis 1:26 is derived from regal vocabulary, which serves to elevate the king above the ordinary run of men. In the Bible this idea has become democratized. All human beings are created 'in the image of God'; each person bears the stamp of royalty," Nahum Sarna, *Genesis* (Philadelphia: JPS, 1989), 12.

11. Eugene Peterson, *The Pastor* (New York: HarperCollins, 2011), 137.

12. D. J. A. Clines, *What Does Eve Do to Help?* (Sheffield, UK: Sheffield Academic, 1990), 31–40; Kenneth Mathews, *Genesis 1:1–11:26* (Nashville: Broadman & Holman, 1996), 221; Thomas Schreiner, "An Interpretation of 1 Timothy 2:9–15," in *Women in the Church*, ed. Andreas Köstenberger and Thomas Schreiner, 2nd ed. (Grand Rapids: Baker, 2005), 106.

13. Mathews, *Genesis 1:1–11:26*, 220.

14. In ancient Israel and in other ancient Near Eastern cultures, the king was perceived to have a priestlike relationship with the deity, so the blending of kingly and priestly roles in descriptions of Adam and Eve in Genesis was not unique. See, e.g., M. E. Aubet, *Commerce and Colonization in the Ancient Near East* (Cambridge: Cambridge University Press, 2013), 279–286; Mario Liverani, *The Ancient Near East* (New York: Routledge, 2014), 80. In Israel, however, the king's priestly role did not necessarily authorize him to perform the ritual duties of the priest. D. W. Rooke has suggested that the king held an ontological status of priest while the high priest's priesthood was functional. Although this distinction as expressed by Rooke unnecessarily pits a hypothetical P source against other portions of the Old Testament,

it still may provide a helpful set of categories by which to understand the king's priestlike status in relation to Yahweh that, among the Israelites, did not include the privilege of performing ritual duties in the tabernacle or temple. See D. W. Rooke, "Kingship as Priesthood," in *King and Messiah in Israel and the Ancient Near East*, ed. John Day (Sheffield, UK: Sheffield Academic, 1998), 187–208; "Jesus as Royal Priest," *Biblica* 81 (2000): 81–94.

15. כָּבַשׁ ("subdue," Gen 1:28) can suggest violent conquest or subjugation (Num 32:33; Josh 18:1; 2 Chr 28:10; Neh 5:5; Esth 7:8; Jer 34:11–16; Mic 7:19; Zech 9:15); however, the more likely implication here seems to be breaking up the surface of the earth for agriculture, paralleling the references to tilling in Gen 2:5, 15.

16. "Unrestricted freedom" did not exist even in the garden of Eden, Sarna, *Genesis*, 21.

17. "Enjoyment of God's good land is contingent on 'keeping' (*lismor*) God's commandments (*miswot*, cf. Deuteronomy 30:16). The similarity between this condition for enjoying God's blessing and that laid down for Israel at Sinai and in Deuteronomy is transparent. . . . To enjoy the 'good,' humankind must trust God and obey him," John Sailhamer, "Genesis," in *The Expositor's Bible Commentary*, vol. 1, rev. ed., ed. David Garland and Tremper Longman (Grand Rapids: Zondervan, 2008), 79–80.

18. Hamilton, *The Book of Genesis*, 138.

19. Timothy Keller, *Every Good Endeavor* (New York: Penguin, 2012), with Katherine Leary Alsdorf, ebook, chapter 2.

20. Eric Mason, *Manhood Restored* (Nashville: B&H, 2013), 12.

21. In his essay "Equality," C. S. Lewis eloquently affirmed both the goodness of hierarchical structures in God's design and the essential equality of human beings that functions in a fallen world as a corrective (a "medicine") to prevent hierarchy from becoming abusive. "When equality is treated not as a medicine or a safety-gadget but as an ideal we begin to breed that stunted and envious sort of mind which hates all superiority. That mind is the special disease of democracy, as cruelty and servility are the special diseases of privileged societies. It will kill us all if it grows unchecked. The man who cannot conceive a joyful and loyal obedience on the one hand, nor an unembarrassed and noble acceptance of that obedience on the other, the man who has never even wanted to kneel or to bow, is a prosaic barbarian. . . . Hierarchy within can alone preserve egalitarianism without," C. S. Lewis, "Equality," *The Spectator* (August 27, 1943): 8.

22. C. S. Lewis, *Prince Caspian* (New York: Harper, 1951), 233.

23. J. R. R. Tolkien, "On Fairy Stories," *The Tolkien Reader*, ed. P. S. Beagle (New York: Ballantine, 1986), 69.

24. The focus here is intentionally on the provision and providence of God, not on the practices of Moses. It seems, even from the perspective of ancient Israel, that Moses was perceived as a unique leader raised up for a particular purpose at a particular time whose role would not be replicated. For discussions of Moses's uniqueness as a leader and the unlikelihood that he is intended to serve as a model for leaders to imitate, see Arthur Boers, *Servants and Fools* (Nashville: Abingdon, 2015), Kindle edition, chapter 3; Robert Karl Gnuse, *No Tolerance for Tyrants* (Collegeville, MN: Liturgical Press, 2011), 39–53; Derek Tidball, *Skillful Shepherds* (Grand Rapids: Zondervan, 1986), 36.

25. The opening verses of Exodus "are to be read as theological fulfillment of God's ongoing faithfulness, kindness, and provision for Abraham, Isaac and Jacob. The promise-keeping God continues to act across centuries, keeping pledges to men and women now long dead," Paul House, *Old Testament Theology* (Downers Grove, IL: InterVarsity, 1998), 89.

26. For Adam as priest and king, see G. K. Beale, *The Temple and the Church's Mission* (Downers Grove, IL: InterVarsity, 2004), 66; Gnuse, *No Tolerance for Tyrants*, 108–109.

27. Philip Graham Ryken, *Exodus: Saved for God's Glory* (Wheaton: Crossway, 2005), 92–93.

28. Brevard Childs, *The Book of Exodus* (Louisville: WJK, 1974), 73.

29. This statement expresses "the nature, character, and essence of the promise in v. 12: 'I will be with you' (*'ehyeh 'immak*). What, then, is his name? The answer is: '[My name in its inner significance is] I am for I am/will be [present]," Walter Kaiser, "Exodus," *The Expositor's Bible Commentary*, 371.

30. Gerhard von Rad, *Old Testament Theology*, trans. D. M. G. Stalker (New York: Harper and Row, 1965), 2:57. See also Andrew Davis, "Leading the Church in Today's World," in *Shepherding God's Flock*, ed. Thomas Schreiner and Benjamin Merkle (Grand Rapids: Kregel, 2014), 334.

31. Ryken, *Exodus*, 1028.

32. Ibid., 93.

33. Wesley Feltner, "The relationship between pastoral influence tactics, follower outcome levels, and types of congregational change" (Ed.D. diss., The Southern Baptist Theological Seminary, 2009), 12-27. Feltner provides helpful insight regarding God's power and his empowerment of humanity.

34. "Simply stated, there is no other deity to stop, rebuke, or oppose God, and it is this 'simple' theological issue that Moses attempts to teach the ancient audience and that constitutes the foundation for the Bible's enduring message for today. . . . [The plagues] are Yahweh's means for instructing Moses, Pharaoh, and their respective peoples about God's identity and sole claim to deity," House, *Old Testament Theology*, 88, 101.

35. Douglas Stuart, *Exodus* (Nashville: B&H, 2006), 159. Names of around forty Egyptian gods and goddesses are known, and many were known by more than one name. See E. Ray Clendenen, "Religious Background of the Old Testament," in *Foundations for Biblical Interpretation*, ed. David Dockery et al. (Nashville: Broadman & Holman, 1994), 284; Duane Garrett, *A Commentary on Exodus* (Grand Rapids: Kregel, 2014), 206–207.

36. Boers, *Servants and Fools*, location 476.

37. John Piper, *Brothers, We Are Not Professionals*, rev. ed. (Nashville: B&H, 2013), 70.

38. Paraphrased from Eugene Peterson, "My Soul Waits," *God's Message for Each Day* (eBook; Nashville: Nelson, 2004).

39. Ryken, *Exodus*, 380.

40. Ibid., 382.

41. Ibid., 381.

42. Quoted in George Stevens, *Conversations at the American Film Institute with the Great Moviemakers* (New York: Random House, 2012), 284.

43. Bede, *Exodus, Leviticus, Numbers, Deuteronomy*, Ancient Christian Commentary on Scripture: Old Testament 3, ed. Joseph T. Lienhard (Downers Grove, IL: InterVarsity, 2001), 72.

44. Alice Cooper and Bob Marlette, "I Just Wanna Be God," *Dragontown* (Spitfire, 2001).

45. Prophecy was more a function than an office and frequently functioned in relation to the office of king. See Joseph Blenkinsopp, *Sage, Priest, Prophet* (Louisville: WJK, 1995), 116; Marty Stevens, *Leadership Roles of the Old Testament* (Eugene, OR: Cascade, 2012), 31. As such, instead of developing a separate chapter devoted to the role of prophet, this role has been addressed throughout chapters 3 and 4.

46. Thomas Oden, *Pastoral Theology* (San Franscisco: Harper, 1983), 49; Derek Tidball, *Builders and Fools* (Leicester, UK: Inter-Varsity, 1999), 133; Tidball, *Skillful Shepherds*, 45.

Part Two: Old Covenant Precedents for Leadership through Followership

1. "Abusive church leaders often distort their role and authority by claiming to speak for God. This type of environment provides no accountability for those in leadership. . . . Such environments produce parishioners (adults and children) who are initially unwilling to report criminal behavior and are uncooperative with criminal investigations," Victor Vieth and Boz Tchividjian, "When the Child Abuser Has a Bible": http://www.netgrace.org /resources/2015/2/12/when-the-child-abuser-has-a-bible-investigating-child-maltreatment -sanctioned-or-condoned-by-a-religious-leader-center-piece. Any failure on the part of pastoral leaders to report abuse or to hold abusive leaders accountable represents a shameful, disgraceful, and disqualifying abdication of their God-given role as shepherds called to care for the vulnerable and oppressed. Leaders who foster church cultures that fail to report such abuse should be held accountable, even if they were not personally aware of the abuse. For guidance on how to prevent and respond to suspected abuse in the church, see Deepak Reju, *On Guard* (Greensboro: New Growth, 2014).

2. God, having planned before time began what Christ would do and be, formed these three offices to foreshadow Christ. Thus—when looking at Old Testament prophets, priests, and kings—"we must not derive from their offices what Christ was, but must rather infer from Christ what their offices were. They were anointed because he would be anointed; he was not anointed because they had been," Geerhardus Vos, *Christology*, vol. 3 of *Reformed Dogmatics*, trans. and ed. Richard Gaffin (Bellingham, WA: Lexham, 2014), 11.

3. Particularly in the case of priests, kings, and occasionally prophets, "the act of anointing confers כָּבוֹד; it is thus to be regarded as an act of enablement," Walter Grundmann, "χρίω," in *TDNT*, ed. Gerhard Kittel and Gerhard Friedrich, trans. Geoffrey Bromiley (Grand Rapids: Eerdmans, 1964), 9:498. Those who were anointed in the Old Testament became, according to Eusebius of Caesarea, "Christs in type, so that all these have reference to the true Christ," *Historia ecclesiastica* 1:3:8. Anointing of prophets (1 Kgs 19:16) seems to have occurred less frequently than the anointing of kings and priests; however, prophets were perceived as directly anointed by the Spirit of God even if they were not physically anointed (cf. Luke 4:18–24; Acts 10:34–38). In 11Q13 (11QMelch) in the Dead Sea Scrolls, a prophetic messenger—expected to accompany the priest-king Melchizedek in an end-times conflict—is identified as one "anointed by the Spirit." For further exploration of the relationship between Melchizedek and the messenger in 11Q13, see Florentino Martinez, "Las tradiciones sobre Melquisedec en los manuscritos de Qumran," *Bib* 81 (2000): 70–80. In some instances, ritual anointing could indicate purification rather than (or, in some cases, in addition to) empowerment. See Yair Lorberbaum, *Disempowered King* (New York: Continuum, 2011), 22.

4. See 1QS 9 and 4Q175 in the Dead Sea Scrolls. The triad of prophet, priest, and king occurs only in these two texts from Qumran, both of which were written by the same scribe. One scholar suggests this may mean that the triad "was [the] personal opinion and invention" of this solitary scribe, Geza Xeravits, *King, Priest, Prophet* (Leiden: Brill, 2003), 224, 228. It is certainly true that messianic expectations at Qumran were not consistent or canonized; however, given that this triad appears early and widely in ancient Christian tradition, it also seems unlikely that the triad may be dismissed as the invention of an isolated scribe at Qumran. 4Q175 links the "prophet like [Moses]" (Deut 18:18–19) with a prophet yet to come; the "scepter . . . out of Israel" (Num 24:15–17) with a coming king; and the blessing of the Levites (Deut 33:8–11) with a coming priest. The Damascus Document (CD) also attests to Jewish expectation both of a priest and of a king. This document mentions a teacher but does not mention a prophet—perhaps because it was understood that prophecy had ceased in this era (see 1 Macc 9:27; 14:41)—and envisions a singular Messiah who

would be both priestly ("Messiah of Aaron") and kingly ("Messiah . . . of Israel"): "Those that remain shall be delivered up to the sword when there comes the Messiah of Aaron and Israel," 19b; see also CD 14a; 20b. Josephus, writing near the end of the first century AD, referred to John Hyrcanus as prophet, priest, and king: "τρία γοῦν τὰ κρατιστεύοντα μόνος εἶχεν, τὴν τεάρχὴν τοῦ ἔθνους καὶ τὴν ἀρχιερωσύνην καὶ προφητείαν" ("He alone had three of the most desirable things—rulership of his nation, high priesthood, and prophecy"), *Bellum Judaicum* 1:2:8. The triad of prophet, priest, and king may also be found in *Testament of Levi* 8:11–15, with the kingly role perhaps descriptive of John Hyrcanus: "A king shall arise in Judah and shall establish a new priesthood according to the type of the nations [κατα τύπον των εθνών]. . . . His presence is beloved, as a prophet of the Most High, of the seed of Abraham our father." The reference to the nations may suggest a priesthood in which intercession would be made not only for Israel but also for the nations.

    5. "Μόνον ἀρχιέρεα τῶν ὅλων καὶ μόνον ἀπάσης κτίσεως βασιλέα καὶ μόνον προφητῶν ἀρχιπροφήτην τοῦ πατρὸς τυγχάνοντα," ("the only High Priest of the whole [world], the only King over creation, and—among the prophets—the only High Prophet of the Father"), Eusebius of Caesarea, *Historia ecclesiastica* 1:3:8. Justin Martyr referred in the second century AD to Christ having received from God the Father the titles of "king and messiah and priest and messenger," *Dialogus cum Tryphone Judaeo*, 86. For references to *munus triplex* in the writings of John Chrysostom and Peter Chrysologus, see Geoffrey Wainwright, *For Our Salvation* (Grand Rapids: Eerdmans, 1997), 110–112. See also Robert Crouse, "Church as Priest, King, Prophet" (presentation, Evangelical Theological Society Annual Meeting, Atlanta, 2015). In the *Summa theologiae* of Thomas Aquinas, the triad is not prophet, priest, and king but lawgiver, priest, and king ("*legislator . . . sacerdos . . . rex*," *Summa theologica* 3, q. 22, a. 1, ad. 3), though Aquinas does elsewhere recognize Christ as prophet (*Summa theologica* 2, q. 174, a. 5, ad. 3) and may not have been at this point attempting to present the *munus triplex*. See Juan Alfaro, "Die Heilsfunktionen Christi als Offenbarer, Herr, und Priester," in *Mysterium Salutis* 3 (Einsiedeln: Benzinger, 1970), 680.

    6. See, e.g., John Calvin, *Institutio Christianae Religionis* 2:15; Westminster Confession of Faith 8:1; Westminster Larger Catechism 41–45; Westminster Shorter Catechism 23–26; Heidelberg Catechism 31; First London Confession of Faith 10–20; Basil Manly, "The Abstract of Principles of The Southern Baptist Theological Seminary," article 7. Karl Barth also extensively utilized the munus triplex but, as Adam Johnson has demonstrated, the munus triplex functions primarily in Barth's theology as "a traditional gloss on his own christological framework. . . . [Barth] does not rely upon the munus triplex for the material or formal content of his doctrine of reconciliation," Adam Johnson, "The Servant Lord," *SJT* 65 (2012): 164. On the basis of the prevalence of the munus triplex in the Reformed tradition, Robert Banks and Bernice Ledbetter identify prophet, priest, and king as "the Presbyterian model" of leadership, *Reviewing Leadership*, 2nd ed., (Grand Rapids: Baker, 2016), 36; unfortunately, their presentation utterly misconstrues the function of the *munus triplex* in the broader Reformed tradition and seems to suggest, incorrectly, that it was the *munus triplex* that gave rise to the three offices of ministers of the Word, ruling elders, and deacons.

    7. Dogmatic Constitution on the Church (*Lumen Gentium*), 8–12; Catechism of the Catholic Church, 783–786, 901–913, 1581.

    8. Counseling professor Dan Allender suggests that every church leader has "skills and gifts that place" him or her "primarily in one category—prophet, priest, or king." Although Allender treats these clustered sets of skills as inevitable, he does not expect that any Christian leader should remain within a single category. Unlike many who treat the triad as a leadership typology, Allender urges leaders to develop the capacity to lead from all three vantage points. "We are to be all three, all at once," he writes. "To lead is to mirror Jesus in all three of

these capacities," Dan Allender, *Leading with a Limp* (Colorado Springs: Waterbrook, 2006), 186–187. In a similar appropriation of the munus triplex, Owen Strachan contends that it is "rather commonsense" that the *munus triplex* should shape our understanding of a pastor's work, suggesting that "essential elements of the work of the old covenant prophet, priest, and king have transferred to the pastorate in the new covenant." No biblical or theological support is, however, offered for these claims other than the assertion that a pastor holds "the office of covenant minister," Owen Strachan, "Of Prophets, Priests, and Kings," in *The Pastor as Public Theologian*, ed. Kevin Vanhoozer and Owen Strachan (Grand Rapids: Baker, 2015), 39. Richard Belcher emphasizes prophecy, priesthood, and kingship as offices fulfilled through the church and recognizes certain expressions of these offices as uniquely fulfilled by the church's leadership; however, he does so without attempting either to ascribe the offices in varying degrees based on individual gifts or to make any direct connection between leadership offices and church leadership offices; Richard Belcher, *Prophet, Priest, and King* (Phillipsburg, NJ: P&R, 2016), 159, 164–166, 169–170, 175–176. For a further example of a similar appropriation of the *munus triplex*, see Nicholas Ostermann, "A Triperspectival Approach to Shared Pastoral Leadership Based on the Munus Triplex Christi" (EdD thesis, SBTS, 2014), 68–70. Such applications of the *munus triplex* represent wiser appropriations than those that attempt to link particular personality traits or particular new covenant offices to these old covenant offices, due to a clear and helpful recognition that church leaders should not seek to function in only one of the three offices. Nevertheless, these applications of the *munus triplex* to the distinct roles of pastors or other church leaders still lack sufficient biblical support to be sustained.

9. Building on this typology, one pastor and conference speaker has promoted the three offices as leadership personality types, identifying prophets as those leaders who are gifted as teachers, priests as those who care for people's needs, and kings as planners and organizers. See, e.g., Drew Goodmanson, "Triperspectival Leadership," presentation, Acts 29 Boot Camp, Raleigh, 2008, and "How Multiperspectivalism Shapes Church Leadership and How You Staff a Church," https://www.goodmanson.com/church/how-mutliperspectivalism-shapes-church-leadership-and-how-you-staff-a-church [sic]. See also David Fairchild, "Prophet, Priest, and King," presentation, Acts 29 Boot Camp, Raleigh, 2008.

10. John Frame, "A Primer on Perspectivalism," https://frame-poythress.org/a-primer-on-perspectivalism/.

11. Vern Poythress, "Modern Spiritual Gifts as Analogous to Apostolic Gifts," *JETS* 39 (1996): 73–75. While not disputing that these gifts "can be" classified as prophetic, kingly, or priestly, I question whether they *should* be so classified, and I particularly question whether such classifications can be derived exegetically from the roles themselves or from the lists of spiritual gifts. When applied to spiritual gifts, the categories into which each gift might fit overlap significantly, and a threefold division of gifts seems to be a structure that is imposed on the lists rather than a structure that emerges naturally from the lists.

12. Duane Covrig et al., "Integrating Four Types of Moral Leadership," *Journal of Applied Christian Leadership* 6 (2012): 41–42, 61–62.

13. The earliest appearance that I have discovered of the appropriation of prophet, priest, and king as a typology for capacities that different church leaders possess in differing degree is in R. B. Kuiper, *The Glorious Body of Christ* (Edinburgh: Banner of Truth, 1967). On the one hand, Kuiper admits that "every living member of the body of Christ is undeniably a partaker of Christ's anointing and hence a prophet, priest and king," 131; however, he then goes on to state that "the minister or teaching elder represents [Christ] as prophet, the deacon represents him as priest, and the ruling elder represents him as King," 134.

14. Steve Timmis makes much the same point in *Gospel-Centred Leadership* (Surrey, UK: Good Book, 2012), 34.

15. Adam Johnson has contended—with reference to the use of the *munus triplex* as a schematic conceptualization of Christ's work of atonement—that, "despite its elegance and usefulness (particularly for integrating the theocratic aspects of Israel into Christ's work), this framework is simply too constricting to be of abiding service to the church in offering sufficient conceptual unity to Christ's saving work. . . . The *munus triplex* is an important though limited conceptual device. . . . We should be cautious in our use of this schema lest it take on a life of its own and outstrip the biblical foundation upon which it rests," Adam Johnson, "The Servant Lord," *SJT* 65 (2012): 171–173. The same might be said with reference to the use of this schema as a typological paradigm for church leadership.

16. "Deuteronomy is to be designated as the middle point of the Old Testament," Gerhard von Rad, *Studies in Deuteronomy*, trans. David Stalker (London: SCM, 1953), 37. See also Walter Brueggemann, *Deuteronomy* (Nashville: Abingdon, 2011), 17; Peter Gentry and Stephen Wellum, *Kingdom through Covenant* (Wheaton: Crossway, 2012), 363–366; Patrick Miller, *Deuteronomy* (Louisville: WJK, 2011), 16; Frederick Prussner, *Old Testament Theology* (Louisville: WJK, 1985), 259. Deuteronomy is not, of course, the middle of the Old Testament in terms of chronology or canonical location, regardless of what order one follows for the Old Testament canon; Deuteronomy does, however, stand at the center of the theology and metanarrative of the Old Testament. The first four books of the Torah look forward to Deuteronomy, with Israel standing poised at the entrance to the land; this marks the fulfillment of God's promise to Abraham, the goal of God's powerful rescue in the exodus, and the proof of God's promised preservation in the wilderness. Historical and prophetic texts such as Joshua, Judges, Samuel, and Kings point back to Deuteronomy as the standard by which Israel's faithfulness is to be assessed. The faithfulness of fathers is assessed by the standards in Deuteronomy 6, the justice of judges by Deuteronomy 16, the fidelity of kings by Deuteronomy 17, and the authenticity of prophets by Deuteronomy 18.

Chapter Three: The Quest for Justice

1. "The way in which an author arranges his statements and structures his thoughts contributes significantly to the communication as a whole," Peter Gentry, *How to Read and Understand the Biblical Prophets* (Wheaton: Crossway, 2017), 125.

2. The arrangement followed here is based on a structure proposed by Peter Gentry; however, for the purposes of this chapter, the structure of Deuteronomy in relation to Hittite suzerain-vassal treaties is not determinative for the points being made. In virtually every proposal related to the relationship between suzerain-vassal treaties and the structure of Deuteronomy, chapters 12–26 provide detailed stipulations and the Ten Commandments form the broad order and framework for these stipulations. See, e.g., Peter Craigie, *The Book of Deuteronomy* (Grand Rapids: Eerdmans, 1976), 24; Peter Gentry and Stephen Wellum, *Kingdom through Covenant* (Wheaton: Crossway, 2012), 357–363; Steven Guest, "Deuteronomy 26:16–19 as the Central Focus of the Covenantal Framework of Deuteronomy" (PhD diss., SBTS, 2009), 55; Kenneth Kitchen, *Ancient Orient and Old Testament* (Downers Grove, IL: InterVarsity, 1966), 93–97; Kenneth Kitchen, "The Fall and Rise of Covenant, Law, and Treaty," *TynBul* 40 (1989): 126; Eugene Merrill, *Deuteronomy* (Nashville: Broadman & Holman, 1994), 38–40. Steven Guest specifically argues that the distinct literary styles of the three sermons in Deuteronomy 1:6–30:20 demonstrate the high probability that a Hittite treaty formula provided the organizational principle for Deuteronomy ("Deuteronomy 26:16–19 as the Central Focus of the Covenantal Framework of Deuteronomy," 32–71). For chapters

12–26 as theological center of Deuteronomy, see Peter Vogt, *Deuteronomic Theology and the Significance of Torah* (Winona Lake, IN: Eisenbrauns, 2006), 29.

    3. "A covenant is not merely a legal structure, but proceeds from love and gives structure to love," Peter Leithart, *A Son to Me* (Moscow, ID: Canon, 2003), Kindle edition, location 1093.

    4. J. G. Millar and J. G. McConville, eds., *Time and Place in Deuteronomy* (Sheffield, UK: Sheffield Academic, 1994), 47, 69.

    5. Judges, prophets, priests, and kings were not constituted or created by Moses's description in Deuteronomy; they were, instead, situated in the context of God's covenant with Israel: (1) Judges prior to Deuteronomy: Judges had been appointed soon after the Israelites left Egypt (Exod 18:13–26). (2) Prophets prior to Deuteronomy: In the centuries that preceded the people's entrance into the Promised Land, Abraham and Aaron, Moses and Miriam, and the elders Eldad and Medad had all been identified as prophets (Gen 20:7; Exod 7:1; 15:20; Num 11:25–30; Deut 18:15). (3) Priests prior to Deuteronomy: While Moses was on Mount Sinai, God commanded him to appoint Aaron and his sons as priests for Israel (Exod 28:1–5). Earlier in the Old Testament, Melchizedek and Jethro had already been recognized as priests (Gen 14:18; Exod 2:16). (4) Expectation of a king prior to Deuteronomy: God's promises to Abraham clearly anticipated a king through whom God's blessings would be mediated to every nation (Gen 17:6). See T. D. Alexander, "Royal Expectations in Genesis to Kings," *TynBul* 49 (1998): 202–203. The threefold blessing of land, descendants, and covenant relationship with God are entwined in Genesis with the promise of a royal offspring who would defeat the primal serpent (Gen 3:15; 12:3; 22:18; see also 17:6, 6; 35:11; 49:10). Additionally, soon before Moses addressed his people on the plains of Moab, Balaam attempted to curse the Israelites but instead foresaw a future king who would "smash the forehead of Moab" (Num 24:17–19). For the kingly implications of this oracle of Balaam, see Katherine Doob Sakenfeld, *Journeying with God* (Edinburgh: Handsel, 1995), 133. The imagery of crushing the head of Moab suggests a typological link between the Messiah's predicted triumph over the serpent (Gen 3:15) and a future king's defeat of nations that reject God's reign.

    6. In Exod 18:21–26, judges were chosen from the wise and able men and constituted as "commanders" or "officials" (שָׂרֵי, derived from שַׂר) over thousands, hundreds, fifties, and tens. The term שַׂר ("official") could refer to a broad range of military and civic leadership roles, ranging from chief butlers and bakers (Gen 40:9, 16, 20) to battle commanders (Josh 5:14–15; Judg 4:2; 1 Sam 22:2) appointed by tribal officers over groups of hundreds and thousands (Deut 20:5–9; Num 31:48; 1 Chr 13:48). Moshe Weinfeld has highlighted the differences between the accounts in Exodus 18 and Deuteronomy 1 and argued that Deuteronomy 1 represents the perspective of a scribal school in a later nationalizing program in which the judiciary became secularized. Weinfeld identifies the timing of the appointment of judges in Deuteronomy 1 with the appointing of the elders in Numbers 11 but links the office described in Exodus with the secularized judiciary in Deuteronomy. The differences in emphasis between Exodus 18 and Deuteronomy 1 may be better explained, however, by recognizing that Deuteronomy 1 was not intended to be strictly chronological and that Exodus 18 and Deuteronomy 1 describe the same developments from different perspectives. The focus of Deuteronomy is on Moses's unique role as Yahweh's representative, and the function of the book is to celebrate Yahweh's supremacy in a manner that calls Israel to covenant faithfulness. For discussion, see Vogt, *Deuteronomic Theology and the Significance of Torah*, 107–112; Moshe Weinfeld, *Deuteronomy 1–11* (New York: Doubleday, 1991), 137–140; Moshe Weinfeld, *Deuteronomy and the Deuteronomic School* (Winona Lake, IN: Eisenbrauns, 1992), 233–281.

7. Regarding the relationship of שָׁפַט ("judge") in this context to the judges described in the book of Judges, it has been suggested that the role of the judges described in Deuteronomy was broader than mere judicial decision-making and included the establishment of justice through deliverance as well as decision making; thus, the judges in the book of Judges brought justice but not through judicial decisions. The judges in the book of Judges thus (according to this line of thinking) brought justice by delivering the people from oppressors and by governing the people justly—and, perhaps, at times by discerning God's will through divine charism. See Daniel Block, *Judges, Ruth* (Nashville: Broadman & Holman, 1999), 22–25; J. Clinton McCann, *Judges* (Louisville: WJK, 2011), 4; H. C. Thomson, "Shophet and Mishpat in the Book of Judges," *Glasgow University Oriental Society* (1963): 76–77. Another possibility is that the judges in the book of Judges represent an altogether different category of leader from the judges described in Deuteronomy. It seems more likely to me, however, that judicial leadership may not have been strictly separated from military leadership, so that שָׁפַט did indeed refer to judicial leadership but that these individuals not infrequently also served as military officials. In instructions to Hittite officers and commanders in the time of Tudhaliya IV, roles of judges and military officers seem to have overlapped, suggesting that (at least in other ancient Near Eastern cultures) judges could serve in a military function as well. If this was the case in Israel, when the people of Israel failed in the pursuit of justice, God raised up individuals who were already applying the Torah by means of judicial decisions or who would be expected to embrace this role after being raised up; these divinely empowered individuals were now also called to deliver Israel from external oppressors. Not every judicial official in Israel was a military deliverer, of course; however, it seems quite conceivable that the divinely empowered military deliverers in the book of Judges were also judges who handed down judicial decisions. "In Judges 4:4, where we are told that Deborah was judging (שֹׁפְטָה) Israel, it is clear that the author means she was giving case decisions. Yet, according to the story which follows, she was also a military heroine. . . . [The] editor of [Judges] believed . . . that, like Deborah, these men [the judges] filled both a military and a judicial role," Donald McKenzie, "The Judge of Israel," *VT* 17 (1967): 119. See in particular 2 Kgs 23:22, which seems to suggest that judges in the era prior to the kings not only ruled and rescued but also handed down judicial decisions—they were "judging ones who judged." If so, the deliverer judges in the book of Judges were unique in that they were directly raised up by Yahweh himself for the purpose of delivering the people; they may have already been judges or they may have been directly designated by Yahweh as judges in the judicial sense by means of the same empowerment by which he raised them up as deliverers (Judg 2:16; 3:9, 15; 6:15; 8:22; 10:1; 13:5). If so, perhaps their responsibility—after having delivered Israel from their oppressors—was intended to have been to solidify Israel's return to Yahweh by handing down righteous judgments from the Torah. For references and further discussion, see A. D. H. Mayes, *Deuteronomy* (Grand Rapids: Eerdmans, 1981), 124–125; Moshe Weinfeld, "Judge and Officer in Ancient Israel and the Ancient Near East," *IOS* 7 (1977): 65–88; Weinfeld, *Deuteronomy 1–11*, 140–141.

8. The "officer" (שֹׁטֵר) seems to have served as a tribal leader among or closely connected to the elders (Num 11:16; Deut 31:28; Josh 8:33). The officer (שֹׁטֵר) apparently outranked the military "commander" or "official" (שָׂר), given that the tribal officer was charged with appointing the official (Deut 20:9). In the exodus and later, this same term (שֹׁטֵר) referred to tribal officers who were responsible to urge potential soldiers to withdraw from the military force if they might not be fully committed to the battle (Deut 20:5–8); the text seems to draw some distinction between the tribal officer and the military commander, suggesting that the officer may not have been primarily a military leader (Deut 20:9), Alexander Rofe, "The Organization of the Judiciary in Deuteronomy," in *The World of the Arameans*,

ed. J. W. Wevers et al. (Sheffield, UK: Sheffield Academic, 2001), 98. The Akkadian and Syriac roots from which שֹׁטֵר developed described scribal activity, suggesting that the range of this officer's duties might have included record keeping, G. T. Manley, "'Officers' in the Old Testament," *EvQ* 29 (1957): 149. The range of this term seems to have expanded in time to describe a variety of administrative roles, although the translators of the Septuagint still took שֹׁטֵר to refer to a teaching and scribal role, as evidenced by their translation of שֹׁטֵר as "schoolmasters" or "instructors" (γραμματοεισαγωγεῖς) in Deut 1:15; 16:18; 29:9; and, 31:28. Previous to the exodus, שֹׁטֵר referred to Hebrews who tracked the people's production of bricks for their Egyptian masters (Exod 5:6, 10, 14–19). In general, it seems שֹׁוטֵר may have described a class of scribal leaders, overlapping with the more fluid leadership category of eldership (Num 11:16); the communities of Israel—perhaps represented by their tribal elders—may have appointed judges from this class (Deut 16:18), though Yahweh could and did sovereignly select and empower judges as well.

9. Alexander Rofe treats "officers" as a high-ranking class of scribes and takes the two nouns in the hendiadytic sense of "judges who belong to the professional status of 'scribes,'" Alexander Rofe, *Deuteronomy: Issues and Interpretation* (Edinburgh: T&T Clark, 2002), 109; for further discussion of this text and related texts, see Rofe, "The Organization of the Judiciary in Deuteronomy," 92–112. "Hendiadys" is the use of multiple words joined by conjunctions to describe a single entity or reality.

10. In Hebrew, צֶדֶק צֶדֶק ("Justice, justice") expresses God's expectation for judicial offices in Israel (16:20). צֶדֶק described the active principle by which God rules his world (Job 8:3; 36:3; Jer 11:20). צֶדֶק is enacted by persons living in covenant with Yahweh when they do good to those who cannot repay their acts of kindness (Ps 82:3). צֶדֶק has been rendered in other translations as "fairness," "goodness," "right," "righteousness" (see, e.g., Common English Bible, Easy-to-Read Version, Today's English Version). צֶדֶק ("justice") and מִשְׁפָּט ("righteousness," "judgment," "justice"), while certainly not identical in meaning, could function in parallel and overlapping relationships with each other (Eccl 3:16). צֶדֶק in conjunction with מִשְׁפָּט could convey God's faithfulness in the keeping of his covenant (Ps 33:5; Isa 9:7; 33:5; Hos 2:19–20; Amos 5:15). Independent of צֶדֶק, forms of מִשְׁפָּט could describe the righteous statutes of Yahweh as well as judicial decisions based on those statutes (see, e.g., Lev 26:15; Deut 1:17).

11. Moses referred to the judges and officers in third-person plural ("they are to judge the people," Deut 16:18), but the prohibitions of injustice, partiality, and bribery appear in second-person masculine singular and seem to be directed to the whole people of Israel, particularly to fathers as representatives of their households (16:19–20). For further discussion, see Jeffrey Tigay, *Deuteronomy* (Philadelphia: JPS, 2003), 160. For possible echoes of these prohibitions in the New Testament, see Jas 1:27–2:4.

12. In the Torah, laws for daily living—no less than guidelines for worship and leadership—were gifts given by God to cultivate justice and faithful love. For this reason, rules for right worship (Deut 16:21–17:5) intertwine by design in this text with guidelines for pursuing righteous judicial decisions by selecting trustworthy judges and seeking evidence in criminal cases (16:18–20; 17:6–7). Viewed in this manner, Deut 17:2–7 is not an interpolation or a misplaced text, contrary to commentators who see these various segments as "entirely unrelated" to the judges and "displaced from their original position" in the text; Samuel Driver, *A Critical and Exegetical Commentary on Deuteronomy* (New York: Scribner's 1895), 201. Instead, Deut 17:2–7 defined rules of evidentiary certainty for Israel and stands as an original and integral part of Deuteronomy 16–17. For further discussion from a critical perspective, see Bernard Levinson, *Deuteronomy and the Hermeneutics of Legal Innovation* (Oxford: Oxford University Press, 1997), 108–116.

13. Christopher J. H. Wright, *Deuteronomy* (Grand Rapids: Baker, 1994), 27; Vogt, *Deuteronomic Theology and the Significance of Torah*, 112.

14. Regarding Israel's need for a king, see Stephen Dempster, *Dominion and Dynasty* (Downers Grove, IL: InterVarsity, 2003), 132–134, and Thomas Schreiner, *The King in His Beauty* (Grand Rapids: Baker, 2013), 117–118. In the early chapters of Judges, the Israelites turned back to God after each judge delivered them, and the land rested (Judg 3:11, 30; 5:31; 8:28). In the final chapters of the book, the people no longer returned, the land received no rest, and their persistence in injustice birthed a brutal contagion of breaking covenant with one another and with God (Judg 19:30–20:48). Unlike the office of king, the office of judge was not hereditary and, in the instances in which the offspring of a judge did become leaders in the land, this arrangement did not result in justice for the people (Judg 8:29–9:57; 1 Sam 8:1–3). In addition to being chronologically limited to the judge's lifetime, the judge's influence seems to have been regionally limited as well. Judges were appointed in each town, suggesting that a judge's role was limited to the regions surrounding his particular municipality (Deut 16:18). Even among the deliverer judges in the book of Judges, leadership seems to have been regionally limited. Ehud's leadership in his struggle against Moab was supported by the tribe of Benjamin and limited to the central region of Israel (Judg 3:12–15); Barak's campaign against the Canaanites occurred in the north, supported by the tribes of Ephraim, Benjamin, Zebulun, Naphtali, and Issachar (4:1–2, 6, 10; 5:14–15, 18); Gideon led the tribes of Naphtali, Asher, Manasseh, Zebulun, and later Ephraim against the Midianites in the heartland of Israel (6:35; 7:23–24), and so on. The tribal and regional limits of judgeship are also evidenced by the apparent chronological overlap among the judges in the book of Judges. Since one judge's rule apparently overlapped with the rule of other judges, no single judge seems to have ruled all of Israel all at once. Rest in one region of Israel was very likely coterminous with periods of oppression and conflict in other regions. For further discussion, see Block, *Judges, Ruth*, 59–64.

15. For an exploration of patriarchal promises and precedents of kingship, see Daniel Diffey, "The Royal Promise in Genesis," *TynBul* 62 (2011): 313–316. The people's desire was not merely to have a king like other nations had but to set up a king in the same manner and for the same purposes as the nations around them. Grammatically, "like all the nations" in Deut 17:14 could refer to the king, in which case the desire was to have "a king like all the nations have"; however, it is more likely that the phrase refers to the rationale for and the process of installing a king as the nations did, in which case the request reflected a desire to be like the nations. This interpretation seems to be supported by the way the elders of Israel presented their demand that Samuel give them a king (1 Sam 8:5): "No, there shall be a king over us, that we may also be like the nations," Daniel Block, "The Burden of Leadership," *BSac* (2005): 262–263. Yahweh was Israel's supreme shepherd and king (Exod 15:13, 18; Num 23:21–22; Deut 33:5), but Yahweh's supremacy never precluded the possibility of a human vicegerent who would mediate Yahweh's rule and model covenant faithfulness for the people. God was the supreme Judge (Gen 18:25; Judg 11:27; Pss 50:6; 75:7; 94:2; Isa 33:22); this divine judicial supremacy relativized but did not preclude human judges who mediated God's justice (Deut 16:18–20). Likewise, God's supreme kingship relativized but did not preclude the possibility of a human king who would mediate God's reign and serve as an exemplar of covenant faithfulness.

16. John Woodhouse, *1 Samuel: Looking for a Leader* (Wheaton: Crossway, 2008), 145. For a description from the prophets of the incapacity of Israel's kings to rescue the people, see Hos 13:10–11.

17. "The judges in many cases acted as miniature kings, so perhaps the distinction between judge and king was a small one," Lester Grabbe, *Priests, Prophets, Diviners, Sages*

(Valley Forge, PA: Trinity, 1995), 21. Moses was a judge and yet Philo described his divinely designated role in kingly terms: "Since Moses had abandoned the chief authority in Egypt, which he might have had as the grandson of the reigning king . . . it seemed good to the Ruler and Governor of the universe to recompense him with the sovereign authority over a more populous and more powerful nation, which he was about to take to himself out of all other nations and to consecrate to the priesthood," Philo of Alexandria, *De vita Mosis*, 1:27 (149).

18. T. H. White, *The Once and Future King* (New York: Putnam, 1965), 421.

19. For the king of Israel as a son of God and the relationship of this role to Jesus as the Son of God, see Artur Malina, "Image of God the Father in Matthew 1–4," in *Perche Stessero con Lui,* ed. Lorenzo de Santos and Santi Grasso (Rome: Gregorian and Biblical, 2010), 60–62.

20. In the table "Right Judgments, Right Offerings, Right Testimony," the positioning of kingship as the heading of the second section, as well as the contrast between the king and the presumptuous nation of Israel, suggests that the section on kingship should be treated as supremely significant in this passage of Scripture. Daniel Block has suggested the following structure for Deut 16:18–18:22:

> A. Instructions for communal judges as guardians of justice and orthodoxy (16:18–17:7)
> > B. Instructions for Levitical priests as supreme court, maintainers of justice (17:8–13)
> > > C. Instructions for king (17:14–20)
> > B'. Instructions for Levitical priests as worship leaders, maintainers of orthodoxy (18:1–8)
> A'. Instructions for prophets as spokespersons for orthodoxy and justice (18:9–22)

This structure, although different from the structure I have suggested, also treats kingship as central in this text. In Block's arrangement, the most centralized and formal role is embedded at the center of the text, while less centralized and less formal roles mark the beginning and the end, Block, "The Burden of Leadership," 260.

21. Rahab and Ruth are two of the clearest examples of the possibility of incorporation of Gentiles into the congregation and covenants of Israel. Rahab was a Canaanite, and Ruth was a Moabite (Josh 2:1; Ruth 1:4); yet both women turned to Israel's God and were incorporated into God's covenant with Israel (Josh 6:25; Ruth 1:16; 4:13–17; Matt 1:5–6; see also Heb 11:31; Jas 2:25).

22. This understanding of Israel may also be found in deuterocanonical texts: "Have mercy . . . on Israel, whom you likened to a first born," Sir 36:17.

23. For an example from seventh-century BC Assyria, see James Pritchard, ed., *Ancient Near Eastern Texts Relating to the Old Testament*, 3rd ed. (Princeton: Princeton University Press, 1969), 289. For further discussion in reference to Israel, see Bernard Levinson, "The Reconceptualization of Kingship in Deuteronomy and the Deuteronomistic History's Transformation of Torah," *VT* 51 (2001): 512–514.

24. "The covenant carefully defined the king's limitation and demanded obedience to the will of God, the Suzerain (Deuteronomy 17:14–20). God governed and ruled the nation with his laws, defeated the king's enemies, set up the standards for justice, and received all worship. The sanctity of human kingship never developed because the covenant with God, the Great Suzerain, cemented God and the people together long before the monarchy was accepted as normative," Gary Smith, "The Concept of God/the Gods as King in the Ancient Near East and the Bible," *TrinJ* 3 (1982): 37.

25. Block, "The Burden of Leadership," 263.

26. One source for gaining the finest warhorses was trade with Egypt (1 Kgs 10:28–29; 2 Chr 1:16–17; 9:28; Isa 31:1–3; 36:9), though Anatolia was a supplier of horses as well. See Craigie, *The Book of Deuteronomy*, 255. The clause "send the people back" may refer to sending Israelites as slaves to purchase horses; this clause probably either explains the prohibition on horse trading with Egypt ("otherwise he might send people back to Egypt for this purpose") or qualifies the prohibition ("to the point that he would send people back to Egypt"), Jeffrey Tigay, *Deuteronomy* (Philadelphia: JPS, 1996), 167. Either way, Yahweh had promised his people would never see the Egyptians again (Exod 14:13; Deut 28:68); to return to Egypt willingly would be to disdain Yahweh's promise.

27. This is not to suggest that this text only disallowed marriage alliances with pagan nations or that only marriage alliances were in view; Moses clearly saw a large harem as incompatible with Israelite kingship, regardless of the purpose of the marriages. According to 11QTemple 57:17–18, this prohibition limited the king to one wife, though this interpretation of the text does not seem to have been universally accepted. See Jonathan Burnside, *God, Justice, and Society* (Oxford: Oxford University Press, 2011), 399.

28. Part of the reason for the division of the kingdom after the death of King Solomon may have been Solomon's disproportionate imposition on the northern kingdom of responsibilities for the support of the royal court and the army (1 Kgs 4:7–28). For further discussion, see Marvin Sweeney, *1 and 2 Kings* (Louisville: WJK, 2007), 169–170.

29. For further exploration of the connection between the written record of the covenant and the covenant itself in the ancient Near East, see Meredith Kline, *The Structure of Biblical Authority*, 2nd ed. (Eugene, OR: Wipf and Stock, 1997), 27–44. In kingdoms surrounding Israel, covenant documents might be kept in a temple so that a priest could read the treaty to the king at designated times. Statements of deposition may be found in several surviving Hittite treaties: "A duplicate of this tablet is deposited before the Sun-Goddess of Arinna since the Sun-Goddess of Arinna governs kingship and queenship," reads one such document. "A duplicate of this tablet is deposited in the land of Mittani before the Storm-God," another text declares. "It shall be read repeatedly forever and ever, before the king of the land." For these and other examples, see Gary Beckman, *Hittite Diplomatic Texts* (Atlanta: Scholars' Press, 1996), 42–48. Moses prescribed a similar practice for Israel each year at the Feast of Tabernacles (Deut 31:9–13) in addition to the requirement that the king copy and keep a copy of the Torah; however, Moses called for a reading of the Torah not merely in the hearing of Israel's leaders but in the presence of everyone in Israel ("men, women, children, and foreigners").

30. For discussion of the radicality of this text in the ancient world, see Robert Karl Gnuse, *No Tolerance for Tyrants* (Collegeville, MN: Liturgical Press, 2011), 41–46. See also Levinson, "The Reconceptualization of Kingship in Deuteronomy and the Deuteronomistic History's Transformation of Torah," 514. Although Nero reigned centuries later, his words summarize well the attitude toward kingship that this text rejects: "Remember that I am permitted to do anything to anybody," Suetonius, *Vita Caligulae*, 29.

31. Jason Weaver, Rowan Atkinson, and Laura Williams, "I Just Can't Wait to Be King," *The Lion King* (Buena Vista, 1994).

32. Donald Murray, *Divine Prerogative and Royal Pretension* (New York: Bloomsbury, 1998), 299. See also Jeong Kim and D. J. Human, "Nagid: A Reexamination in the Light of the Royal Ideology in the Ancient Near East," *HTS* 64 (July–September 2008).

33. "The king will get the Deuteronomic law from the levitical priests, who will have custody of it," Jack Lundbom, *Deuteronomy* (Grand Rapids: Eerdmans, 2013), 541.

34. "Kings were to listen to the voice of Father Yahweh by heeding the guidance of the father-prophet," Leithart, *A Son to Me*, location 721. The prophet was in relation to the king

"the pebble in the shoe, the goad in the hide, a courtier who doesn't always have to be courtly, because it's understood that he serves a higher power," Geraldine Brooks, "The King and I," *New York Times*, December 11, 2015, https://www.nytimes.com/2015/12/13/books/review /the-king-and-i.html.

35. For discussion of contractuality and consensuality in Israel's model of kingship, see Murray, *Divine Prerogative and Royal Pretension*, 306. Deuteronomy 16:18–18:22 distributed and limited the functions of power by means of a constitutional scheme that defined power relationships in Israel. The Torah functioned as the ultimate authority, and all offices—even the king's—were subject to the Torah. Whenever there is a true distribution of functions, "no one authority is simply a delegation from a superior authority, . . . and delegation of the separate, distributed powers must be made in accord with an antecedent constitutional law that exists for these powers. Precisely such a law is found in the laws concerning offices in Deuteronomy," Norbert Lohfink, "Distribution of the Functions of Power," in *A Song of Power and the Power of Song*, ed. D. L. Christensen (Winona Lake, IN: Eisenbrauns, 1993), 347–348. For distribution of powers in Israel through the replacement of Moses's role with a multiplicity of offices, see Vogt, *Deuteronomic Theology and the Significance of Torah*, 112.

36. Gnuse, *No Tolerance for Tyrants*, 41.

37. In some sense, Israel's monarchy began to fall short of God's standard before God had even selected their first king. In the era of the judges, the people begged Gideon the judge to take the office of monarch, but Gideon refused (Judg 8:23). Gideon's son Abimelech was neither appointed by God nor anointed by a prophet or a priest, yet he claimed for himself the office that his father had refused (Judg 9:2). This pretender king's reign ended when a woman rolled a millstone from the top of a tower and crushed his skull (Judg 9:53–54; compare Gen 3:15). Later Israelites never viewed Abimelech as a legitimate monarch—but the authors of the Old Testament did draw from the successes and shortfallings of Gideon and Abimelech to make sense of the reigns of later kings. See Leithart, *A Son to Me*, locations 1768–1772, 2530–2533, 3039, 3051–3065, 3934.

38. Saul seemed humble and well-intentioned at first (1 Sam 10:22–24; 11:6, 11, 15), but he was also impetuous, unwilling to listen, and obsessed with others' perceptions of him (1 Sam 13:8–14; 14:24–33; 15:30). In time, power became Saul's primary concern—to the point of seeking supernatural power over life and death (1 Sam 28:7–15). In the end, he was more obsessed with his own honor and position than he was concerned for the people he was called to lead (1 Sam 22:8). Saul began like Gideon but died like Abimelech. See Leithart, *A Son to Me*, location 111.

39. Dennis McCarthy, "2 Samuel 7 and Deuteronomistic History," *JBL* 84 (1965): 133.

40. "Kue" was the region known in the New Testament as "Cilicia." The people of Kue, like the people of Tyre, might have imported horses from Beth Togarmah (see Ezekiel 27:14). See Walter Elwell, "Kue," *Baker Encyclopedia of the Bible,* vol. 2, ed. Walter Elwell (Grand Rapids: Baker, 1988), 1294–1295.

41. The focus on divine kingship in Isa 2:2–4 and 4:2–6 leaves little room for any merely human king; Gregory Goswell, "Isaiah 1:26: A Neglected Text on Kingship," *TynBul* 62 (2011): 244. Additionally, Isaiah repeatedly emphasizes the death of kings and their heirs (6:1; 7:1; 39:6–8).

42. After the exile from Jerusalem, Isaiah's prediction of righteous judges was—as the church father Jerome recognized—partially fulfilled through Zerubbabel, Ezra, Nehemiah, and later leaders of Israel. "Zorobabel, Esdram, et Neemiam et caeteros principes, qui usque ad Hircanum populo praefuerunt, cui Herodes successit in regnum" ("Zerubbabel, Ezra, and Nehemiah and the rest had princes up to Hyrcanus, whom Herod succeeded as king"),

Jerome, "Commentariorum in Isaiam Prophetam, Sancti Eusebii Hieronymi Stridonensis Presbyteri Opera Omnia," *PL* 1:2:28. Yet this fulfillment under the postexilic leaders of Israel ultimately fell short and was merely a foretaste of the ultimate fulfillment of this promise in Jesus Christ.

43. It is conceivable that Isaiah recognized in 1:26–27 the failure of the monarchy and was calling here for a return to judges. See Christopher Seitz, *Isaiah 1–39* (Louisville: WJK, 1993), 35. It seems more likely, however, that Isaiah was referring to a past time in which judges appointed by the king pursued righteousness. Isaiah may have seen judges under King Hezekiah as exemplars of justice and the judges under King Manasseh as perverters of justice.

44. The priests emerged as political leaders under the Persians, and the position of high priest became corrupted through bribery, political machinations, even murder. According to Josephus (*Antiquitates Iudaice* 11:7), Bagoses—one of the generals in the army of Artaxerxes—promised the high priesthood to Joshua son of Jehoiada; Joshua's brother John became high priest instead and murdered Joshua to maintain his position. Later, a kingship of sorts emerged briefly in the late second century BC, uniting the offices of priest and king under the Hasmonean ruler Aristobulus I, a descendant of the Maccabees. This kingdom came to an end in 63 BC when Pompey conquered the province of Syria on behalf of the Roman Republic.

45. "It is on the basis of this union with the One who perfectly fulfilled the Law for us that we can have confidence for vindication at the judgment," Douglas Moo, *James* (Leicester, UK: Inter-Varsity, 1985), 99.

46. Mark Driscoll, *On Church Leadership* (Wheaton: Crossway, 2008), 68.

47. Michael Cafferky, "Honor the King. Yes, but Emulate the King?" *Journal of Applied Christian Leadership* 4 (2010): 33. In a bizarre application of Deut 17:17, the biblical command not to "acquire many wives" becomes in this leadership article the "principle of structurally minimizing the interorganizational entanglements . . . when upper-echelon leaders participate in interlocking directorates," 45. Whatever that means, it seems quite likely that it was not what Moses or the Holy Spirit had in mind when the book of Deuteronomy was inspired and inscribed.

48. Duane Covrig et al., "Integrating Four Types of Moral Leadership," *Journal of Applied Christian Leadership* 6 (2012): 48, 61–62.

49. This is not to suggest that the kingliness claimed by this faction in the Corinthian church was the same as the kingly leadership proposed by those who see prophet, priest, king, and judge as typological categories for church leaders. It is simply to point out that, when the imagery of kingship was applied to particular persons in the church separate from others, the imagery was being used to describe an ungodly pattern of behavior; Paul's response was to call church members to return to unity with the corporate body, awaiting the full revelation of their kingship in union with Christ at the end of time. The foundations of the Corinthians' pretensions of kingship probably had to do with their over-realized eschatology. See Anthony Thiselton, *The First Epistle to the Corinthians* (Grand Rapids: Eerdmans, 2000), 357–358.

50. "Christ alone will be the sovereign and will yield his kingship to [the Father] . . . and arguably . . . the corporeity of believers characterized by being-in-Christ in this derivative sense share in Christ's acts and declarative speech-acts," Thiselton, *The First Epistle to the Corinthians*, 431.

51. Jonathan Leeman, *Church Discipline* (Wheaton: Crossway, 2012), 33.

52. Even in the healthiest churches with the best of intentions, discipline can be handled poorly. Unfortunately, instead of correcting unhealthy practices and pursuing healthy church discipline, many churches have replaced poor church discipline with no church discipline.

To help churches pursue restorative and Christ-honoring church discipline, Robert Cheong has helpfully provided a list of common abuses of church discipline: (1) Leaders may use church discipline to flaunt their authority; (2) leaders may threaten removal in an attempt to manipulate someone to repent without doing the hard work of understanding and address-ing the sinner's struggles; (3) leaders may remove someone prematurely due to a legalistic assumption that no real Christian could have committed a particular sin in the first place; (4) leaders may prematurely remove someone because they want to set an example for others; (5) leaders or members may threaten church discipline to hurt or to manipulate someone who has wronged them or resisted their leadership. See Robert Cheong, *God Redeeming His Bride* (Ross-Shire, UK: Christian Focus, 2012), Kindle edition, location 2554.

53. Ibid., location 342.

54. Friedrich Schleiermacher recognized the implications of Christ's kingship in the munus triplex for the practice of church discipline: "In the power of the keys . . . we have . . . the continuation of the kingly activity of Christ." However, Schleiermacher ultimately understood church discipline as defining "the place taken in the community by each indi-vidual as a consequence of his inward state" and determining "whether much or little can be entrusted to him." As a result, he denied the binding capacity of creeds and rejected the practice of excluding unrepentant sinners, basing this rejection in part on his claim that Jesus never excommunicated the scribes and Pharisees. See Friedrich Schleiermacher, *Der christliche Glaube: Nach den Grundsätzen der evangelischen Kirche* (Halle, Germany: Hendel, 1897), sections 127, 144–145. For critical evaluation of Friedrich Schleiermacher's treatment of church discipline, see Eric Bargerhuff, *Love That Rescues* (Eugene, OR: Wipf and Stock, 2010), 41–46.

55. For further discussion of this aspect of church discipline, see Gregg Allison, *Sojourners and Strangers* (Wheaton: Crossway, 2012), 181–182, 199–201.

56. For first-century Christians, this refusal to practice partiality in judgments stood in stark contrast to the judicial practices of their culture. "To the wealthy, well-born, and well-connected went the chief rewards of the legal system," Ben Witherington, *Conflict and Community in Corinth* (Grand Rapids: Eerdmans, 1995), 163. Judgments before pagan judges in Corinth would likely have resulted in legal victories for privileged individuals in the Corinthian church; judgments in the church on the basis of the Word of God would have placed those who were more and less privileged on equal footing. This may, in part, explain the desire of certain individuals in the church to deal with their legal issues "before the unrighteous, and not before the saints" (1 Cor 6:1–8).

57. Paul's words in 1 Tim 5:19 should be taken to mean that a rebuke of an elder must be based on substantial evidence, not that a rebuke should occur only when there have been two or three eyewitnesses to his misdeeds; "μαρτύρων" ("witnesses") requires the presence of trustworthy testimony, not necessarily eyewitness evidence. If two or three eyewitnesses of an errant elder's misdeeds had been the intent, it seems likely that Paul would have been led to select instead some form of ἐπόπτης ("eyewitness") when he wrote these words.

58. For a summary of connections between proscriptions in Deuteronomy and Paul's descriptions of church discipline in the Corinthian correspondence, see E. G. Perona, "The Presence and Function of Deuteronomy in the Paranaesis of Paul in 1 Corinthians 5:1–11:1" (PhD diss., Trinity Evangelical Divinity School, 2005); Brian Rosner, *Paul, Scripture, and Ethics* (Leiden: Brill, 1994); Brian Rosner, "Deuteronomy in 1 and 2 Corinthians," in *Deuteronomy in the New Testament*, ed. Steve Moyise and Maarten J. J. Menken (London: T&T Clark, 2007), 122–126; and G. P. Waters, "Curse Redux?" *WTJ* 77 (2015): 237–250. Paul's clear connections between the appointment of judges in the old covenant and the church's discipline of members in the new covenant undergirds the movement I have made

in this chapter from the appointment of judges in Deuteronomy to the church's participation through union with Christ in the judgments of Christ. For specific correspondences between the appointment of judges and Paul's call for church discipline in 1 Corinthians, see Roy Ciampa and Brian Rosner, "1 Corinthians," in *Commentary on the New Testament Use of the Old Testament*, ed. D. A. Carson and G. K. Beale (Grand Rapids: Baker, 2007), 707–713. Paul seems to have seen his own circumstances as a reflection in his own experience of the overwhelming burden that Moses faced when he served as the sole judge of Israel; in the same way that Moses delegated judgment to trustworthy judges, Paul delegated judgment to the whole people of God, guided by the Spirit of Christ, under the authority of the trustworthy message of Christ. "Both Moses and Paul are overwhelmed by the judicial problems of the people of God. Both leaders decide to handle the more difficult cases themselves, with the Lord's help (cf. Exodus 18:19b and 1 Corinthians 5:3–5), and appoint judges to adjudicate the lesser cases (see Exodus 18:21–22; Deuteronomy 1:15; 1 Corinthians 6:1b, 4, 5b) by deciding between their brothers. There are also impressive terminological links between [1 Corinthians] 6:1–11 and Exodus 18/Deuteronomy 1 LXX (and related passages). A total of eight terms, some of which occur rarely in both the LXX and Paul's letters, can be traced from 6:1–8 to the tradition of Moses appointing judges," Ciampa and Rosner, "1 Corinthians," in Carson and Beale, *Commentary on the New Testament Use of the Old Testament*, 711. Andrés Vera has argued that Paul's dependence on the Deuteronomic covenant exclusion and curse formulas suggests that, even though calling the man who was committing incest with his father's wife to repentance was certainly one aspect of Paul's purpose, the apostle's focus was on preserving the holiness of the Corinthian church, Andrés Vera, "Removal from the Covenant Community" (paper presentation, Evangelical Theological Society Southeast Meeting, Louisville, 2017).

59. Gregg Allison, "Article XIV, The Church," in *Confessing the Faith*, ed. R. Albert Mohler (Louisville: SBTS Press, 2016), 98.

60. The church father Jerome understood the apostles and the church that had been founded on the apostles' proclamation to constitute the new covenant fulfillment of Isaiah's prediction of future righteous judges in Isa 1:26: "Apostolos . . . ecclesiarumque principes constituti sunt" ("the apostles—they believed—were appointed rulers of the church"), *Commentariorum in Isaiam Prophetam, Sancti Eusebii Hieronymi Stridonensis Presbyteri Opera Omnia, PL* 1:2:28.

61. Stephen Wellum and Kirk Wellum, "The Biblical and Theological Case for Congregationalism," in *Baptist Foundations*, ed. Mark Dever and Jonathan Leeman (Nashville: B&H, 2015), Kindle edition, locations 1181, 1508. Steve Timmis uses the term "consensus leadership" to describe leadership that guides the church toward this type of congregationalism: "Consensus leadership is a process that shapes the life of the whole church. It is important for leaders to open up an issue for wide-ranging discussion, as it allows the Spirit of God to be at work in the people of God," Steve Timmis, *Gospel-Centred Leadership* (Surrey, UK: Good Book, 2012), 104.

62. Dietrich Bonhoeffer, *Life Together*, trans. J. W. Doberstein (New York: Harper, 1954), 107.

63. This clause has provided the title for two popular rap songs, one by Tupac Shakur ("All Eyez on Me," Death Row Records, 1996) and the other by Master P ("Only God Can Judge Me," EMI Records, 1999). Tupac Shakur's performance depicts an individual speaking these words as he dies in an emergency room after being shot, rightly noting that—at this point—his judgment is in God's hands; the lyrics wrestle deeply with the struggles of an urban African American male. In Master P's lyrics, however, the same clause becomes an apparent refusal to accept responsibility and consequences for one's choices and actions.

This second meaning from Master P seems to reflect the dominant function of the clause in contemporary culture.

64. R. Albert Mohler, "Church Discipline," in *Polity*, ed. Mark Dever (Washington, DC: CCR, 2001), 43.

65. For a historical description of the decline of church discipline in Baptist churches, see Gregory Wills, *Democratic Religion* (Oxford: Oxford University Press, 2003), particularly chapter 8. In 1923, Gaines S. Dobbins—professor of church efficiency at SBTS—suggested that, if churches simply increased the intensity of their programming and refused to listen to persons who talked about others' sins, difficulties that once would have resulted in church discipline would disappear on their own, Gaines S. Dobbins, *The Efficient Church* (Nashville: Baptist Sunday School Board, 1923), 194. Many Southern Baptist churches seem to have done exactly what Dobbins encouraged, with disastrous results.

66. John L. Dagg, *A Treatise on Church Order* (Charleston: Southern Baptist Publication Society, 1858), 274. One evidence of the church's tendency to fall short in the pursuit of justice—and thus to bring harm to the church and reproach on the cause of Christ—is Dagg himself, who would rightly be disciplined today in any church that recognizes the implications of the Gospel for racial justice, due to his disgusting and gospel-denying perspectives on African American persons. See John L. Dagg, *The Elements of Moral Science* (New York: Sheldon, 1860).

67. Rachael Denhollander, "Response to Sovereign Grace Churches," March 1, 2018, https://www.facebook.com/notes/rachael-denhollander/response-to-sovereign-grace-churches/1720170721396574/.

Chapter Four: A Devoted Community

1. This individual was apparently unaware that the Roman Catholic Church does allow deacons to distribute the elements of Holy Communion (see Code of Canon Law, canons 907–910). However, in many Roman Catholic congregations, only the priest partakes of the cup. Perhaps she had only witnessed that practice and was unaware that deacons may, even in the Roman Catholic Church, distribute both the bread and the cup.

2. Drew Goodmanson, "How Multiperspectivalism Shapes Church Leadership and How You Staff a Church," https://www.goodmanson.com/church/how-mutliperspectivalism-shapes-church-leadership-and-how-you-staff-a-church. According to Goodmanson, the primary concern of a priestly leader is who might be hurt by a circumstance. "Often they will avoid the 'authority' or 'the way it should be implemented' if it causes too much emotional damage. . . . A priest has a tremendous understanding of the needs of the people."

3. Mark Driscoll, *On Church Leadership* (Wheaton: Crossway, 2008), 67; Drew Goodmanson, "Leadership Conflict Resolution," http://www.thespiritlife.net/79-spirit/spirit-reflection/3226-leadership-conflict-resolution-prophet-priest-king-by-drew-goodmanson, and "How Multiperspectivalism Shapes Church Leadership and How You Staff a Church."

4. John Frame, "A Primer on Perspectivalism," https://frame-poythress.org/a-primer-on-perspectivalism/.

5. H. S. MacGillivray, *The Influence of Christianity on the Vocabulary of Old English*, part 1 (Halle: Max Niemeyer, 1902), 70–71.

6. The clause could be translated "the priests who are Levites or the judge" (Deut 17:9), indicating that either priests or a judge could hand down a decision. However, it is more likely that referred cases were handled "by both priests and judges," Peter Craigie, *Deuteronomy* (Grand Rapids: Eerdmans, 1976), 252. "While [17:9] speaks of priests in the plural, [17:12] refers to 'the priest' in the singular. So while priests may be involved in the process, the final

decision belongs to the chief judge and high priest," Ajith Fernando, *Deuteronomy: Loving Obedience to a Loving God* (Wheaton: Crossway, 2012), 443.

7. "Priests were educated, with civil and criminal law forming part of their knowledge. According to [Deut 17:18] and 31:9 and 24, they have charge of the scroll of God's teaching, and according to Leviticus 10:11, their tasks include teaching the people all of God's laws," Jeffrey Tigay, *Deuteronomy* (Philadelphia: JPS, 2003), 164. See also Derek Tidball, *Skillful Shepherds* (Grand Rapids: Zondervan, 1986), 42.

8. In some circumstances and situations, the Torah was not sufficiently explicit or the priest did not possess enough knowledge to be certain of the right decision, hence the provision of Urim and Thummim (Exod 28:30; Lev 8:8; Num 27:21; Deut 33:8; 1 Sam 23:9–12; 28:6; 30:7–8; Ezra 2:63; Neh 7:65). For discussion of the Urim and Thummim, see Philip Graham Ryken, *Exodus: Saved for God's Glory* (Wheaton: Crossway, 2005), 881–887.

9. Appointment to priesthood involved consecration, the promise of physical provision, and anointing (Exod 28:41). "The crucial difference between prophet and priest is that the former is called while the latter is appointed to office and therefore dispenses salvation by virtue of the office, rather than through personal charismatic endowment. From a strictly religious point of view, installation in the priestly office is described as an act of consecration . . . (1 Sam 7:1; Exod 28:3; 30:30), but the expression 'filling the hand' is also used (Judg 17:5, 12; 1 Kgs 13:33), suggesting the conferring of the benefice that went with the office," Joseph Blenkinsopp, *Sage, Priest, Prophet* (Louisville: WJK, 1995), 79–80. Blenkinsopp rightly notes the difference between appointment of a priest and the personal charismatic endowment of a prophet; however, it is possible that some sort of organized prophetic guild existed during the era of the divided kingdom ("sons of the prophets," 2 Kings 2–6).

10. See also 2 Macc 1:10, where a letter from Judas Maccabeus refers to Aristobulus as "a member of the family of anointed priests and teacher of King Ptolemy" ("Ιουδας Ἀριστοβούλῳ διδασκάλῳ Πτολεμαίου τοῦ βασιλέως ὄντι δὲ ἀπὸ τοῦ τῶν χριστῶν ἱερέων γένους").

11. "The priest was also a teacher, and in the first place a teacher of the law," Blenkinsopp, *Sage, Priest, Prophet*, 82. One might say that Leviticus 10:10–11 provides at least a partial job description for the priesthood: "You must distinguish between the holy and the common, and the clean and the unclean, and teach the Israelites all the statutes that the Lord has given to them through Moses." See also Marty Stevens, *Leadership Roles of the Old Testament* (Eugene, OR: Cascade, 2012), 82.

12. Not only in Israel but also in ancient Near Eastern contexts beyond Israel, the priests who maintained temples to the people's gods were also responsible for maintaining documentation of covenants. See, for example, the treaty between ruler of the Hittites and the ruler of Mitanni: "A duplicate of this tablet has been deposited before the Sun-goddess of Arinna, because the Sun-goddess of Arinna regulates kingship and queenship. In the Mitanni land [a duplicate] has been deposited before Tessub, the lord of the [shrine] of Kahat. At regular intervals shall they read it in the presence of the king of the Mitanni land and in the presence of the sons of the Hurri country," James Pritchard, ed., *Ancient Near Eastern Texts Relating to the Old Testament*, 3rd ed. (Princeton: Princeton University Press, 1969), 205. See also Daniel Block "The Burden of Leadership," *BSac* (2005): 271.

13. "The designations the 'priests,' the 'Levites,' and the 'whole tribe of Levi' indicate that the priests and Levites were not always coextensive terms; the 'priests' were those Levites who were the descendants of Aaron, and the 'Levites' included all those who belonged to the tribe of Levi, whether or not they were descendants of Aaron (Num 18:20, 23–24)," Earl Kalland, "Deuteronomy," in *The Expositor's Bible Commentary* (Grand Rapids: Zondervan, 1992), 3:118.

14. Although the teaching role of priests would be particularly important in the place chosen for God's tabernacle, the teaching responsibilities of the priests were not limited to this single locale. By divine design, priests and Levites possessed no unified territory. Instead, priests and Levites were distributed throughout the land so that the Torah might be taught in every place. Centuries earlier, the patriarch Jacob had predicted on his deathbed that, due to the bloodlust he had glimpsed in his son Levi, Levi's descendants would be scattered throughout the land (Gen 49:5–7). Later, the family of Aaron within the tribe of Levi was selected to serve as Israel's priesthood, and the entire tribe of Levi received the responsibility of assisting the priesthood (Exod 28:1–5; 32:26–39; Num 1:47–53), but Jacob's words were still fulfilled. Before the people crossed into Canaan, Yahweh commanded the Israelites to set aside four dozen villages, scattered throughout the land, as the property of priests and Levites (Num 35:1–8). Through this scattering of the Levites, Jacob's curse on the descendants of one of his sons became a blessing for the descendants of all his sons. The Levites' lands were limited to a narrow tract that skirted each of their scattered villages, but the Levites received a far greater provision than fields or pastures. Yahweh's "fire offerings"—and, ultimately, Yahweh himself—became the inheritance of the tribe of Levi (Deut 18:1–2; see also Num 18:20–24). The sovereign Lord was the Levites' allotment, and they lived as guests at his table. Whenever offerings were brought to Yahweh, the priests and Levites received produce from the worshipers' fields and specified portions from the sacrifices of cattle, oxen, and sheep (Deut 18:3–4). If the people failed to worship Yahweh at the place of his choosing, the priests and Levites could not continue to serve at Yahweh's altar; the livelihood of the tribe of Levi depended, therefore, on the covenant faithfulness of all the tribes of Israel.

15. "'The man who shows contempt' . . . may not only be the local judge who does not want to exact the punishment decided by the priests and the judge in the place the Lord would choose; such a man may be anyone in Israel," Kalland, "Deuteronomy," 115. For any Israelite, to reject these righteous judgments was to swerve off the path of faithfulness to God's covenant (Deut 17:11; compare Prov 2:20–3:1). Anyone who veered from the verdicts that the priest declared was behaving "presumptuously" by rejecting God's revelation and forging a pathway to destruction (Deut 17:12 NASB). In the old covenant, only the death of the offender could purge such presumption from the land and prevent others from following the covenant-breaker's path; the purpose of this sentence of death was to renew the people's fear of God (Deut 17:12–13). And so when a son of Israel turned against the Torah in the old covenant, the result was a death sentence for one Israelite that was intended to result in the return of all Israel to God's Torah; in the new covenant, the Son who never violated God's Torah or offended God's justice purged his chosen people's sin by embracing the full penalty for their sin on the cross. In this way, the sacrificial death of one single Israelite now results in the return of every authentic believer to God's righteous way.

16. When the Assyrians settled pagan populations in Israel, wild beasts tormented the new inhabitants of the land until a priest was sent to teach "how they should fear" the LORD (2 Kgs 17:24–28)—a phrase that seems to have suggested obedience to the Torah (see parallels between fear of the LORD and the precepts of the Torah in Pss 112:1; 119:38, 63). "Ancient Israel . . . could apprehend genuine wisdom and 'fear of the Lord' by keeping and studying Torah. . . . The 'fear' of Yahweh reflects a loyal response to the covenant (Deuteronomy 6:2, 13, 24) and is closely identified with wisdom. It also designates observance of the Torah (Psalm 119:63; Ecclesiastes 12:13–14)," Sheri Klouda, "The Dialectical Interplay of Seeing and Hearing in Psalm 19 and Its Connection to Wisdom," *BBR* 10 (2000): 184.

17. It was the priest Jehoiada who not only taught Joash but also crowned him (2 Kgs 12:1–2; 2 Chr 23:1–11). The moment Jehoiada died, however, Joash listened to the voices

of powerful leaders and abandoned the temple as well as the Torah (2 Chr 24:15–19). "The verb 'abandon' ('*āzab*) is a characteristic one of the Chronicler (2 Chronicles 12:1; 15:2; 21:10; 24:20; 28:6; 29:60," J. A. Thompson, *1, 2 Chronicles* (Nashville: B&H, 1994), 317. Apparently the faithfulness of Joash depended more on the presence of the teacher who crowned him than on the God who had called him.

18. The author of Hebrews describes the priesthood of believers and union with Christ in different terms than Paul, but the doctrines are no less clear in Hebrews than in the rest of the New Testament. After having established that Jesus is the great and consummate high priest, for example, the author of Hebrews writes, "Let us draw near with a true heart in full assurance of faith, our hearts sprinkled clean from an evil conscience and our bodies washed in pure water" (Heb 10:22). Ritual sprinkling and washing in water were associated with priesthood (Exod 29:4; 40:12; Lev 8:6; 16:4, 24, 26; Num 19:7–8), suggesting both unity with Christ the great high priest and a comprehensive priesthood of all who believe. "As at their consecration the Levitical priests were washed with water and sprinkled with the blood of the sacrifice (Exodus 29:4, 21), so now sprinkling and washing are obligatory for all who belong to this 'holy priesthood,'" Philip Edgcumbe Hughes, *A Commentary on the Epistle to the Hebrews* (Grand Rapids: Eerdmans, 1977), 410–411. A clearer expression of union with Christ may be present in Heb 3:14, depending on whether μέτοχοι is translated "partners with" or "participants in." For the rendering "participants in," see Harold Attridge, *The Epistle to the Hebrews* (Philadelphia: Fortress, 1989), 117. For further discussion of union with Christ in Hebrews, see Grant Macaskill, *Union with Christ in the New Testament* (Oxford: Oxford University Press, 2014), 178–187, particularly 185–186.

19. Dietrich Bonhoeffer, *Life Together*, trans. J. W. Doberstein (New York: Harper, 1954), 33.

20. Robert Peterson, *Salvation Applied by the Spirit* (Wheaton: Crossway, 2015), 417.

21. "Here for the first time two fundamental concepts appear together: that of the *b'rith* [covenant] of JHWH [Yahweh] with the people which is to supersede his *b'rith* with the fathers (2:24; 6:4ff), and that of the *melekh*-ship [kingship] of JHWH, in the form of the *mamlakha* [kingdom], of the domain of the kingly rule," Martin Buber, *Kingship of God*, 3rd ed., trans. Richard Scheimann (New York: Harper, 1967), 129.

22. In Exodus 19, Moses provides "the background to the Book of the Covenant (Exodus 19–24)"; this chapter "acts as a bookend on the opening side of the covenant document," Peter Gentry and Stephen Wellum, *Kingdom through Covenant* (Wheaton: Crossway, 2012), 309. Verses 3–8 function as a self-contained unit in which verbs shift from third-person plural to second-person singular and the emphasis is placed on God's purpose in his establishment of a covenant with Israel. The conditional statement here is read as a speech-act condition; in a speech-act condition, the result (holy priesthood, in this instance) expresses what is inherent in the reality declared by the speaker (covenant relationship). The imagery from *The Lord of the Rings* comes from a conversation with my colleague Peter Gentry.

23. Stephen Dempster, *Dominion and Dynasty* (Downers Grove, IL: InterVarsity, 2003), 101–102.

24. Jesus was the representative Israelite in whom the covenant was kept on behalf of anyone who is united with him through faith. For Jesus as the true Israel and representation of the nation in the fulfillment of the covenant, see Graeme Goldsworthy, *According to Plan* (Downers Grove, IL: InterVarsity, 1991), 204–206, and N. T. Wright, "Jesus, Israel, and the Cross," SBLSP (Chico, CA: Scholars' Press, 1985), 75–95.

25. *The Works of the Reverend John Newton* (Philadelphia: Uriah Hunt, 1839), 1:62.

26. Driscoll, *On Church Leadership*, 67; Frame, "Primer on Perspectivalism"; Goodmanson, "Leadership Conflict Resolution" and "How Multiperspectivalism Shapes

Church Leadership and How You Staff a Church; Vern Poythress, "Modern Spiritual Gifts as Analogous to Apostolic Gifts," *JETS* 39 (1996): 73–75. The implication that prophecy is to be identified primarily with teaching may also be found in a broad range of Reformed theologians, including, e.g., John Calvin, *Institutio Christianae Religionis*, 2:15:2; James Petigru Boyce, *Abstract of Systematic Theology* (1887; repr. ed., Louisville: SBTS Press, 2014), 261–262; Emil Brunner, *The Christian Doctrine of Creation and Redemption*, trans. Olive Wyon (Philadelphia: Westminster, 1952), 275–281. Friedrich Schleiermacher identified the prophetic office of Christ with the church's proclamation of the Word, the priestly office of Christ with administration of the sacraments, and the kingly office of Christ with church discipline, *Der christliche Glaube: Nach den Grundsätzen der evangelischen Kirche* (Halle, Germany: Hendel, 1897), section 127.

27. Duane Covrig et al., "Integrating Four Types of Moral Leadership," *Journal of Applied Christian Leadership* 6 (2012): 40–41.

28. The temple and temple courts in Jerusalem—the domain overseen by the priests and Levites—constituted not only a space set aside for rituals, sacrifice, and prayer but also a space for teachers and teaching. "From time immemorial, the priests and the Levites had been the authoritative teachers of the law, and even later rabbis recognized that the Temple Mount had been the supreme seat of authoritative Torah teaching," Oskar Skarsaune, *In the Shadow of the Temple* (Downers Grove, IL: InterVarsity, 2002), 93–95. For discussion of the significance of the temple in the teaching ministry of Jesus and his apostles (see Luke 2:46; 19:47; 20:1; 21:37; John 7:14; Acts 5:21–25), see Birger Gerhardsson, *Memory and Manuscript with Tradition and Transmission in Early Christianity* (Grand Rapids: Eerdmans, 1998), 219.

29. Frederick Buechner, *Beyond Words* (New York: HarperCollins, 2004), 325.

30. For discussion of overlap between prophecy and teaching in Acts 13:1, see Craig Keener, *Acts: An Exegetical Commentary*, vol. 2 (Grand Rapids: Baker, 2013), Kindle edition, locations 24223–24237. When the people acclaimed Jesus as a prophet, it was only rarely in response to his teachings and, even then, the words may have been perceived more as prophetic oracle than as teaching or proclamation (John 7:37–44). Most often the people's acclamations were in reaction to his miraculous signs or supernatural knowledge, again suggesting a weakness in the claim of direct linkage between prophecy and teaching (Luke 7:11–17; John 4:16–20; 6:1–15; 9:17). John the Baptist was a prophet (Matt 21:26; Mark 11:32; Luke 20:6) but he seems not to have been widely known for teaching, apart from teaching his followers how to pray (Luke 11:1). For the prophet as a person of prayer, see also Gen 20:7.

31. Karl Barth, *This Christian Cause* (New York: MacMillan, 1941), letter 1. For Barth, the church's pursuit of justice and the church's prophetic cries against oppressive powers were to be grounded in a theological confession of humanity's incapacity to achieve righteousness in our own power. The justice of God is enacted not through human effort or violence but through prophetic witness to divine truth and justice. "The church . . . will not preach a crusade against Hitler. He who died upon the Cross died for Hitler too, and, even more, for all those bewildered men who voluntarily or involuntarily serve under his banner. But precisely because the church knows about justification which we men cannot attain by any means for ourselves, she cannot remain indifferent. . . . Where [justice] is at stake, there the church cannot withhold her witness" (letter 1).

32. "The priesthood of all believers has an easy habit of becoming a discussion of the priesthood of each believer, individually and independently, in which each of us is considered our own priest. In that way, the doctrine falls victim to the very thing it seeks to avoid: individuals appropriate the very thing which the work of Christ ends, and which is only continued as the believer participates in the body of Christ, in the whole life of the church.

The priesthood of all believers is a doctrine that states that priesthood is no longer individual (whether in relation to ministers or the total number of individuals in the church), but corporate in the narrow sense of the term, relating to the body of Christ. . . . [In the New Testament,] the term *hiereus* is only ever used in the singular (with the exception of referring to temple priests) of one person—Jesus Christ," Tom Greggs, "The Priesthood of No Believer," *International Journal of Systematic Theology* 17 (2015): 377.

33. This stands in stark contrast to the teachings of the Roman Catholic Church, which admits a priesthood of the laity but then proceeds to teach that the priesthood of ordained individuals differs from the people's priesthood not only in degree but also in essence (*Lumen Gentium* 2:1:36): According to the *Catechism of the Catholic Church*, "the whole Church is a priestly people. Through Baptism all the faithful share in the priesthood of Christ. . . . The ministerial priesthood differs in essence from the common priesthood of the faithful because it confers a sacred power for the service of the faithful. The ordained ministers exercise their service for the People of God by teaching (*munus docendi*), divine worship (*munus liturgicum*) and pastoral governance (*munus regendi*). Since the beginning, the ordained ministry has been conferred and exercised in three degrees: that of bishops, that of presbyters, and that of deacons," *Catechism of the Catholic Church*, 1591–1593. It is worth noting the degree to which this triad is similar to the *munus triplex* leadership typology suggested by some Reformed theologians. *Munus docendi* and *munus regendi* would seem to be respectively analogous to prophetic leadership and kingly leadership in a leadership typology based on the *munus triplex*. If not for the fact that proponents of the *munus triplex* leadership typology have identified priestly leadership with mercy ministry instead of worship ministry, *munus liturgicum* could be linked to priestly leadership in the *munus triplex* leadership typology.

34. One other instance in which Paul drew a possible parallel between old covenant priests and new covenant church leaders was in his first letter to the Corinthians: "Don't you know that those who perform the temple services eat food from the temple, and those who serve at the altar share in the offerings of the altar? In the same way, the Lord has commanded that those who preach the gospel should earn their living by the gospel" (1 Cor 9:13–14). However, this comparison is part of a sequence of metaphors that also includes references to soldiers, vinedressers, shepherds, and oxen (1 Cor 9:7–12). Paul was drawing examples from a wide range of familiar patterns wherein an individual was allowed to receive provisions from the goods gained through service. The reference to priesthood seems to be as applicable to a Greco-Roman pagan priest as to a Levitical priest in the old covenant. As such, it seems unlikely that this reference supports any individualized role as a priest or a priestly leader. For further discussion of this text, see Anthony Thiselton, *The First Epistle to the Corinthians* (Grand Rapids: Eerdmans, 2000), 661–663, 691–692.

35. Although "bodies" is plural, "sacrifice" is singular, suggesting a community united as one in Christ. N. T. Wright captures the sense well: "Offer God the true worship; be transformed by having your minds renewed, because you should be thinking as one people in the Messiah," N. T. Wright, "Romans," in *The New Interpreter's Bible*, ed. Leander Keck (Nashville: Abingdon, 2002), 708. "In keeping with the rest of the New Testament, Paul assumes an eschatological transformation of the Old Testament cultic ministry in which animal sacrifices are replaced by the obedience of Christians (cf. Romans 12:1) and praise offered to God (Hebrews 13:15)," Douglas Moo, *Epistle to the Romans* (Grand Rapids: Eerdmans, 1996), 891. "The terms ἁγίαν ["holy"] and εὐάρεστον ["acceptable"] have cultic associations. . . . The former term denotes the idea that the sacrifice is dedicated to God, while the latter evokes Old Testament notions of sacrifices that are pleasing and fragrant to God. . . . The word λατρειαν ["service," "act of worship"] is another cultic term. What is

remarkable is that Paul has applied the language of the cult to everyday existence," Thomas Schreiner, *Romans* (Grand Rapids: Baker, 1998), 644, 646.

36. Paul saw himself as part of a priesthood performing priestly duties but not as a priest individually. The word "priest" in the clause "serving as a priest of God's good news" (Rom 15:16) does not represent a singular noun in the Greek text but contributes to the translation of a function described by a verb (ἱερουργοῦντα, "working in a priestly capacity"). Later in the same chapter, Paul described the sacrificial giving of the Roman church in terms of λειτουργῆσαι (15:27). In the Septuagint, some form of λειτουργεῖν ("to serve," "to worship") was the typical translation of שֵׁרֵת ("serve") whenever שֵׁרֵת described cultic service. Given the clear function of λειτουργεῖν in the Septuagint as well as the function of the verb in Heb 10:11, it seems most reasonable that λειτουργεῖν conveys priestly implications in Rom 15:27 as well. In Acts 13:2, the term similarly seems to point to the community's engagement in worship and prayer as a priestly activity. The verb that Luke employed in Acts 13:2 "could include any kind of public service, but it clearly bears a narrower sense here. The [Septuagint] usually applies it to priestly, cultic worship, an activity difficult to perform without the temple. The term also, however, included the Levitical temple worship of thanks and praise (1 Chronicles 6:32; 16:4; 2 Chronicles 31:2). To the extent that it retains its frequent cultic associations from the [Septuagint], it is helpful to think of spiritual sacrifices of worship," Keener, *Acts: An Exegetical Commentary*, vol. 2, location 24411. In Acts 13:2, "λειτουργούντων . . . καὶ νηστευόντων" ("serving [worshiping] . . . and fasting") may convey much the same sense as "προσευξάμενοι μετὰ νηστειῶν" ("praying and fasting") in Acts 14:23. Together, these patterns seem to suggest that Paul did not view his priestly service in Rom 15:16 as an office that he held individually but as an identity in which he participated with the members of the church through union with Christ.

37. "Part of the newness of Jeremiah's covenant seems to be a democratization of the teaching office ('from the least to the greatest' in Israel) in the latter days so that every Israelite will be in the knowledgeable position of the priests (and likely also prophets) and thus will have no need to be taught by any leader or caste of priests. . . . The likely reason for this democratization is that in the new age all will have more access to revelation than did even the teaching priests and prophets of the former age," G. K. Beale, *A New Testament Biblical Theology* (Grand Rapids: Baker, 2011), 734–735.

38. The suggestion that certain church leaders might be more priestly than others calls to mind the famous lines from George Orwell, "All animals are equal, but some animals are more equal than others," which one might paraphrase in this context as, "All believers are a priesthood, but some believers are more priestly than others." See George Orwell, *Animal Farm*, chapter 10.

39. Although the topic of cessationism and continuationism is relevant to the issue of prophecy in the new covenant, any detailed discussion of cessationism and continuationism stands beyond the scope of this study. For further exploration of this topic, see Wayne Grudem, ed., *Are Miraculous Gifts for Today?* (Grand Rapids: Zondervan, 1996), and C. Samuel Storms, *Practicing the Power* (Grand Rapids: Zondervan, 2017). It should be noted, on the topic of prophecy, that some continuationists allow for the possibility of fallible prophecy in the new covenant. Another possibility, which seems to be a better appropriation of the biblical evidence, is to recognize both that prophecy has persisted into the present age and that authentic prophecy is never in error. New covenant prophecy, no less than old covenant prophecy, is to be rejected as false if it fails to come to pass or if it is incongruent with God's previous revelation (see Deut 18:15–22). If the supposed prophecy of a church member turns out to be untrue, the result is not a death penalty but church discipline, beginning with an individual confrontation and escalating—if the individual remains unrepentant

regarding his or her errant claim to have received and spoken a divine message—to expulsion from the community of faith.

40. Beale, *A New Testament Biblical Theology*, 735.

41. Richard Baxter, *Reformed Pastor* (1656; repr., Glasgow: William Collins, 1829), 120.

42. In Exod 19:22, Yahweh called for the consecration of a priesthood prior to the setting apart of the tribe of Levi or the establishment of the Aaronic priesthood. Some have taken this as an anachronism in which a redactor placed this text out of order; see, e.g., J. I. Durham, *Exodus* (Waco: Word, 1987), 272–273. A more likely suggestion, on the basis of Exod 13:11–15, is that the firstborn son in each family functioned as a priest at this time; Walter Kaiser, "Exodus," in *The Expositor's Bible Commentary*, rev. ed., ed. David Garland and Tremper Longman (Grand Rapids: Zondervan, 2008), 1:476. It is also conceivable that Yahweh was referring to the whole community as a collective priesthood or that certain persons in the Israelite community other than firstborn sons functioned in a priestly role prior to the establishment of the Aaronic priesthood, much like Melchizedek and Jethro had in earlier times (Gen 14:18; Exod 2:16).

43. "Human holiness is not to be found in separation in the sense of withdrawal, and certainly not in moral prudishness, but in distinctiveness of lifestyle that does not eclipse compassionate and open-hearted reaching out to those who are not fit for God's presence," James Robson, "Forgotten Dimensions of Holiness," *HBT* 33 (2011): 146. Although Robson focuses on love as an overlooked dimension of holiness, he rightly emphasizes distinctiveness and devotion rather than separation as most central in the definition of holiness.

44. Peter Gentry, "The Meaning of 'Holy' in the Old Testament," *BSac* 170 (2013): 417. Gentry goes on to point out that "the notion of divine transcendence in Isaiah 6 is there to demonstrate that the holiness of Yahweh—his dedication to social justice in this particular situation—cannot be manipulated, and judgment is certain. That explains the coincidence of holiness and divine transcendence in this text."

45. "L'idee de separation n'apparait dans aucun de ces textes; c'est la notion de relation, d'appartenance, qui predomine" ("The idea of separation does not appear in any of these texts; it is the notion of the relationship, the devotion, which predominates"), Claude-Bernard Costecalde, *Aux Origines du Sacre Biblique* (Paris: Letouzey and Ane, 1986), 137. The commonly cited (but not quite accurate) definitions of "holiness," such as "purity" or "separation," are attributed by Costecalde to an incorrect etymology in the nineteenth-century work of W. W. Baudissin (see Costecalde, 23–30). Baudissin did indeed support these definitions by suggesting an etymology that traced קָדוֹשׁ ("holy") back to a root that meant "to cut." Costecalde is correct, therefore, to critique Baudissin's contribution to an incorrect etymological understanding of קָדוֹשׁ. Defining holiness in terms of purity or separation, however, reaches back farther than a misconstrued etymology from the nineteenth century. In Martin Luther's lectures on Romans, for example, Luther—following early medieval pope Gregory the Great—took "holy" when applied to human beings to mean cleanness, chasteness, or separation, understanding the word to point to the purity that every human being owes to God; Martin Luther, *Lectures on Romans*, ed. Wilhelm Pauck (Philadelphia: Westminster, 1961), 324. Baudissin's incorrect understanding of the origins of קָדוֹשׁ seems to have provided etymological support for a misunderstanding of "holiness" that preceded Baudissin's research. Nevertheless, Costecalde is correct that the more correct meaning of "holiness" is "devotion." Costecalde's work, unfortunately, remains available only in French and thus has only minimally impacted the broader world of evangelical scholarship.

46. "The priestly function of the whole people of God is to be holy and offer sacrifices to God, and only in that context to mediate between God and fallen humanity. Christians are to offer themselves in loyal consecration to God, offering spiritual sacrifices that are

'coextensive with the lives of the faithful,' by which the church 'brings the kingdom of God into being here below,'" D. A. Carson, "1 Peter," in *Commentary on the New Testament Use of the Old Testament*, ed. D. A. Carson and G. K. Beale (Grand Rapids: Baker, 2007), 1031. See also the discussion in Karen Jobes, *1 Peter* (Grand Rapids: Baker, 2005), 161.

47. In the mind of the author of Hebrews, "there is a Christian altar . . . that . . . is quite distinct from that of the levitical cultus," Paul Ellingworth, *The Epistle to the Hebrews* (Grand Rapids: Eerdmans, 1993), 719. In Hebrews 13:15, the biblical author identifies "as Christian sacrifices (1) praise, and (2) good deeds," ibid. "The term translated *do good* is a noun that appears nowhere else in the Greek Bible. . . . In this context it probably denotes 'acts of kindness' that are concrete expressions of concern for others," P. T. O'Brien, *The Letter to the Hebrews* (Grand Rapids: Eerdmans, 2010), 528.

48. This sentence is adapted from a point in a sermon shared by my friend and fellow pastor Justin Karl with college students at the Midtown congregation of Sojourn Community Church in Louisville.

49. Although the saving benefits of Christ's death are efficacious only for believers, certain temporal benefits of Christ's death extend beyond the community of faith so that all humanity is blessed. "It is not denied by the advocates of particular redemption . . . that mankind in general, even those who ultimately perish, do derive some advantages or benefits from Christ's death. . . . Important benefits have accrued to the whole human race from the death of Christ, and . . . in these benefits those who are finally impenitent and unbelieving partake," William Cunningham, *Historical Theology* (1870; repr., Edmonton, AB: Still Waters, 1991), 2:332–333. One expression of these temporal benefits is the church's redemptive pursuit of justice, peace, and beauty for the benefit not only of believers but also of society and culture as a whole, not merely for the sake of a platform for proclamation of the gospel but for the glory of God and for the flourishing of societies and communities.

50. Paul made much the same point in a different way when he referred to his proclamation of the gospel as a priestly act whereby people from many ethnicities were being devoted to God as a living sacrifice (Rom 15:16). God called Paul to serve as a "minister . . . to the Gentiles" for "the offering up" of the nations to God (Rom 15:16 KJV; see also Isa 66:20–21; Rom 12:1–2; Heb 13:15).

51. "There are a thousand ways to magnify Christ in life and death. None should be scorned. All are important. But none makes the worth of Christ shine more brightly than sacrificial love for other people in the name of Jesus. If Christ is so valuable that the hope of his immediate and eternal fellowship after death frees us from the self-serving fear of dying and enables us to lay down our lives for the good of others, such love magnifies the glory of Christ like nothing else in the world," John Piper, *Risk Is Right* (Wheaton: Crossway, 2013), 15.

52. Amy Hubbard, "Celebrating 100 Years or More of T-Shirts," *Los Angeles Times*, June 15, 2013, http://articles.latimes.com/2013/jun/15/news/la-fe-atr-t-shirt-100-years-old -20130528.

53. "Every financial transaction in which we engage must be done as if the money was God's (which it is). While we are careful with all funds, we have to be extra-careful with money that has been designated as belonging to God. Just as the failure to give God his due is viewed in the Bible as robbing God, the failure to use God's funds responsibly could be viewed as defrauding God," Fernando, *Deuteronomy*, 459.

54. Paul House, *Bonhoeffer's Seminary Vision* (Wheaton: Crossway, 2015), 139.

55. Bonhoeffer, *Life Together*, 27–28.

56. D. A. Carson, *A Call to Spiritual Reformation* (Grand Rapids: Baker, 1992), 58.

57. For κλῆρος (translated as "those entrusted" in 1 Pet 5:3) as portions of land allotted to tribes of Israel, see, e.g., Deut 18:1, 2; Josh 19:1, 2, 10, 17, 24, 32, 40, 49 LXX. For further discussion, see Edmund Clowney, *The Message of 1 Peter* (Leicester, UK: Inter-Varsity, 1989), 202.

58. The emphasis in this chapter on the church as the property of God was inspired in part by the phrase from the Barmen Declaration *sie allein sein Eigentum ist* ("she [the church] is his [God's] property alone"), thesis 3.

59. Although this radio address given by Bonhoeffer in in 1933 primarily concerned political leadership, his words are also applicable in this context: "The true leader must always be able to disappoint. If a leader . . . does not continually tell his followers quite clearly of the limited nature of his task and of their own responsibility, if he allows himself to surrender to the wishes of his followers, who would always make him their idol—then the image of the leader will pass over into the image of the misleader, and he will be acting in a criminal way not only towards those he leads, but also towards himself," Dietrich Bonhoeffer, *The Bonhoeffer Reader,* ed. Clifford Green and Michael DeJonge (Minneapolis: Fortress, 2013), 368.

60. Effective followership requires followers who are not only accountable but also willing to hold their leaders accountable. See discussion of Ira Chaleff's book *The Courageous Follower* in Mary Uhl-Bien et al., "Followership Theory," *Leadership Quarterly* 25 (2014): 90. In an unhealthy organization, followers may see their purpose as enacting the vision of a senior leader instead of seeking to do what is right for the sake of others. In such organizations, the senior leader tends not to be held accountable even when he or she is clearly in the wrong. A clear example of this phenomenon may be observed in a response to *Star Wars: Episode I—The Phantom Menace* from effects supervisor Rob Coleman, who oversaw the creation of the most despised CGI character in the history of cinema, Jar Jar Binks. When asked about his complicity in this cinematic travesty, Coleman replied that he never challenged or critiqued George Lucas's vision for Jar Jar Binks because "I only had one audience member to please and that was George Lucas. . . . If he was happy with what we were doing with Jar Jar, then I was happy," Eric Harrison, "Even an Insider Found Jar Jar, Well, Jarring" *Los Angeles Times,* June 21, 1999, http://articles.latimes.com/1999/jun/21/entertainment/ca-48611. The next time you are watching *The Phantom Menace,* remember: this disaster happened due to an organizational culture that saw pleasing the senior leader as a greater goal than doing what was right by holding him accountable and letting him know that Jar Jar Binks was a terrible idea. Be accountable in your leadership, or you could end up creating your own Jar Jar Binks. For a more serious description of how followers can challenge their leaders and of why they should hold leaders accountable, see Ira Chaleff, *The Courageous Follower* (Kindle edition; San Francisco: Berrett-Koehler, 2009), chapter 4.

61. Robert Fryling, *The Leadership Ellipse* (Downers Grove, IL: InterVarsity, 2010), 19.

62. Paul Cannings, *African American Church Leadership*, ed. Lee June and Christopher Mathis (Grand Rapids: Kregel, 2013), 97.

63. Baxter, *Reformed Pastor*, 93. See also Gregory the Great on the pastor's personal reading of the Scriptures: "All this is duly executed . . . if, inspired by the spirit of heavenly fear and love, he meditate daily on the precepts of Sacred Writ, that the words of Divine admonition may restore in him the power of solicitude and of provident circumspection with regard to the celestial life, which familiar conversation with men continually destroys. . . . For hence it is that Paul admonishes his disciple who had been put over the flock, saying, Till I come, give attendance to reading," *Liber regulae pastoralis* 2:11.

64. Paraphrased from Steve Timmis, *Gospel-Centred Leadership* (Surrey, UK: Good Book, 2012), 62.

65. John M. Perkins and Wayne Gordon, *Leadership Revolution* (Ventura: Regal, 2012), 35.

66. This point derives in part from Richard Baxter's admonition: "Is not every true Christian a member of the body of Christ, and therefore, partakes of the blessings of the whole, and belongs to each particular member? And does not every man owe thanks to God for his brethren's gifts, not only as having himself a part in those gifts as members of one body, but also because his own ends may be attained by his brethren's gifts, as well as by his own gifts?" *Reformed Pastor*, 67.

67. *The Complete Works of Andrew Fuller*, ed. J. Belcher (Harrisonburg, VA: Sprinkle, 1988), 1:142; see also 1:482, 484, 498, 501, 505, 507, 517. My colleague David Prince pointed me to Andrew Fuller's observations on this matter. For a brief introduction to Andrew Fuller's life, see Matthew Haste, "Marriage and Family in the Life of Andrew Fuller," *Southern Baptist Journal of Theology* 17 (2013): 28–34. Martyn Lloyd-Jones made a similar point when he wrote, "The moment in your study you cease to come under the power of the truth, you have become a victim of the devil. I must apply that to myself as a preacher. If I can study the Bible without being searched and examined and humbled, without being lifted up and made to praise God, and to feel as much of a desire to sing when I am alone in my study as when I am standing in the pulpit, I am in bad shape," D. Martyn Lloyd-Jones, *The Christian Warfare* (Grand Rapids: Baker, 1998), 180.

68. According to Roman Catholic teaching on the priesthood, formalized at the Council of Florence and promulgated in 1439 in the bull *Exultate Deo*, ordination to the priesthood results in *character indelebilis* upon the soul of the ordinand, such that the priest differs from laypeople both in essence and in degree of participation in priestliness. Responding to this claim of character indelebilis, Martin Luther summarized the doctrine of the priesthood of all believers in this way: "Now they have invented characteres indelebiles, and prate that a deposed priest is nevertheless something different from a mere layman. . . . There is really no difference between laymen and priests, princes and bishops, 'spirituals' and 'temporals,' as they call them, except that of office and work, but not of 'estate'; for they are all of the same estate. . . . Those who are now called 'spiritual'—priests, bishops or popes—are neither different from other Christians nor superior to them, except that they are charged with the administration of the Word of God and the sacraments, which is their work and office," Martin Luther, "An Open Letter to the Christian Nobility" (1520), in *Works of Martin Luther* (Philadelphia: Holman, 1915), 2:68–69.

69. Dayton Moore with Matthew Fulks, *More Than a Season* (Chicago: Triumph, 2015), ebook, chapter 5.

70. It is understood here that "pastor/shepherd," "elder/presbyter," and "overseer/bishop" are different terms, each with a distinct and identifiable nuance, that described one office in the New Testament churches. Pastor/shepherd does seem to be a gift rather than an office in Paul's letter to the Ephesians (4:11); however, the function of pastor/shepherd is closely tied to the office of elder/presbyter and overseer/bishop in Acts 20:28 and 1 Pet 5:2. As such, I am using "pastor" interchangeably with "elder." For further discussion, see Benjamin Merkle, "The Scriptural Basis for Elders," in *Baptist Foundations*, ed. Mark Dever and Jonathan Leeman (Nashville: B&H, 2015), 245–252. The two divinely authorized offices among the new covenant people of God are elders (pastors/shepherds/bishops/overseers) and deacons (servants). The Qumran community also envisioned a community with two distinct leadership offices, though their two designated offices were priests and elders. See Gerhardsson, *Memory and Manuscript with Tradition and Transmission in Early Christianity*, 245. Very soon after the New Testament era, the term "overseer/bishop" came to

describe an elder who ruled multiple churches in a particular city or region and who oversaw other elders. See, e.g., Ignatius of Antioch, *Pros Magnetas Ignatios*, 2:1–3:2.

71. Peterson, *Working the Angles*, 3–5.

72. "The designation of all Israel as a 'royal priesthood' did not preclude, a few chapters later, the establishment of a Levitical priesthood. . . . The designation of Christian believers as a 'royal priesthood' does not preclude the existence of pastors/elders/overseers," Carson, "1 Peter," in Carson and Beale, *Commentary on the New Testament Use of the Old Testament*, 1031.

Chapter Five: The Shepherd Leader

1. A possible precedent for the Christian linkage of the functions of "overseer/bishop" (ἐπίσκοπος) with "pastor/shepherd" (ποιμην) in, e.g., 1 Pet 2:25, may be found in the Damascus Document. In this text, the מבקר ("guardian") was charged with caring for community members "in all their distress, like a shepherd carries his sheep," Damascus Document 13:7; compare 1QS, e.g., 6:20; the מבקר ("overseer")seems to have been a teacher who oversaw admissions to and expulsions from the community. It is possible that the role of the מבקר in the Damascus Document provides some background for the New Testament office of ἐπίσκοπος ("overseer"). Ἐπισκεπτομαι ("I oversee," the verb form of ἐπίσκοπος) is not the most frequent translation of בקר ("inspect," "inquire regarding," "care for," the verb from which מבקר derives) in the Septuagint. This rendering does, however, appear in Ezek 34:11. Similar verbal connections between shepherding language (ποιμην ["shepherd"], ποιμαινω ["I shepherd"]) and careful oversight (ἐπισκέπτομαι) may also be observed in Jer 23:2; Zech 10:3; 11:16. This is not to suggest that the New Testament terms or offices were borrowed directly from earlier Jewish practices; the point is simply that some link between the responsibilities associated with ἐπίσκοπος and ποιμην seems to have preceded the Christian usage of these terms. See Herbert Braun, *Qumran und das Neue Testament* (Tübingen: Mohr, 1966), 2:331. Compare also Barbara Thiering, "Mebaqqer and Episkopos in the Light of the Temple Scroll," *JBL* 100 (1981): 59–74.

2. For the *munus triplex* as a conceptual device to conceive more effectively the relationship of roles in the old and new covenants, see Adam Johnson, "The Servant Lord," *SJT* 65 (2012): 159–173. The focus of Johnson's work is the function of the *munus triplex* in the doctrine of atonement, but the principle is relevant in relation to its usage in the practice of leadership as well.

3. Timothy Laniak, *Shepherds after My Own Heart* (Downers Grove, IL: InterVarsity, 2006), 58. In Sumerian royal inscriptions, the king was described as a divinely appointed shepherd. In Babylon and Assyria, "shepherd" was a common epithet for rules, and the verb "pasture" could serve as a metaphor for "rule." See Joachim Jeremias, "ποιμην, αρχιποιμην, ποιμανω, ποιμνη, ποιμνιον," in *TDNT*, ed. Gerhard Kittel and Gerhard Friedrich, trans. Geoffrey Bromiley (Grand Rapids: Eerdmans, 1964), 6:486–487.

4. Enlil-Suraše, lines 154–155. See William Hallo, *The World's Oldest Literature* (Leiden: Brill, 2009), 425.

5. James Pritchard, ed., *Ancient Near Eastern Texts Relating to the Old Testament*, 3rd ed. (Princeton: Princeton University Press, 1969), 164, 289. See also Young Chae, *Jesus as the Eschatological Davidic Shepherd* (Tübingen: Mohr Siebeck, 2006), 19–94; Donald Murray, *Divine Prerogative and Royal Pretension* (New York: Bloomsbury, 1998), 264; Karin Schopflin, "The Composition of Metaphorical Oracles within the Book of Ezekiel," *VT* 55 (2005): 113.

6. Victor Hamilton, *The Book of Genesis: Chapters 18–50* (Grand Rapids: Eerdmans, 1995), 603–604.

7. David Silverman, *Ancient Egypt* (Oxford: Oxford University Press, 2003), 104, 157.

8. Papyrus Leiden I 344, as translated in R. O. Faulkner, "The Admonitions of an Egyptian Sage," *JEA* 51 (1965): 59, 60. For the shift in perception of the pharaoh's position from a distant supremacy over the people to a shepherding role with a responsibility to guard the people, see John Wilson, *The Culture of Ancient Egypt* (Chicago: University of Chicago, 1956), 120–122. A century after the exodus, Pharaoh Amenhotep III referred to himself as "the good shepherd," David O'Connor, "The City and the World," in *Amenhotep III*, ed. David O'Connor and Eric Cline (Ann Arbor: University of Michigan Press, 2001), 138. This reconstruction assumes a mid-fifteenth-century BC date for the exodus. For a discussion of the date of the exodus, see Bryant Wood, "The Rise and Fall of the Thirteenth-Century Exodus-Conquest Theory," *JETS* 48 (2005): 475–489. For further references and reflections on the relationship of this imagery to Jesus as the good shepherd, see Michael Bird, *Jesus Is the Christ* (Downers Grove, IL: InterVarsity, 2013), 126–127.

9. Laniak, *Shepherds after My Own Heart*, 44. After they inhabited the land, the Israelites developed into a dimorphic society, combining agricultural patterns of permanence with persistent patterns of impermanence in the form of shepherding. Still, they did not forget their nomadic roots. Each year, they recalled together that their ancestor Abraham had been "a wandering Aramean" and that they themselves were "aliens and sojourners" (Deut 26:5; Lev 25:23). According to M. B. Rowton, the necessity of seasonal migration for shepherds is key to understanding how tribal identity persisted in a dimorphic social structure: "Seasonal migration had a curious dual, and to some extent contradictory, effect. By bringing the tribesmen seasonally within the reach of the state and its law it tended to incorporate the migratory group within the state. But just as regularly, year by year, the group would leave the realm of effective state control. Thereupon, whether high on the mountain ranges or out in the steppes, the nomad would revert from subject to independent tribesman," M. B. Rowton, "Enclosed Nomadism," *Journal of Economic and Social History of the Orient* 17 (1974): 28.

10. For "his bow remained firm" (NASB) as preservation of Joseph against his enemies, see Hamilton, *The Book of Genesis*, 684–685.

11. Writings from Second Temple Judaism classified Joshua "among the prophets" ("ἐν προφητείαις," Sir 46:1) as well as identifying him as one who had been "a judge in Israel" ("κριτὴς ἐν Ἰσραηλ," 1 Macc 2:55).

12. Central to Saul's downfall was his persistent insistence on modifying God's commands to maintain his own popularity instead of following God's commands and entrusting the results to God; e.g., offering a sacrifice instead of waiting for Samuel because he feared that his army would abandon him (1 Sam 13:8–11). See Peter Leithart, *A Son to Me* (Moscow, ID: Canon, 2003), Kindle edition, locations 853–868.

13. Ibid., location 737.

14. One of the most important tasks that an ancient king could undertake, as a perceived mediator between the divine and human realms, was the construction or repair of a temple. For discussion, see Philip Satterthwaite, "David in the Books of Samuel," in *The Lord's Anointed*, ed. Philip Satterthwaite et al. (Grand Rapids: Baker, 1995), 53–54.

15. Stephen Dempster has pointed out how the extraordinary importance of humanity is demonstrated through the number of words allotted to humanity's creation compared to the rest of the created order in Gen 1:1–2:3. A similar observation holds true in 2 Samuel 7, where—after summarizing at least a decade in six chapters—the narrator commits an entire chapter to a series of events that seem to have happened over the course of a couple of days. See Stephen Dempster, *Dominion and Dynasty* (Downers Grove, IL: InterVarsity, 2003), 57.

16. Antti Laato, "Second Samuel 7 and Ancient Near Eastern Royal Ideology," *CBQ* 59 (1997): 244. "The account of Nathan's prophecy to David is at the center of the David stories, both literarily and thematically," Gerald Gerbrandt, *Kingship according to the Deuteronomistic History* (Atlanta: Scholars' Press, 1986), 160. This text is the "theological highlight" of the books of Samuel, according to A. A. Anderson, *2 Samuel* (Dallas: Word, 1989), 112. "It has been compared to the Magna Carta or the United States Declaration of Independence, texts that inspire a whole people and engender a national identity," Bill Arnold, *1 and 2 Samuel* (Grand Rapids: Zondervan, 2003), 472.

17. Yahweh had been, so to speak, moving from place to place with his people and with David (2 Sam 7:6–7, 9), and Yahweh had led David and his people to a place of rest and protection from enemies (7:10–11). If a future descendant of David became a preying beast instead of serving as a shepherd in submission to Yahweh the shepherd, Yahweh would discipline him using a shepherd's "club" (בְּשֵׁבֶט, 7:14; compare Lev 27:32; Ps 23:4; Ezek 20:37; Mic 7:14). These images of shepherding seem to suggest a turn in the text not only from David planning a house for Yahweh to Yahweh promising a house for David but also from David being a shepherd to Yahweh becoming David's shepherd.

18. Arguments related to the tense and aspect of the verbs in 2 Sam 7:10 fall outside the parameters of this study. The Masoretic text of 2 Sam 7:10 may be read "dwell beneath it" instead of "dwell in their own place"; if that reading is followed, the text conveys a sense of divine protection. See David Vanderhooft, "Dwelling beneath the Sacred Place," *JBL* 118 (1999): 625–633. David Tsumura treats both 2 Sam 7:8b–9a and 7:9b–11a as referring to Yahweh's past dealings. Seen in this way, the text serves structurally as a transition from Yahweh's past dealings with David in 7:8b–9a to his future dealings with David in 7:12–16. In three stages of providential guidance, Yahweh "took" David, "was" with him, and "cut off" his enemies (7:8b–9a). How Yahweh did this is explicated in a procedural discourse (7:9b–11a). See David Tsumura, "Tense and Aspect of Hebrew Verbs in 2 Samuel 7:8–16 from the Point of View of Discourse Grammar," *VT* 60 (2010): 641–651; also A. A. Anderson, *2 Samuel* (Dallas: Word, 1989), 121. Antti Laato has gathered parallel texts roughly contemporaneous with the reigns of David and Solomon that demonstrate that the promise of an eternal dynasty in 2 Samuel 7 would not have been anachronistic. See Laato, "Second Samuel 7 and Ancient Near Eastern Royal Ideology," 248–269.

19. Many of these themes may also be found in Psalm 89, which appears to be dependent on 2 Samuel 7 and specifically denotes the divine establishment of a covenant with David (89:3). For a discussion of the relationship between these two texts, see Knut Heim, "The (God-) Forsaken King of Psalm 89," in *King and Messiah in Israel and the Ancient Near East*, ed. John Day (Sheffield, UK: Sheffield Academic, 1998), 296–322, and Nahum Sarna, "Psalm 89," in *Biblical and Other Studies*, ed. Alexander Altmann (Cambridge, MA: Harvard University, 1963), 29–46. David and his descendants were recognized as sons of God and representatives of Israel by means of this covenant that is rich with shepherding motifs. For implications of sonship in this text, see Anderson, *2 Samuel*, 122.

20. The clause commonly rendered "he restores my soul" (Ps 23:3) might also be rendered "he brings me back" or "he causes me to repent," suggesting rescue as well. See Kenneth Bailey, *The Good Shepherd* (Downers Grove, IL: InterVarsity, 2014), 44–45.

21. "In the Old Testament world, to eat and drink at someone's table created a bond of mutual loyalty, and could be the culminating token of a covenant," Derek Kidner, *Psalms 1–72* (Downers Grove, IL: InterVarsity, 1973), 110, 112.

22. "450 Sheep Jump to Their Deaths in Turkey," *USA Today*, July 8, 2005, https://usatoday30.usatoday.com/news/offbeat/2005-07-08-sheep-suicide_x.htm.

23. Jason Molinet, "Sheep Chased by Unleashed Dog Gets Pinned to Edge of Cliff," *New York Daily News*, June 23, 2015, http://www.nydailynews.com/news/world/sheep-chased-unleashed-dog-plunges-cliff-death-article-1.2267593.

24. "No one can make a sheep lie down. Sheep will only lie down when they have had plenty to eat, have quenched their thirst and are not threatened by any wild animal or disturbed by biting insects," Bailey, *The Good Shepherd*, 40.

25. Laniak, *Shepherds after My Own Heart*, 55.

26. F. B. Meyer, quoted in L. B. Cowman, "He Putteth Forth His Own Sheep," *Streams in the Desert*, ed. James Reimann (Grand Rapids: Zondervan, 1997), 32.

27. In Jer 10:21, the "shepherds" seem to have included Judah's leaders—not only the kings but also other leaders both political and religious (see Jer 2:8). In Zech 10:3, the corrupt shepherds included Judah's faithless leaders—not only the kings in the people's recent memory but also their present leaders in exile. In Ezekiel, "shepherds" similarly refers to Israel's entire ruling class. See Elizabeth Achtemeier, *Nahum–Malachi* (Atlanta: John Knox, 1986), 155; Wayne Baxter, "Healing and the 'Son of David,'" *NovT* 48 (2006): 42; Anja Klein, "Prophecy Continued," *VT* 60 (2010): 576; J. A. Thompson, *The Book of Jeremiah* (Grand Rapids: Eerdmans, 1980), 335.

28. Don Henley and Stan Lynch, "Learn to Be Still," sung by the Eagles, *Hell Freezes Over* (Geffen, 1994).

29. "Ezekiel seems to have had Jeremiah's oracle before him and presented his 'Shepherd Address' as an exposition of his contemporary's prophecy. But his adherence to Jeremiah is not slavish. Signs of adaptation and reinterpretation are evident in his downplaying the status of David while highlighting the role of Yahweh," Daniel Block, *The Book of Ezekiel: Chapters 25–48* (Grand Rapids: Eerdmans, 1998), 275–276. Compared to Jeremiah, the charges in Ezekiel are less severe; the crime in Ezekiel is not active dispersal of the flock but neglect of the flock, with an emphasis on the saving work of Yahweh. See Klein, "Prophecy Continued," 576–578.

30. When Jesus sent out his first followers as sheep among "wolves" (Matt 10:16–18), he seems to have applied the imagery of wild beasts from Ezekiel 34 to the religious leaders of Israel in his own day. If indeed the wild animals in Ezekiel 34 were Gentile rulers, Jesus was identifying religious leaders in his day as the equivalent of the Gentile kings who destroyed Israel and sent the people into exile. See John Paul Heil, "Ezekiel 34 and the Narrative Strategy of the Shepherd and Sheep Metaphor in Matthew," *CBQ* 55 (1993): 702–703. Leslie Allen, however, sees "every wild animal" as a reference to Israel's failed shepherds, Leslie Allen, *Ezekiel 20–48* (Nashville: Word, 1990), 162.

31. Allen, *Ezekiel 20–48*, 161.

32. For Ezek 34:3 as expression of necrophagia, see Nathanael Warren, "A Cannibal Feast in Ezekiel," *JSOT* 38 (2014): 506–507.

33. "There is no thought in these prophecies of the resurrection of the historical king. . . . [Ezekiel] envisions a single person, who may embody the dynasty but who occupies the throne himself," Block, *The Book of Ezekiel*, 298.

34. This human shepherd would reign not as a human sovereign but as a "prince" of God (Ezek 34:24). "Ezekiel's use of the archaic title *nasi* ["prince"] contrasts with Hosea and Jeremiah, who had both spoken explicitly of 'David their king.' It is consistent, however, with his efforts elsewhere to downplay the roles of Israel's monarchs, and harks back to 1 Kings 11:34, which says of Solomon, 'I will make him *nasi* all the days of his life.' . . . Ezekiel's preference for *nasi* over *melek* [king] . . . is not intended to deny this person's true kingship but to highlight the distinction between them and the recent occupants of the

office," Block, *The Book of Ezekiel*, 299–300. See also Daniel Block, "Bringing Back David," in *The Lord's Anointed*, ed. Satterthwaite et al., 183–188, and Paul Joyce, "King and Messiah in Ezekiel," in *King and Messiah in Israel and the Ancient Near East*, ed. John Day (Sheffield, UK: Sheffield Academic, 1998), 336.

35. Jews of the Second Temple era such as Joshua son of Sirach saw God as Israel's supreme shepherd (Sir 18:13, early second century BC), but they still seem to have longed for a human shepherd to gather the people as well. In the fictional book of Judith, the eponymous heroine promised the general Holofernes that, through her treachery, he would be able to make the Jews "like sheep that have no shepherd" (Judith 11:19, late second century BC). In the story, Judith tricked the general and triumphed over him, but the author of this tale may have been expressing a recognition of what Israel had become as well as hope for a time when Israel would no longer be without a shepherd.

36. Laniak, *Shepherds after My Own Heart*, 171.

37. William Greenhill, a non-Conformist member of the Westminster Assembly, provides another perspective, taking the plant in Ezek 34:29–30 to signify Christ and the church: "This 'plant of renown' is, by some expositors, interpreted to be the Christian church, gathered out of all the nations and planted in Christ. . . . Others expound it of Christ. We may take both: Christ and the church, which springs up out of him," William Greenhill, "A Plant of Peace," *Ezekiel, Daniel*, ed. Carl Beckwith, Reformation Commentary on Scripture (Downers Grove, IL: InterVarsity, 2012), 171.

38. The structure of Ezekiel hints at this movement from death to resurrection. In Ezek 34:1–31, there is a death of the nation typified by the dismissal of the shepherds with only a hint of new life; in Ezek 37:15–28—a text with significant verbal parallels to the shepherd oracle—there is a resurrection of the nation. See David Morgan, "Ezekiel and the Twelve," *BBR* 20 (2010): 382–383.

39. "All human authority is ultimately determined as legitimate or illegitimate based on its faithfulness in relation to God with the Holy Spirit as indicator of God's presence and approval," Quentin Kinnison, "Shepherd or One of the Sheep," *Journal of Religious Leadership* 9 (2010): 74.

40. The words of Jesus in Matt 26:31–32 echo Ezek 34:12–13 in the Septuagint. See Heil, "Ezekiel 34 and the Narrative Strategy of the Shepherd and Sheep Metaphor in Matthew," 706.

41. In the Qumran community, this text may have contributed to the expectation of a messianic healing shepherd. 4Q521 clearly draws from Isaiah (26:19; 42:7; 61:1–3) but seems to make a connection between healing and shepherding, which is characteristic of Ezekiel's prophecy: "He will release the captives, make the blind see, raise up the do[wntrodden]. When he [come]s he will heal the sick, raise the dead, and announce good news to the poor; he will lead the [hol]y ones; he will shepherd [th]em." For further discussion, see Baxter, "Healing and the 'Son of David,'" 46.

42. Steve Timmis, *Gospel-Centred Leadership* (Surrey, UK: Good Book, 2012), 64.

43. Henri J. M. Nouwen, *In the Name of Jesus* (Spring Valley, NY: Crossroad, 1992), 61–62.

44. Eddie Gibbs, *Followed or Pushed?* (Bromley, UK: MARC, 1987), 20.

45. Eugene Peterson, *The Pastor* (New York: HarperCollins, 2011), 86–87.

46. These commitments represent a covenantal approach to leadership in contrast to a business-driven model, which results in a contractual approach. For discussion of the distinction between covenantal and contractual approaches to pastoral leadership, see Derek Tidball, *Builders and Fools* (Leicester, UK: Inter-Varsity, 1999), 8–9.

47. Augustine of Hippo, *Sermo* 46:15.

48. John M. Perkins, interview with Charles Marsh, "Let Justice Roll Down," in *Mobilizing for the Common Good*, ed. Peter Slade et al. (Jackson: University Press of Mississippi, 2013), 198.

49. D. A. Carson, *The Cross and Christian Ministry* (Downers Grove, IL: InterVarsity, 1993), 109.

50. Brian Croft and Bryce Butler, *Oversee God's People* (Grand Rapids: Zondervan, 2015), 43.

51. Jesus fulfilled his role as shepherd not only through preaching and teaching but also through healing and feeding. For the connection between these tasks and Ezekiel 34, see Young Chae, *Jesus as the Eschatological Davidic Shepherd*, 247–326, and Heil, "Ezekiel 34 and the Narrative Strategy of the Shepherd and Sheep Metaphor in Matthew," 701. For the elder as one who nourishes the sheep, see also Alexander Strauch, *Biblical Eldership*, 3rd ed. (Colorado Springs: Lewis and Roth, 1995), 29–31.

52. Eric Mason, *Manhood Restored* (Nashville: B&H, 2013), 138.

53. Walter Brueggemann, *Sabbath as Resistance,* rev. ed. (Louisville: WJK, 2017), 6, 30.

54. The selection of sheep to serve as shepherds has an analogy in actual practices of shepherding, though it is uncertain whether such a practice was known to biblical authors: "In the context of herding, shepherds sometimes choose other sheep to help steer the herd (the Bedouin 'bell' sheep), sheep which are chosen based on their love for and loyalty to the shepherd and obedience," Kinnison, "Shepherd or One of the Sheep," 74.

55. Martin Bucer, *Concerning the True Care of Souls,* trans. Peter Beale (Carlisle: Banner of Truth, 2009), 181–182.

56. Richard Baxter, *Reformed Pastor* repr. ed. (London: Ward, 1656), 18.

57. J. I. Packer, "Introduction," in Richard Baxter, *Reformed Pastor* (eBook; Carlisle: Banner of Truth, 1974).

Part Three: New Covenant Practices for Leadership through Followership

1. Timothy Laniak, *Shepherds after My Own Heart* (Downers Grove, IL: InterVarsity, 2006), 248..

2. Derek Tidball, *Skillful Shepherds* (Grand Rapids: Zondervan, 1986), 337.

Chapter Six: The Shepherd's Call

1. When compared to other literature in the ancient world, the Gospels are most similar to the didactic and historical subtypes within the *bios* genre of writing. The didactic subtype in particular focused on a leader's way of life with the intention of calling readers to imitate that way of life. For further discussion, see Jonathan Pennington, *Reading the Gospels Wisely* (Grand Rapids: Baker, 2012), 26–31.

2. The words of Jesus in Mark 1:17 echo Jer 16:15–19. In Jeremiah's prophecy, the "fish" were being caught for judgment; in Mark, they are caught for salvation. See R. T. France, *The Gospel of Matthew* (Grand Rapids: Eerdmans, 2007), 109.

3. "[Jesus] saw the need for quiet prayer, time alone with his Father, before the terrible ordeal he was facing," Leon Morris, *The Gospel According to Matthew*, PNTC (Grand Rapids: Eerdmans, 1992), 667.

4. "Εκθαμβεῖσθαι (*ekthambeisthai*) is peculiar to Mark (1:27; 9:15; 16:5–6). It is a difficult word to translate. Swete has 'terrified surprise'; Rawlinson, 'shuddering awe'; Taylor, 'amazement amounting to consternation,'" Walter Wessel, "Mark," in *Matthew, Mark, Luke,* vol. 8 of *The Expositor's Bible Commentary,* ed. Frank Gaebelein (Grand Rapids: Zondervan, 1984), 765. See also James Brooks, *Mark* (Nashville: Broadman & Holman, 1991): "Mark's

description of Jesus is shocking. Mark employed words that express the strongest possible anguish. . . . 'Horror and dismay came over him,'" 234.

5. Craig Blomberg, *Matthew*, NAC 22 (Nashville: Broadman & Holman, 1992), 394. Blomberg writes, "Jesus knows of his coming death and the gruesome method of his execution. Spiritually he recognizes the even greater agony involved in bearing the sins of the world. Luke 22:44 describes the extent of his physical suffering in the garden, hence Matthew's 'to the point of death.'" See also Morris, *The Gospel According to Matthew*, 667. Morris writes, "Matthew does not leave his readers to think that Jesus was troubled in the same way as we all are from time to time. In Gethsemane he underwent a most unusual sense of being troubled that we must feel is connected not only with the fact that he would die, but that he would die the kind of death he faced, a death for sinners. Jesus was a brave man, and lesser people by far, including many who have owed their inspiration to him, have faced death calmly. It is impossible to hold that it was the fact of death that moved Jesus so deeply. Rather, it was the kind of death that he would die that brought the anguish."

6. "He fell face downward, an expression that means that Jesus adopted the lowliest posture for this very significant prayer. . . . ἔπεσεν ἐπὶ πρόσωπον, literally 'fell on face'; it indicates prostration, the adoption of the lowliest position of all. Only Matthew has the reference to the face; Mark speaks of his falling 'on the ground,' while Luke speaks of his falling to his knees. This is the only occasion on which Jesus is said to have prostrated himself," Morris, *The Gospel According to Matthew*, 668.

7. "The Apostles are so sure of their own strength that they will not allow the possibility of failure, even when they are forewarned of it by Christ. The Son of Man is so conscious of the weakness of His humanity that He prays to the Father that He may be spared the approaching trial. He feels the need of being strengthened by prayer," Alfred Plummer, *An Exegetical Commentary on the Gospel to S. Matthew* (London: Elliot Stock, 1910), 368.

8. A. C. Dixon, quoted in G. M. Cocoris, *Evangelism* (Chicago: Moody, 1984), 108.

9. "The Spirit's way of relating to the Father and the Son follows a complex but consistent pattern: the Spirit descends from the Father to rest and remain upon the Son so that, through the Son, he may come to rest and remain upon Jesus' disciples as well. . . . According to John, the Spirit is given by the Father to the disciples at Jesus' request in order to empower them for their mission and to abide with them forever (14:16–17; 15:26–27)," Andreas J. Köstenberger and Scott R. Swain, *Father, Son and Spirit: The Trinity and John's Gospel*, New Studies in Biblical Theology, ed. D. A. Carson (Downers Grove, IL: InterVarsity, 2008), 136. See also 93–103, 135–148 on the role of the Spirit in John.

10. "The Spirit is a driving force for Luke's portrait of salvation, energizing and guiding events both in Luke and especially in Acts," Darrell L. Bock, *A Theology of Luke and Acts* (Grand Rapids: Zondervan, 2012), 211. Luke mentions the Holy Spirit sixteen times compared with six references in Mark and twelve in Matthew. Acts contains no fewer than fifty-seven references to the Spirit.

11. Bruce Ware, *The Man Christ Jesus* (Kindle edition; Wheaton: Crossway, 2013), locations 451, 457.

12. Ibid., location 499.

13. Regarding the emphasis on the power of the Spirit in the ministry of Jesus in Luke's Gospel, see Bock, *A Theology of Luke and Acts*, 218.

14. "Hebrew Scripture would be read in a standing position in one- to three-verse units. Then the text was translated into Aramaic. . . . After the reading came an invitation for someone to instruct the audience," Darrell L. Bock, *Luke*, BECNT (Grand Rapids: Baker, 1996), 1:403.

15. Bock, *Luke*, 1:404.

16. The binding up of the brokenhearted is not mentioned (Isa 61:1); more notable is the omission of "the vengeance of our God" (Isa 61:2). "For Luke the present day, i.e. the 'today' of Luke 4:21, was a day of salvation, the time of opportunity (cf. 2 Corinthians 6:2)," Robert Stein, *Luke*, NAC (Nashville: B&H), 156.

17. Bock, *Luke*, 1:405; G. K. Beale and D. A. Carson, eds., *Commentary on the New Testament Use of the Old Testament* (Grand Rapids: Baker, 2007), 287–290.

18. Bock, *Luke*, 1:406–407. See also D. A. Carson and Douglas J. Moo, *An Introduction to the New Testament* (Grand Rapids: Zondervan, 2005), 199; Köstenberger and Swain, *Father, Son and Spirit*, 137.

19. Ware, *The Man Christ Jesus*, location 491.

20. Brandon Crowe, *The Last Adam* (Grand Rapids: Baker, 2017), ebook, chapter 6.

21. Gerald Hawthorne, *The Presence and the Power: The Significance of the Holy Spirit in the Life and Ministry of Jesus* (Dallas: Word, 1991), 35.

22. Karl Barth, *Dogmatics in Outline* (New York: Harper and Row, 1959), 141–142.

23. John's Gospel introduces the footwashing scene with these words: "Now before the Feast of the Passover, when Jesus knew his hour had come to depart out of this world to the Father" (13:1). "Theologically, the clause alerts the readers to the Passover theme developed throughout the book (2:13, 23; 6:4; 11:55; 12:1; cf. 18:28, 39; 19:14), inviting them to see in the footwashing an anticipation of Jesus' own climactic Passover act as the Lamb of God who takes away the sin of the world," D. A. Carson, *The Gospel According to John*, PNTC (Grand Rapids: Eerdmans, 1991), 460–461.

24. Herman Ridderbos calls it "'love to the last breath' and 'love in its highest intensity' that was exemplified by 'the concrete expression of this love in the footwashing and in his self-giving 'to the end,'" Herman Ridderbos, *The Gospel of John* (Grand Rapids: Eerdmans, 1997), 452.

25. Timothy Cochrell, "Slaves of the Most High God: A Biblical Model of Servant Leadership in the Slave Imagery of Luke-Acts" (PhD diss., SBTS, 2015), 135.

26. George Raymond Beasley-Murray, *John*, WBC (Nashville: Thomas Nelson, 1999), 233; Carson, *The Gospel According to John*, 462; Köstenberger, *John*, 403–404; Leon Morris, *The Gospel According to John*, NICNT (Grand Rapids: Eerdmans, 1995), 548.

27. Alan Kerr, *The Temple of Jesus' Body* (London: Sheffield, 2002), 283.

28. Gerald L. Borchert, *John 12–21*, NAC 25b (Nashville: B&H, 2002), 78.

29. Cochrell, "Slaves of the Most High God," 115.

30. Ibid., 257, 263, 272, 284, 286, 290–291.

31. "This is true humility, to feel and to behave as if we were low; not, to cherish a notion of our importance, while we affect a low position . . . . As the world uses the word, 'condescension' is a stooping indeed of the person, but a bending forward, unattended . . . with the slightest effort to leave by a single inch the seat in which it is so firmly established. It is the act of a superior, who protests to himself, while he commits it, that he is superior still, and that he is doing nothing else but an act of grace towards those on whose level, in theory, he is placing himself," John Henry Newman, *The Idea of a University*, 3rd ed. (London: Basil Montagu Pickering, 1873), 205–206.

32. Robert Greenleaf, "Servant Leadership," in *The Leader's Companion*, ed. J. Thomas Wren (New York: Simon and Schuster, 2013), 22.

33. Timothy Paul Jones, "Scripture and the Long Shadow of American Slavery," September 27, 2016, www.timothypauljones.com/church-history-problem-american-slavery. David Nystrom has provided a helpful summary of four distinct forms of slavery that existed in the first-century Roman Empire; urban household slavery was the form of slavery that was most likely in the minds of New Testament authors when they utilized the slave metaphor. See David Nystrom, *James* (Grand Rapids: Zondervan, 1997), 34-36.

34. Timothy Keller, *Every Good Endeavor* (New York: Penguin Books, 2012), with Katherine Leary Alsdorf, 280–283.

35. "Enslavers" or "manstealers" in 1 Tim 1:10 can hardly imply anything other than the taking of persons for the purpose of selling them into slavery. The verb form of this term appears in the *Historiai* of Herodotus with precisely this meaning (ἠνδραπόδισαν . . . ἐόντας ὁμαίμους ["its people were enslaved by their own"], 1:151:2). In Thucydides's account of the Peloponnesian War, the term even encompassed the trade of persons who had been conquered in a time of war (Ἠιόνα τὴν ἐπὶ Στρυμόνι Μήδων ἐχόντων πολιορκίᾳ εἷλον καὶ ἠνδραπόδισαν ["they took Eion upon the river Strymon from the Medes by siege and carried away the inhabitants captives" to be enslaved], 1:98:1–2)

Chapter Seven: The Shepherd's Commission

1. Andreas J. Köstenberger, "Jesus the Good Shepherd Who Will Also Bring Other Sheep (John 10:16): The Old Testament Background of a Familiar Metaphor," *BBR* 12 (2002): 93; Kenneth E. Bailey, *The Good Shepherd: A Thousand-Year Journey from Psalm 23 to the New Testament* (Downers Grove, IL: InterVarsity, 2014), Kindle edition, locations 400–410.

2. Matt 2:6; 7:15; 9:36; 10:5–6, 16;18:10–14; 26:31; Mark 6:34; Luke 12:32; 15:4–7; John 1:29, 36; 10:1–30; 21:15–19. "The Gospels provide an important bridge from the Old Testament to the teaching on shepherding in the New Testament epistles and the book of Revelation," Andreas J. Köstenberger, "Shepherds and Shepherding in the Gospels," in *Shepherding God's Flock: Biblical Leadership in the New Testament and Beyond*, ed. Benjamin L. Merkle and Thomas R. Schreiner (Grand Rapids: Kregel, 2014) 36.

3. The Gospel of John is structured with a prologue (John 1:1–18) and an epilogue (John 21), with two major sections in between, commonly understood to be the "Book of Signs" (John 2–12) and the "Book of Glory" (John 13–20). For further discussion of the structure of John, see Gerald L. Borchert, *John 1–11*, NAC 25a (Nashville: Broadman & Holman, 1996), 95–98; D. A. Carson, *The Gospel According to John*, PNTC (Grand Rapids: Eerdmans, 1991), 102–111.

4. "John draws broadly from other Old Testament traditions. Like the synoptic authors, he looks to Zechariah in the framing of his passion narratives. Branch (Zechariah 3:8; 6:12) and shepherd (Zechariah 9–12) symbolism echo in the fourth Gospel. Like Ezekiel and Jeremiah before him, Zechariah emphasized that the coming branch and shepherd would be a Davidic ruler. This association was present in the more developed royal traditions of the Psalms. John sees in Jesus both the fulfillment of God's promise to shepherd his people personally and the fulfillment of his promise to appoint a Davidic shepherd ruler," Timothy Laniak, *Shepherds after My Own Heart* (Downers Grove, IL: InterVarsity, 2006), 211.

5. "John makes it clear elsewhere that Jesus is ultimately training his followers to be like him in his life and death (4:34–38; 14:12; 17:20; 20:21–23; 21:15–19). They will eventually take care of his flock and risk their lives like their master (21:15–23)," ibid.

6. Köstenberger notes that the audience for John 10 is the same as the audience for John 9, the Pharisees, *John*, 298. The "truly, truly" verbal construction "never begins a discourse in this Gospel, which suggests that the present pericope represents a continuation of the events recounted in the previous chapter," 300.

7. Other Old Testament allusions include Jer 23:1–2 and Ezek 34:2–3 in John 10:8; Ps 23:1, Isa 40:1, and Ezek 34:15 in John 10:11; and Isa 56:8, Ezek 34:23, 37:24 in John 10:16. See Laniak, *Shepherds after My Own Heart*, 210; Köstenberger, "Jesus the Good Shepherd," 70. "Some of the language of this section borrows from Moses or David, but most of it points to God shepherding his flock, which fits a primary allusion to Ezekiel 34 (34:11–12) and especially John's overall Christology," Craig Keener, *The Gospel of John*, 2 vols. (Peabody, MA: Hendrickson, 2003), 1:802.

8. In John 10:7–9, Jesus makes another "I am" statement—"I am the door of the sheep" (ESV). This statement was certainly a declaration of entering eternal life exclusively through Jesus Christ, but it was also a rebuke to the religious leaders who seemed to think that they solely controlled access to God (John 9:34). "Jesus . . . alone represents lawful access to the sheepfold," Herman Ridderbos, *The Gospel of John* (Grand Rapids: Eerdmans, 1997), 356.

9. This "figure of speech," as it is labeled in John 10:6, is "actually a symbol-laden discourse employed by Jesus to communicate a certain message," Köstenberger, "Jesus the Good Shepherd," 73. See also Carson, *The Gospel According to John*, 449. The word παροιμία ("figure of speech") appears only in John 10:6 and 16:25–29 in John's Gospel.

10. Köstenberger, "Jesus the Good Shepherd," 74.

11. "Jesus here combines the figure of the messianic shepherd with that of the suffering servant. The true model for pastors must be to keep both in mind. Here in a nutshell is the essence of all John's understanding of pastoring. Ministry is self-giving sacrifice," Derek Tidball, *Skillful Shepherds* (Grand Rapids: Zondervan, 1986), 87. "The pattern of leadership the Old Testament contributes to the New can be summarized in the phrase: the suffering righteous shepherd," James M. Hamilton, "Did the Church Borrow Leadership Structures from the Old Testament or Synagogue?" in *Shepherding God's Flock*, ed. Benjamin L. Merkle and Thomas R. Schreiner (Grand Rapids: Kregel, 2014), 25. Hamilton traces this theme and its roots in Moses and David as the ones who "'typologically' anticipate the role of Christ as the ultimate shepherd. . . . Jesus himself is the ultimate fulfillment of the typological pattern of the suffering righteous shepherd," 30.

12. Köstenberger, "Shepherds and Shepherding in the Gospels," in Merkle and Schreiner, *Shepherding God's Flock*, 43. "Essentially, then, salvation-historical developments were matched by developments in shepherd typology. The decisive point is the exile, where the promise of a coming Davidic shepherd emerges more clearly. In the end, all 'good shepherd' motifs, both human and divine, converge in Jesus. Still faint in Joshua's day, more explicit in David's time, yet clearer at the time of the Babylonian exile, the motif of a messianic shepherd-king, who gathers God's 'scattered flock' and delivers his people, finds its fulfillment and most pronounced revelation in Jesus the Messiah," Köstenberger, "Jesus the Good Shepherd," 90–91.

13. Köstenberger, "Shepherds and Shepherding in the Gospels," in Merkle and Schreiner, *Shepherding God's Flock*, 49. "The repeated reference to Jesus' sacrifice in 10:11–18 makes this the focal point of the characterization of the 'good shepherd,'" Köstenberger, *John*, 308.

14. The phrase "to lay down one's life" is rare in Greek and may reflect the Hebrew idiom "to hand over one's life," Andreas J. Köstenberger, "John," in *Commentary on the New Testament Use of the Old Testament*, ed. G. K. Beale and D. A. Carson (Grand Rapids: Baker, 2007), 463. "[Jesus's] consciousness of his impending violent cross-death and its substitutionary significance (John 10:11, 15, 17–18; compare with 15:13) allows him to anticipate the consequences of this pivotal salvation-historical event," Köstenberger, "Jesus the Good Shepherd," 75.

15. "John 10 thus includes a strong polemic as the passage contrasts Jesus the Good Shepherd of God's flock with the current Jewish leadership which is shown to be part of the trajectory of bad shepherds throughout Old Testament history who served and nurtured only themselves and, shockingly, fed on the sheep rather than caring for them," Köstenberger, *Shepherds and Shepherding in the Gospels*, Merkle and Schreiner, "Shepherding God's Flock," 47.

16. "The image of the shepherd is an extremely important biblical picture of a 'leader' (Num 27:17) because it implies not only an intensely personal relationship between God's people and their leaders but a style or model of leadership exemplified by Jesus (cf. Mark

6:34). . . .The shepherd does not issue commands in a pyramid fashion down to subordinates who carry out his wishes like a general or admiral who stays back out of range of the conflict; nor is a shepherd a whip-carrying organizer who drives the sheep into the pen or to a particular pasture. But the shepherd knows the setting, leads the sheep, and they follow him (cf. John 10:4). Sometimes 'leaders' today are like the strangers of this text, whose voices are unknown to the sheep, and they wonder why there are problems in their organizations (cf. 10:5)," Gerald L. Borchert, *John 1–11*, NAC 25a (Nashville: Broadman & Holman, 1996), 332.

17. Tidball, *Skillful Shepherds*, 87.

18. Charles Haddon Spurgeon, "Laid Aside. Why?" *The Sword and Trowel* (May 1876): 1.

19. Ibid.

20. "The use of *idia* ("his own," 10:3–4) is a clear indication of intimate ownership (cf. the *idia* and *idioi* of 1:11)," Borchert, *John 1–11*, 331. This passage "illustrates the close relationship between the flock and the true shepherd," Tidball, *Skillful Shepherds*, 86. "Jesus comes to the sheep pen of Judaism, and calls his own sheep out individually to constitute his own messianic 'flock.' The assumption is that they are in some way 'his' before he calls them," Carson, *The Gospel According to John*, 383.

21. "There is evidence for the practice of Palestinian shepherds giving nicknames to some of their sheep, but the more relevant background is to be found in God's calling of his closest servants and Israel as a whole 'by name' (Ex. 33:12, 17; Isa. 43:1)," Köstenberger, *Shepherds and Shepherding in the Gospels*, Merkle and Schreiner, "Shepherding God's Flock," 43. See also Keener, *The Gospel of John*, 1:805: "It seems likely that shepherds assigned names according to shape, colour, and peculiarities."

22. Köstenberger, *John,* 301–302.

23. Tidball, *Skillfull Shepherds*, 86.

24. Köstenberger, *John,* 300–301.

25. John 1 serves as a prologue and John 21 serves as an epilogue to the Gospel, creating "balance and symmetry of structure. . . . Hence, both the prologue and the epilogue frame the Gospel in such a way that they form an integral part of the theological fabric of the entire narrative," Köstenberger, *John*, 584.

26. Carson, *The Gospel According to John,* 676–677. Carson produces an extensive and convincing argument that the two different verbs translated "love" should not be overemphasized. He notes that the two verbs are used interchangeably in John, and no clear distinction can be identified in the Septuagint. Evidence suggests that the verb ἀγαπάω ("love") was rising into prominence throughout Greek literature from about the fourth century B.C. forward. One of the reasons for this change is that another verb φιλεω ("love") had taken on the additional meaning "kiss" in some contexts. In the New Testament, ἀγαπάω is not "always distinguished by a good object" (see, e.g., 2 Tim 4:10). John regularly varies his word choices for stylistic reasons. It is also worth noting that in this encounter with Jesus, Peter is not set as the head over other apostles or over the church. "As for John 21:15–17, neither founding pre-eminence nor comparative authority is in view. . . . There is nothing intrinsic to the language of John 21:15–17 that suggests a distinctive authority for Peter. . . . In the context of the fourth gospel, these verses deal with Peter's reinstatement to service, not with his elevation to primacy," 678–679.

27. Gerald L. Borchert, *John 12–21*, NAC 25b (Nashville: Broadman & Holman, 2002), 335–336. In response to his own question about whether Peter learned from this experience with Jesus, Borchert writes emphatically, "If the first letter of Peter is any indication, there seems little doubt that this experience seared itself into the consciousness of this well-meaning disciple."

28. 1 Clement 5:2–4, in *The Apostolic Fathers: Greek Texts and English Translations*, 3rd ed., ed. Michael W. Holmes (Grand Rapids: Baker, 2007), 51.

29. Henri J. M. Nouwen, *In the Name of Jesus* (New York: Crossroad, 1989), 29–30, 42–43.

30. Eugene Peterson, *Under the Unpredictable Plant* (Grand Rapids: Eerdmans, 1994), 16, 86.

Chapter Eight: The Shepherd's Identity

1. "Despite the . . . objections to Petrine authorship, good and substantial reasons exist for accepting such authorship. . . .We have no evidence from antiquity that the letter was recognized as pseudonymous or as being written by one of Peter's disciples," Thomas R. Schreiner, *1, 2 Peter, Jude*, NAC 37 (Nashville: Broadman & Holman, 2003), 26–27. See also Peter H. Davids, *The First Epistle of Peter*, NICNT (Grand Rapids: Eerdmans, 1990), 4–9. Davids provides a helpful discussion on both authorship and the recipients of the letter. Davids argues for Silvanus having been entrusted by Peter to pen a letter to those who were facing persecution.

2. This text has been chosen, in part, because it has been frequently overlooked in studies of pastoral leadership. "Since the Reformation the Pauline Epistles have occupied center stage, and in modern NT scholarship the Synoptic Gospels and the Johannine corpus have both been seen as more interesting. This, however, is an unfortunate situation, for 1 Peter is a highly relevant book where the church is suffering." This letter exemplifies how early Christians applied the words of "Jesus and the Old Testament to contemporary concerns and is thus a model for modern church usage of those materials," Davids, *The First Epistle of Peter*, 3–4.

3. Peter writes to the churches in northwest Asia Minor, an area Luke tells us that Paul was forbade by the "Spirit of Jesus" to enter (Acts 16:6–7). We have no record of who first preached the gospel to those in this area, unless it was some of those in attendance at Pentecost (Acts 2:9). Neither do we have a clear record of Peter traveling to this area. Some would even argue that since the recipients were primarily Gentiles and Peter's primary mission was to the Jews, it would make no sense that he would write a letter to these congregations. Yet we have confidence these are Peter's words to these five churches, whatever their relationship with him personally. For differing perspectives on Peter's interactions with these churches, see Mark Edward Taylor, *1 Corinthians*, NAC 28 (Nashville: B&H, 2014), 55; and David E. Garland, *1 Corinthians*, BECNT (Grand Rapids: Baker, 2003), 45.

4. Timothy Laniak, *Shepherds after My Own Heart* (Downers Grove, IL: InterVarsity, 2006), 225.

5. Gregg Allison, *Sojourners and Strangers* (Wheaton: Crossway, 2012), 293.

6. Davids, *The First Epistle of Peter*, 175–176. Davids notes that elders "were not the older people in the church, but the leaders of the community; that is, it is the title of an office rather than a description of seniority."

7. "Household of God" refers back to the Old Testament temple. In Peter's usage, the reference is to be understood as the people of God. "In Ezekiel 9 the judgment literally begins at the temple, but now God's judgment begins not at a building but with his people. The judgment that begins with God's people purifies those who truly belong to God, and that purification comes through suffering, making believers morally fit for their inheritance," Schreiner *1, 2 Peter, Jude*, 227.

8. Peter's choice of words in 1 Pet 4:17 reminds us of Ezekiel's prophecy in Ezekiel 8–11 and, more specifically, of Ezek 9:6. In Ezekiel 8, four vignettes are given: an image of jealousy, seventy elders who are committing idolatry, women participating in cultic practices,

and twenty-five men who are possibly priests worshiping the sun. In Ezekiel 9–10, judgment is dispensed and the presence of the Lord leaves the temple, while in Ezekiel 11, civic authorities are punished.

9. Schreiner argues that the elders are addressed at this point for one or all of the following reasons: (1) they are likely to face the severity of persecution before the people do; (2) judgment of the people begins with the leaders; (3) they are addressed first because they are the leaders; Schreiner, *1, 2 Peter, Jude*, 231.

10. Edmond D. Hiebert, "Counsel for Christ's Under-shepherds: An Exposition of 1 Peter 5:1–4," *BSac* 139 (1982): 330–341.

11. Schreiner suggests that the connection of 5:1–5 to the proceeding passage makes much more sense when it is understood that the "suffering and persecution faced by believers (4:12–19) puts a strain on the entire community. Both leaders and those who are younger must, in such a situation, respond appropriately to others in the church," Schreiner, *1, 2 Peter, Jude*, 231.

12. John H. Elliott, "Elders as Leaders in 1 Peter and the Early Church," *HTS* 64 (2008): 681–695. Elliott rightly notes that Peter's introduction of himself as a fellow elder and one who was a witness of Christ's sufferings and a partaker in the glory to be revealed pointed back to themes that had already been developed in this letter (witness, 1:11; 2:21, 23; 3:18; 4:13; partaker, 1:5, 7–8, 11, 13; 4:13, 14), 685. "These characteristics establish, in rhetorical terms, the ethos of the author, ostensibly the Apostle Peter, and his personal qualifications for addressing the elders as he does. This self-identification expresses both the bond uniting the author with the elders and the basis for his instruction and thus is designed to secure a favorable hearing from his fellow-elders," John H. Elliott, *1 Peter* (New Haven: Yale University Press, 2000), 816.

13. "Papias (A.D. 60–130) wrote of John as an elder and of the other apostles as elders," Hiebert, "Counsel for Christ's Under-shepherds," 332.

14. "Fellow elder" has yet to be found elsewhere in ancient literature, so it was likely coined by Peter. "The unique noun *sympresbyteros* occurs nowhere else in Greek literature. . . . It is likely that *sympresbyteros* was coined by our author to accentuate the responsibility common to the author and the elders addressed," Elliott, *1 Peter*, 816–817.

15. Davids notes the following examples of the use of these terms in Paul's writing: "fellow worker" (Rom 16:3, 9, 21; Phil 2:25; 4:3; Col 4:11; 1 Thess 3:2; Phlm 1, 24); "fellow soldier" (Phil 2:25; Phlm 2); "fellow slave" (Col 1:7; 4:7); "fellow prisoner" (Rom 16:7; Col 4:10; Phlm 23), Davids, *The First Epistle of Peter*, 176.

16. Davids goes on to note that Peter's usage of the term "fellow elder" is "consistent with the tendency among the early church leaders to avoid the use of exalted titles," ibid.

17. "He does not stress his own authority but rather appeals to their own sense of what is right. He avoids any implication of the imposition of a higher authority but uses instead the method of spiritual persuasion," Hiebert, "Counsel for Christ's Under-shepherds," 331.

18. Elliott, "Elders as Leaders in 1 Peter and the Early Church," 685.

19. Derek J. Tidball, *Builders and Fools* (Leicester, UK: Inter-Varsity, 1999), 62.

20. Elliott, *1 Peter*, 819. Elliott delineates different uses of the word "witness" in the New Testament: "eyewitness" or "one who bears witness." In this case, Peter is emphasizing that he is bearing witness to Christ's sufferings. See also George W. Forbes, *1 Peter*, EGGNT (Nashville: B&H, 2014), Kindle edition, location 5175: "A witness is one who testifies to something, not necessarily one who observes it." Hiebert suggests that Peter may have been present at the crucifixion as one among "all of his [Jesus's] acquaintances" (Luke 23:49). If not, Peter "certainly did observe the agony of Christ in Gethsemane, saw Him bound and delivered

into the hands of His enemies, and observed at least some of the injustices heaped on Him in the court of the high priest," Hiebert, "Counsel for Christ's Under-shepherds," 333.

21. "As the author shares with the addressees in Christ's glory (v 5c), so in his own experience of suffering he shares with them and the entire brotherhood in the sufferings of Christ (cf. 4:13; 5:9)," John H. Elliott *1 Peter* (New Haven: Yale University Press, 2000), 820. See also Hiebert, "Counsel for Christ's Under-shepherds," 333.

22. Henri J. M. Nouwen, *In the Name of Jesus* (New York: Crossroad, 1989), 55–56.

23. Forbes, *1 Peter*, location 5183. Forbes argues, "The single art. ὁ ["the"] governs both συμπρεσβύτερος ["co-elder"] and μάρτυς ["witness"], indicating the close linking of the roles in the same person," location 5175.

24. Hiebert, "Counsel for Christ's Under-shepherds," 334.

25. "Verses 2–3 present three contrasting pairs indicating both inappropriate and appropriate attitudes and motives for those who shepherd God's flock," Forbes, *1 Peter*, location 5135. Meekness, understood as strength or power under control, is noted here as the attitude that is expected instead of domineering ways.

26. Hiebert notes that the term "chief shepherd" is used only here in the New Testament. He writes, "The term, once thought to be Peter's own coinage, has been found on an Egyptian mummy label in the sense of the 'master-shepherd,'" Hiebert, "Counsel for Christ's Under-shepherds," 339.

27. Here we take "elder" and "overseer" to refer to the same office (see, for example, Acts 20:17, 28; Titus 1:5, 7; 1 Tim 3:1–2; 5:17). See Schreiner, *1 Peter*, 234.

28. Laniak, *Shepherds after My Own Heart*, 233.

29. Forbes, *1 Peter*, location 5159.

30. Hiebert, "Counsel for Christ's Under-shepherds," 336. "This warning also includes the temptation to use the work of the ministry to gain personal popularity or social influence. When a love for gain reigns, the shepherds are prone to become mere hirelings, feeding themselves at the expense of the flock," 337.

31. Laniak, *Shepherds after My Own Heart*, 234. See also Forbes, *1 Peter*, location 5245, as well as "κλῆρος" ("portion," "allotment") in BDAG, 3rd ed. "The allotment implies responsibility," Hiebert, "Counsel for Christ's Under-shepherds," 337.

32. When Peter referenced the appearance of the Chief Shepherd he was maintaining "eschatological urgency," Schreiner, *1 Peter*, 236.

33. The word "strangers" points toward the "crucial idea in the letter . . . that God's people are pilgrims, sojourners, and exiles on earth," Schreiner, *1, 2 Peter, Jude*, 50. Schreiner argues that Peter's audience "are exiles because they suffer for their faith in a world that finds their faith off-putting and strange," (50). Grudem notes, "Nowhere else in ancient Jewish or Christian literature does a writer qualify 'sojourners' with the adjective 'elect' (*eklektos*), as Peter does here," Wayne A. Grudem, *1 Peter* (Downers Grove: InterVarsity, 1988), 52.

34. Peter uses the term "dispersion," which was a common Old Testament description of Israel, indicating their status as God's people dispersed into foreign lands as a form of punishment for their rebellion against God. When Peter wrote 1 Peter, there were "perhaps a million Jews living in Palestine and two to four million outside of it." These exiles would have hoped to return to their land at some point. It is in this context that we find Peter making a "natural transfer of one of the titles of Israel to the church," Davids, *1 Peter*, 46. Davids goes on to write, "The church consists of communities of people living outside of their native land, which is not Jerusalem or Palestine but the heavenly city," 47.

35. "Peter specifies distinct actions by the different persons in the Trinity yet sees them uniting to bring about a common goal, the eternal, full salvation of these 'chosen sojourners,'" Grudem, *1 Peter*, 55.

36. "There is a conscious balance between God's action in heaven, protecting their future, and his action on earth, protecting them in the present," Davids, *1 Peter*, 53.

37. Karen H. Jobes, *1 Peter* (Grand Rapids: Baker, 2005), 144; Paul J. Achtemeier and Eldon Jay Epp, *1 Peter* (Minneapolis: Fortress, 1996), 149.

38. "Here Peter emphasizes the community of believers . . . in terms of that community's relationship to God, to redemptive history, and to those outside the community," Jobes, *1 Peter*, 142. Jobes also notes that throughout this portion of Scripture, "Peter continues to draw heavily on the Old Testament by quoting or alluding to six LXX passages: Psalm 117:22 (118:22 Eng.); Exo. 19:5–6; Isa. 8:14; 28:16; 43:20–21; and Hos. 2:25 (2:23 Eng.)," 143.

39. "Jesus is doubtless called the 'living' stone because of his resurrection," Schreiner, *1 Peter*, 104. Schreiner goes on to note that it is very likely that Peter took this theme of Jesus as the living stone from Ps 118:22.

40. Schreiner, *1 Peter*, 105. The only place in the New Testament where Christians are called living stones is 1 Pet 2:5. Jobes notes that the "stone image is found in three Old Testament passages (Ps. 118:22–23; Isa. 8:14–15; 28:16), and all three of them are quoted in 1 Peter 2:6–8," Jobes, *1 Peter*, 147.

41. "Prescription Flavoring Services," Walgreens, www.walgreens.com/topic/pharmacy /medication-flavoring.jsp.

42. Gene L. Green, "The Use of the Old Testament for Christian Ethics in 1 Peter," *TynBul* 41 (1990): 289.

43. Schreiner, *1 Peter*, 218.

44. Peter warns his readers in 1 Pet 4:15 not to add to their suffering by sinning. "The suffering presumed in this letter was a result of verbal abuse and public humiliation rather than of official incrimination," Elliott, *1 Peter*, 779. On commitment, see Schreiner, *1 Peter*, 220.

45. The number of "unaffiliated" increased by 6.7% between 2007 and 2014 to 22.8%, while evangelical Protestants decreased by 0.9% to 25.4%, Roman Catholics decreased by 3.1% to 20.8%, and mainline Protestants decreased by 3.4% to 14.7%. "America's Changing Religious Landscape," Pew Research Center, May 12, 2015, www.pewforum .org/2015/05/12/americas-changing-religious-landscape.

Conclusion

1. C. S. Lewis, *Mere Christianity* (1952; repr., New York: HarperOne, 2000), 46.

2. Augustine of Hippo, *De doctrina Christiana* 4:12.

3. The methodological trajectory of this book from positive biblical truth to the exposition, debunking, and reinterpretation of alternative models (whether secular or religious) has been shaped by the first two epistemological priorities articulated in David Powlison, "Questions at the Crossroads," *Care for the Soul,* ed. Timothy Phillips and Mark McMinn (Downers Grove: InterVarsity, 2001), 32–42. We have not attempted in this work to pursue the third epistemological priority proposed by Powlison: "learn what we can from defective models" (34). It is hoped that a future work from one of us or from one of our students will build on this research and apply the final epistemological priority to the practice of pastoral leadership.

4. Henri J. M. Nouwen, *In the Name of Jesus* (Spring Valley, NY: Crossroad, 1992), 62–63.

NAME INDEX

SUBJECT INDEX

SCRIPTURE INDEX

258